To My
"Friendly"
Dennis

"Friendly"
Your
Dan

ALSO BY SANFORD D. HORWITT

Let Them Call Me Rebel: Saul Alinsky, His Life and Legacy

FEINGOLD

A New Democratic Party

Sanford D. Horwitt

Simon & Schuster

NEW YORK   LONDON   TORONTO   SYDNEY

SIMON & SCHUSTER
1230 Avenue of the Americas
New York, NY 10020

First Simon & Schuster hardcover edition July 2007

SIMON & SCHUSTER and colophon are registered trademarks
of Simon & Schuster, Inc.

Lyrics on p. 46 for "I'm Gonna Say It Now," by Phil Ochs
© 1965, renewed 1993 Barricade Music, Inc.
All rights administered by Almo Music Corporation/ASCAP
Used by permission. All rights reserved.

For information about special discounts for bulk purchases,
please contact Simon & Schuster Special Sales at 1-800-456-6798
or business@simonandschuster.com.

Text designed by Paul Dippolito

Manufactured in the United States of America

1   3   5   7   9   10   8   6   4   2

Library of Congress Cataloging-in-Publication Data
Horwitt, Sanford D.
Feingold : a new Democratic Party / Sanford D. Horwitt.
p.   cm.
Includes biographical references and index.
1. Feingold, Russ, 1953–   2. Feingold, Russ, 1953–   —Political
and social views. 3. United States. 4. Congress. 5. Senate—
Biography. 6. Democratic Party (U.S.). 7. Legislators—United
States—Biography. 8. Presidential candidates—United States—
Biography. I. Title.
E840.8.F   2007   2007021473

ISBN-13: 978-1-4165-3492-1
ISBN-10:   1-4165-3492-X

For Joan,
Dusty and Jeff

CONTENTS

FEINGOLD

LIVING IN THE REAL WORLD

Senator Hillary Rodham Clinton was livid. Her face turned red and her angry words were aimed directly at Russ Feingold, the junior senator from Wisconsin. "You're not living in the real world," she told him in front of about twenty of their Democratic Senate colleagues at a closed-door strategy meeting in the Senate's elegantly appointed LBJ Room highlighted by nineteenth-century frescoes.

It was Thursday, July 19, 2002, four months after President George W. Bush had signed into law the McCain-Feingold campaign finance reform legislation, the first major reform of federal campaign laws since 1974. That earlier reform was triggered by Watergate-related big-money scandals. Two decades later, the fund-raising scandals associated with Bill Clinton's 1996 reelection campaign had added fuel to the fire for new reforms. Access to the Clinton White House, and to the president himself, had been for sale. Big-money Clinton contributors were eligible for White House coffees. Even bigger contributors got to stay overnight in the Lincoln Bedroom, or share a ride with the president on Air

Force One. All of this was at least unseemly if not illegal. But what was unquestionably illegal were large foreign campaign contributions that poured into the Clinton reelection campaign from China and elsewhere. In the words of Johnny Chung, who got caught in the foreign money scheme: "I see the White House is like a subway: you have to put in coins to open the gates."

The Watergate reforms of 1974 were intended to outlaw unlimited campaign contributions from corporations, labor unions and wealthy individuals. And for a time, they did. But a loophole emerged by 1988, thanks to creative thinking by campaign operatives and a compliant Federal Election Commission. The fundraising rules had changed. And while Bill Clinton and his friend Terry McAuliffe, the man with the golden touch who became chairman of the Democratic National Committee in 2001, did not invent the practice of collecting six-figure campaign checks, they elevated it, so to speak, to near-perfection.

This had become the "real world" for Democrats: the party of the people, of Jefferson and Jackson, had become dependent on wealthy contributors for its electoral successes—such as they were. Although Bill Clinton was elected twice, he received less than 50 percent of the vote each time, and his party lost control of both the Senate and the House, the House for the first time in some forty years.

By 2002, the real-world Democratic Party was addicted to soft money, the Washington jargon for unlimited, largely unregulated campaign contributions reminiscent of the Watergate era. In fact, the national Democratic Party had become virtually as successful raising money from fat cats as the Republican Party. Surprisingly, the big fund-raising disparity that gave Republicans the money advantage at election time was among small donors. Over many years, the Democratic Party leadership had gotten lazy; it lacked imagination and a vision that could appeal to ordinary Democratic-leaning citizens. Instead of inspiring and mobilizing them, the party's influential Washington leaders—lawyer-lobbyists, campaign consultants and senior members of Congress—decided the easiest path to political success led to the doors of wealthy donors, including those in the corporate world. If this strategy sometimes required changing the Democratic Party's policy and message and moving to the political right, then that is what they would do. It was a strategy that Russ Feingold and other dissenting Democrats began to call scornfully "Republican Lite." On a range of important issues for Feingold, from international trade agreements to corporate power to health care, he felt the Democratic Party's capacity to offer sharp, compelling policy alternatives had been compromised again and again because the party's candidates had become so dependent on corporate lobbyists and their clients for campaign contributions.

Feingold's passion for reform had led him to join forces with the Republican John McCain to pass campaign finance reform legislation. Feingold believed so strongly in changing the system—he called it "legalized bribery"—that he risked his Senate seat in 1998 by following a self-imposed ban on soft money that gave his challenger a big fund-raising advantage. Many observers thought he had made a fatal mistake. On election day, John McCain called Feingold from Arizona. Win or lose, McCain said, he wanted to let his friend know how proud he was of him. Feingold, detecting that McCain had heard some bad news about his prospects, said: "Don't worry. We're going to win this thing."

On election night, when the final votes were tallied, Feingold had won by more than 35,000. He quickly became a hero to a broad range of political observers. *New York Times* conservative columnist William Safire wrote, "Idealism lives. The Democratic victory that did my heart good" was Feingold's. "That new Don Quixote demonstrated how a campaign finance reformer could win by running against soft money and practicing what he preached." A *Washington Post* editorial said that "the country owes Feingold for a welcome lesson and his personal example."

But the Democratic Party establishment in Washington was not impressed. It thought Feingold needlessly risked losing a Democratic seat. And, later, Democratic strategists believed the new McCain-Feingold law was going to be a disaster for the party. So, on July 19 in the LBJ Room, Hillary Clinton and a Democratic Party lawyer began exploring how they could persuade the Federal Election Commission to adopt regulations that, in effect, would gut provisions of the new law and keep the soft-money pipeline flowing to Democrats. Feingold had objected. He said it was a troubling display in a party that supposedly stood for reform. That is when Hillary Clinton told him: "You're not living in the real world." He was surprised and taken off guard by her remarks. He remembers saying to himself, "Stay cool, and everything will work out just fine." Feingold responded to Clinton: "Senator, I do live in the real world, and I'm doing just fine in it."

News of the Clinton-Feingold exchange became public, and the following week, in a *New York Times* editorial titled, "Hillary Clinton's 'Real World,'" she was excoriated for her interest in joining forces with "the troglodytes on the Federal Election Commission who would love to poke all sorts of crippling loopholes in the nation's brand-new campaign finance law." In a final shot at Clinton's "real world" attack on Feingold, the *Times* said: "Americans prefer the world of Senator Feingold. It is also the law of the land."

The disagreement between Russ Feingold and Hillary Clinton symbolizes a critical divide in the Democratic Party—and the divide is about much more than how to fund campaigns. Fundamentally, it is between those who believe the modern Democratic Party should become the party of bold ideas and reform, and those who think it should continue to play it safe and, with rare exceptions, accept the status quo. On foreign policy and national security, the divide is between those Democrats who opposed the Bush administration's decision to invade Iraq, as Feingold did, and those who are fearful of challenging the Republican Party's reckless policies and lapel-pin patriotism. On civil liberties in post–September 11 America, the divide is between those Democrats who are loud-and-clear critics of the Bush administration's expansion of executive power, and those who are near-voiceless in the face of the administration's disregard of the rule of law and democratic traditions.

Russ Feingold caught my attention because he represents the progressive side of the Democratic divide more clearly and authentically than any successful politician on the national stage. His roots run deep into the Progressive Era of the early twentieth century, a period personified by two men, Theodore Roosevelt and Wisconsin's legendary governor and later U.S. senator, Robert M. La Follette.

While Roosevelt is one of John McCain's heroes, La Follette is Feingold's role model. On Feingold's late-night tours of the U.S. Capitol that he conducts for old friends who visit him in Washington, one of his highlights is a stop in the Senate Reception Room, where there are portraits of the five greatest senators of the republic's first 150 years selected by a commission created by then-senator John F. Kennedy. One is La Follette. He was called "Fighting Bob" not least because he battled tirelessly against big-money interests of his own Republican party in pursuit of honest, effective government and policies that improved the lives of millions of ordinary Americans. And not surprisingly, La Follette was much more popular with ordinary Americans than he was with his party's establishment leaders.

★ ★ ★

Introduction

After Feingold's celebrated 1998 reelection victory, I began observing him more closely when I periodically returned to Wisconsin, where I grew up. I tried to see Feingold either giving a speech or at one of his listening sessions. When he was first elected to the U.S. Senate in 1992, he made a promise to hold these sessions in each of the state's seventy-two counties every year. I have attended nearly fifty, maybe more than anybody except for Feingold and his staff. It was in these intimate gatherings, typically in small, rural towns all over the state—Bayfield, Coon Valley, Blanchardville—that I began to get a sense of the man.

Small-town America is familiar and fond territory for Feingold. He grew up in Janesville, a blue-collar and agricultural town in Rock County, which had long been a Republican stronghold in southeastern Wisconsin. At these listening sessions, he sounded very much like one of the local civic leaders, and not like the Rhodes Scholar and Harvard Law School graduate that he is.

Russ Feingold is fifty-four years old, still a young man for a senator in the first half of his third term. With a little political luck and good health, he may only be at the midpoint of a long Senate career. So, on the one hand, with his career still unfolding, a definitive biography is premature. On the other hand, Feingold's story is important because he represents the kind of courageous leadership that is so urgently needed in these troubling times.

I began interviewing Feingold well before he was reelected to a third term in 2004. Although he has been generous with his time, this is not an authorized biography. I have examined the public record, interviewed his siblings, friends and foes, journalists and other impartial observers. I hope that I have given him a fair shake—and, in the process, I hope that I have used his story to encourage others—public officials and ordinary citizens alike—to act on their idealism and take risks to transform the "real world" into the kind of world that we would like it to be.

CHAPTER 1

"I'M FOR KENNEDY!"

For much of the twentieth century, the two biggest annual events in Janesville, Wisconsin, were the week-long Rock County 4-H Fair and the Labor Day parade, a fitting tandem for a town surrounded by cornfields and pastures and home to a huge, sprawling General Motors plant.

In August of 1960, when seven-year-old Rusty Feingold and his dad, Leon, went to the fair, as locals called it, there were far more four-legged animals in Rock County than people. In fact, there were three times as many milk cows, hogs and pigs, and sheep and lambs as there were men, women and children. Slightly more than 35,000 of the two-legged variety lived in Janesville, the county seat. Janesville experienced a population explosion of 40 percent between 1950 and 1960, mostly the result of post–World War II births among existing Janesville families. The Feingolds were an example: while Nancy and David were born during the war, the number of Feingold children doubled when Russ was born in 1953 and his sister Dena two years later. So, while the town now had many more people, most of the families who lived there had not changed. In 1960, the "City in the Country," as the *Janesville*

Gazette liked to call it, looked the same and had the same traditions for as long as most could remember.

Going to the fair was one of those traditions. Billed as the country's oldest 4-H county fair, the first was held in 1930 on some thirty-five acres along Milwaukee Street in the heart of Janesville. Throughout Rock County, young people belonged to local 4-H Clubs, which was part of a national leadership and education program for rural youth. They pledged "their allegiance to the improvement of the Head (thinking), Heart (loyalty), Hands (skills) and Health." In the summer, they would come to the fair in Janesville to compete for blue ribbons by exhibiting their calves, pigs, sheep, canned goods, baked items and sewing skills.

There were other attractions at the fair in 1960, such as the music by Red Hedgecock and the Hedgechoppers, the annual horse-pulling contest and the sideshow and carnival rides. Like all children, the Feingold kids looked forward to the rides. But it was not the first thing they were allowed to do. Each of the four children has a clear memory of their parents saying: "No, first you're going to go through the barns. And you're going to see the animals and see the people who really make this area what it is." And it was also made clear to the children, Russ Feingold recalls, that their father's livelihood as a lawyer in town was connected to the hard work and success of the area's farmers. The *Gazette*, the conservative, staunchly Republican daily newspaper, expanded on Leon Feingold's lecture to his children in an editorial on the eve of the 1960 fair. "The big reason for coming to the fair next week is to view once more the products and the work which give this area and the nation its agricultural assets and to renew appreciation . . . of the competitive system which flows through American life." The fair, the *Gazette* noted, will give youth the chance to "experience triumphs and disappointments in preparation for adult life" in the free enterprise system. And so, before they hit the midway, the

Feingold children and their parents would dutifully walk through the dairy barn and the sheep barn and maybe get to talk with an eventual blue-ribbon winner like the girl from Johnstown whose 935-pound Shorthorn steer named Buddy was declared "the champion over all breeds" that year. Another Feingold family tradition was buying a lamb at the county fair auction. The auction was started in 1955; it's always held on Friday and continues to this day. Leon and his wife, Sylvia, would buy a lamb that was being sold by the son or daughter of a friend or a client of Leon's. After the lamb was slaughtered, the Feingolds either shared the meat with friends or froze it and used it throughout the year.

By Tuesday, August 2, the opening day of the 1960 fair, trucks and trailers hauling families and their animals had descended on Janesville from the little towns in Rock County, a nearly perfect square 28 miles across with a southern boundary that touches Illinois. For Janesville and other Rock County residents, the fair was certainly about agriculture and economics, but it was also a celebration of civic and political life. The fair was largely organized and run by volunteers, hundreds of them from every sector of the community—blue-collar workers from the GM plant and the Parker Pen Company, their bosses, small businessmen, bankers and professionals who represented the Kiwanis and Rotary Clubs, and mothers and even their children. Women volunteers helped with the annual "Fashion Fiesta," which attracted some one thousand spectators at the big home economics auditorium tent on Friday night. On Saturday night, three volunteers—the wife of a high school agriculture teacher, a 4-H adult leader and Leon Feingold representing the Janesville Chamber of Commerce—were judges for the gala parade in front of the grandstand. The fair, the grandest event in Janesville year in and year out and the source of great local pride, was dependent on the goodwill, cooperation and participation of its citizens for its success.

The Rock County 4-H Fair was a must-stop event for local politicians and party activists. In an election year such as 1960, it was a good place to pass out campaign literature, schmooze and press the flesh, especially when the weather cooperated. And the weather throughout the 1960 fair was ideal, except for a violent summer storm of high winds and rain that ripped through the fairgrounds on opening day. Although brief, it was the worst storm in the fair's history. Worst hit were the Republican Party's tent and the sideshow tent at the far north end of the midway. There, according to a report, "Coy Mangram, the bearded snake charmer, was sleeping on a cot near his snake pit when the big tent went down." Fortunately, he suffered only minor injuries and, by noon the next day, Mr. Mangram, his snakes and the Republicans were back in business.

When it came to politics in Rock County, whether it was at the fair or at the voting booth on election day, Republicans ruled. For the first sixty years of the twentieth century, only two Democratic presidential candidates carried Rock County or Janesville: Franklin Roosevelt in 1936, and Harry Truman by a whisker in 1948. For most of those sixty years, Wisconsin was a Republican-dominated state, and small farming communities such as Janesville and the rest of Rock County were where the Republican base lived. The political expression "rock-ribbed Republican" did not originate in Rock County, but it was an apt description of the county's politics.

Although Rusty Feingold couldn't have imagined the special scene of a presidential year at the fair before he arrived with his dad, he came that day already possessing a keen, even extraordinary interest in politics. Oh yes, like many other seven-year-old boys, Rusty was interested in baseball because his dad was. But unlike other young boys, Rusty was also soaking up his dad's even greater passion for politics. "He talked about politics incessantly,"

Feingold recalls almost a half-century later. "I knew who the state senator was and the state representative. My dad was nuts about politics, whether it was a [local] judicial election or for president. He'd sit there at dinner, talking about Kennedy, Adlai Stevenson, Gaylord Nelson, the city councilman down the street." Feingold remembers it as a great political feast. "It was like all you could eat," he says. "And I just sat there and listened to it all and remembered it all."

Leon Feingold, a staunch Democrat, may not have realized what kind of life-altering impact he was having on his younger son—that his passion for politics, especially for elective politics, was being transplanted deep into his son's soul. There is an irony here because, many years later when Russ Feingold was in his twenties and telling his dad that he wanted to run for office, Leon tried to discourage him. He himself had run twice for local office as a young man, but as a father he had come to believe it was not a good career choice for one of his children. For Russ, of course, Leon's midlife reappraisal came much too late. "That's where my father made his mistake," Feingold says, recalling the lasting impact of all of those vivid, wonderful political stories his dad told around the dinner table. But it wasn't only the stories; the deal may have been sealed at the 1960 county fair.

To an adult, the political scene at the fair was familiar. The Republican and Democratic tents were separated by a hundred paces, as they always were. And the hand-pumping and backslapping was a time-honored ritual. But to Rusty Feingold, the world that he had only heard about was suddenly vivid and real, with sights and sounds that were beyond his imagination.

On a given day, there was more action at the Republican tent, which that year "centered largely on the Republican congressional primary," the *Gazette* reported. The winner of the three-person contest was assured a seat in Congress. When his Democratic dad stopped by the Republican tent, Russ Feingold remembers the warm, friendly greeting, "Hey, Leon," and soon his dad was shaking hands and chatting with everybody. Even then, Rusty Feingold was struck by the exchange of friendliness and mutual respect. "We walked right in there, and it was the most important thing he ever taught me [about politics]," Feingold recalls. "We shook everyone's hand. They kidded him [because] they were friends. And he introduced me to the state senator. This guy was like a god. He was a state senator! I was impressed by that, like some kids would be impressed if they met a baseball player."

But the real attraction at the fair, the one Rusty had been waiting for, was in the other tent. "I was a little guy with glasses," Feingold says, and "all I wanted to do was go to the Democratic tent because my dad had talked this up." There he saw a big, captivating photo of John F. Kennedy, maybe not life-size but lifelike and inspiring. Kennedy's voice filled the tent, energetic excerpts of his speeches flowing out of the loudspeakers. And when the speeches were not being played, Feingold remembers seeing "one of those old record players. And there was Frank Sinatra's voice coming out: 'He's got high hopes, he's got high hopes, he's got high in the sky, apple pie hopes.' It was John F. Kennedy's campaign song." All of this was immediately thrilling, and on the spot Feingold remembers announcing, "I'm for Kennedy!" And not only that, Feingold admits, but it was around this time that "I was running around telling people I wanted to be president, that I wanted to be the first Jewish president." He recalls this with a good amount of amusement and recounts the teasing he's taken over the years about his childhood presidential ambitions. But he also admits that "it would be impossible for me to pretend that at any point between the ages of seven and twenty-nine that I didn't want to go into politics."

On election day in 1960, John F. Kennedy fared a lot better

nationally than he did in Rusty Feingold's second-grade classroom. In fact, Rusty was the only student who voted for Kennedy. He was crushed and crying when he got home and told his mother what had happened. Clearly, it had not been much of a consolation that his teacher also voted for Kennedy. Maybe she did it to comfort her lone, devastated Democrat. Or maybe she, too, identified with the new president-elect. Rusty Feingold's second-grade teacher just happened to be named Mrs. Kennedy.

Russ's grandfather Max Feingold's journey to Janesville started in a shtetl near the city of Minsk, and included a decade-long layover in Rochester, New York. He came alone, a Yiddish-speaking, Russian-Jewish boy of fourteen, in 1906. By the time his ship docked in New York, he was not only in the New World, but he had adopted a new identity. He boarded the ship as Max Winogradoff and stepped off as Max Feingold. How and why this happened is not entirely clear. The family version that has been handed down over the years is that Max was angry with his uncle who had arranged the trip. In mid-voyage, he decided that he was no longer a Winogradoff and, figuratively speaking, plucked Feingold out of the air. If there was a more earthly inspiration, nobody remembers it.

Either in New York City or in Rochester, where Max stayed with relatives, he met Dina Katz, who came from Minsk. They were married while Max worked a variety of jobs, including a stint at Bausch & Lomb. But his labor-union-organizing activities were not helping his economic prospects, and in 1917, Max, Dina and their two children, Leon and daughter Voltairine, or Volty as she was called, headed to Janesville. Max Feingold's first appearance in the Janesville City Directory lists his occupation as "junk peddler," a job that may have been connected with the small scrap metal business started by two of Dina's brothers who were already living in the town.

When Max Feingold and his family arrived, Janesville was on the cusp of great changes that would reshape the town's economy and government for the remainder of the twentieth century. It was the beginning of a new, transformed Janesville in which Max and Dina's children and many of their grandchildren, including Russ, would grow up.

The old Janesville had been created by the first white settlers in the mid-1830s after the Black Hawk War of 1832. The war, which spread along the Rock River in Illinois and into Wisconsin, was named after the courageous American Indian Black Hawk, leader of the Fox-Sauk. Although Black Hawk was ultimately driven off the land by frontiersmen and the military, his fierce resistance to the brutal, relentless pursuit of him and his people made him a hero in the eyes of many enlightened Americans.

By June of 1836, one of the early settlers who appeared on the scene was Henry F. Janes. He laid claim to land in soon-to-be Janesville that would also become the site of the Rock County seat. Janes "immediately prepared to establish himself as a permanent settler," building a cabin that served as a tavern for a new settlement on the east side of the Rock River. The Rock would become something of a dividing line between the east and west sides of town. But while Henry Janes put the "Janes" into Janesville, his stay was brief. In fact, he turned out to be a peripatetic, promiscuous father of other Janesvilles stretching from Iowa to California.

For much of Janesville's first seventy-five years, the land that surrounded it defined the town's fortunes and fabric. An early, hometown history of the Janesville area noted with pride that "the county of Rock is one of the best agricultural districts in the West, [and] there is scarcely an acre within its limits which cannot be profitably used for farming purposes." The first big crop was wheat, and flour mills soon popped up in Janesville. But before the turn of the century, the wheat had depleted the phosphates in the soil and was replaced by other crops including tobacco, plus dairy farming. Janesville changed accordingly, boasting new tanneries, shoe and cigar makers, dairies and farm implement manufacturers to satisfy the need for plows, threshers and reapers. And for a time in the late nineteenth and early twentieth centuries, one of the largest Janesville industries was the cotton mills, where the majority of workers were women.

Most of Janesville's economic activity was local until the railroads connected the area to a larger world, including Chicago ninety miles southeast and Milwaukee seventy miles to the northeast. Janesville became a big railroad town. By the beginning of the twentieth century, scores of freight trains and passenger trains chugged through each day. Even by the late 1950s, there were still enough trains running through Janesville that they captured the imagination of young Rusty Feingold. Almost a half-century later, he recalls the enchanting sound of the train whistles disappearing into the darkness of a summer night.

The Janesville that Feingold's grandparents, Max and Dina, entered in 1917 was not rich or poor, not boom or bust, not backward but not especially innovative or dynamic either. It was mainly a blue-collar town run by small businessmen who took turns as Janesville's mayor. The population had increased only modestly in recent years to about 14,000. New Englanders such as Henry Janes had founded Janesville, but small waves of German Lutheran, Irish Catholic and some Scandinavian immigrants rolled in throughout the late nineteenth century.

With the Irish low on the socioeconomic ladder, "Janesville's political culture expressed a fusion of New England pietism and German Lutheranism," according to a historical study of early Janesville. In 1917, there were very few Jews in Janesville—for a time, Dina's brothers' families may have been the only ones—and that would not change much even up to the present.

Janesville was not known for having many visionaries. One of the exceptions was Joseph A. Craig, after whom Russ Feingold's high school would be named. By 1918, Craig was the general manager of Janesville's largest business, the Janesville Machine Company. It made farm implements, as did a struggling California company that had been purchased by Detroit-based General Motors and its founder, William C. Durant. Durant tried to entice Craig to Detroit to revitalize his faltering Sampson Tractor operation. Instead, the cagey Craig convinced Durant to move the operation to Janesville and merge with his company. The new operation, GM's Sampson Tractor Division, was up and running by the spring of 1919—and soon new workers poured into Janesville. Within eighteen months, the town's population zoomed from 14,000 to 20,000.

It was around this time that Max Feingold and a partner, Harry Filvaroff, also a Jewish immigrant, opened a small grocery store, the Blackhawk, on Vista Avenue, on Janesville's East Side. They later moved into a somewhat larger location a half-dozen blocks away on Racine Street where Max would stay until the late 1940s.

After what seemed like such a promising start, the Sampson Tractor Division was shut down in 1922, the victim of a farm depression and poor tractor designs. But the Janesville GM factory also started making Chevrolet trucks and, later, Chevrolet cars— and, almost immediately, this operation was a big success.

When J. A. Craig convinced GM's Durant to locate a manufacturing plant in Janesville, part of the deal was that Janesville would improve its schools, housing, roads, bridges—everything that was required to attract and sustain a much larger workforce. Previously, the city fathers' governing philosophy, such as it was, was "the epitome of fiscal conservatism," and that government should do "as little as possible." Janesville's teachers were often among the lowest paid in the state, schools were overcrowded and the city streets and sidewalks were frequently in bad repair. All of this changed in the new, post-GM Janesville when Janesville adopted a city manager form of government and hired Henry Traxler as its first city manager, in 1923. He served in the post for twenty-eight years, the longest of any chief administrator in Janesville history.

Traxler, a Jew born in Milwaukee in 1899, was trained as a civil engineer. His engineering background helped when Janesville embarked on long-delayed public works projects, but he also brought to Janesville a view of government that was typical of the Wisconsin progressive tradition. Improved public services were high priorities, but so, too, were carefully managed, parsimonious budgets. The city streets got cleaned, but at half the old cost. Gas and oil were purchased in bulk to save money. As early as 1924, the Traxler administration could boast, "No new general city bonds have been issued. . . . Everything has been paid for in cash." With Wisconsin progressives, efficient government and fiscal prudence were not empty slogans; they were simply the way government was supposed to work. And honesty and high ethical standards were practical, indispensable ingredients of efficient government because they curbed tendencies toward cronyism, graft and other forms of corruption.

Russ Feingold's father, Leon, was five years old when he came to Janesville with his parents and younger sister, Volty. At home when the children were growing up, the parents spoke Yiddish to each other but mainly English to their children, recalls Volty. Three more girls—Miriam, Lillian and Deborah—would be born in Janesville.

Life for the Feingolds in the 1920s and 1930s revolved around work, family and, for the parents, a strong interest in the larger world of politics and ideas. The store on Racine Street included produce, flour and sugar in bulk and a meat section in the back that was run by Max's partner. For a time, there was one gasoline pump in front of the store. Racine Street was not only a primary east–west street in town, but it was also Highway 14, which you could take to Chicago. The store hours were long; Volty recalls her mother walking to the store after dinner and driving the short distance home with Max in his Chevrolet truck when the store closed. When the children were older, they sometimes worked in the store on weekends and in the summer.

As time-consuming as the store was, and as tenuous as the Feingolds' finances sometimes were, nothing was more important than the family. Volty remembers a home that "was filled with warmth and love." The Feingolds simply enjoyed doing things together. There were summertime picnics at nearby Clear Lake or Lake Geneva, and periodic family meals with their aunts, uncles and cousins in Janesville. For a good number of years, the cohesiveness of the family had much to do with its isolation as a Jewish immigrant family in Janesville. If there was a family problem or crisis, for example, Leon and Volty, even when they were quite young, joined their parents as sort of a "committee of four" to come up with solutions.

Education was a shared family value and took several forms. Doing well in school was important. From an early age, all five children knew they would go to college. All would graduate from the University of Wisconsin in Madison, the beginning of a Feingold family tradition. Leon started college in 1931, and Volty arrived on campus three years later. She remembers that after paying the tuition of $37.50 per semester, she didn't have enough money to live in a dorm. So she rented a room from a Jewish family, one her parents knew.

Having their children learn about Judaism and maintain their Jewish identity were also important to Dina and Max. Some of this happened at family gatherings—for example, one of Dina's brothers in Janesville, who was perhaps the most religiously observant of the extended family, would arrange to have somebody from Chicago conduct Yom Kippur services for the Janesville families. But Dina and Max also arranged to have Jewish college students from Madison come down to Janesville to teach Hebrew to their children. In the Feingold home, the emphasis was not on religion per se, but on the culture, history, language and values of Judaism and what it meant to be a Jew. Interestingly, Dina and Max saw many of their Jewish values and view of social justice reflected in the political leadership of Wisconsin's La Follettes. Volty remembers how much her parents admired them all, Robert M. and his two sons, Bob and Phil.

Both parents, especially Max, also had a lifelong interest in the establishment of a Jewish state. "My dad was so much of a Zionist," says one of Volty's younger sisters, Debbie. Max followed world events through Yiddish language newspapers he received from New York. Dina's reading included the literary classics that were translated into Yiddish. One of her favorite plays, Debbie remembers, was Ibsen's *A Doll's House*. After her death in 1948, the Feingold family donated Dina's collection to the Library of Congress.

Throughout much of the 1920s, Max's Blackhawk grocery store, General Motors and Janesville did well. The store had established itself, in part because of the success of the GM plant. The plant, actually a hybrid of the adjacent Fisher Body and Chevrolet plants, celebrated the production of its 500,000th car on April 9, 1929. It was also the year of record production in Janesville: 125,000 cars were turned out by some 2,200 workers, no doubt many of them and their families customers of the Blackhawk grocery.

But when the Great Depression hit, production plummeted and workers began losing their jobs. A tax dispute between GM

19

and the state of Wisconsin made matters worse. And then the *Janesville Gazette* headlined the worst news of all: "Chevrolet Plant Closing Great Blow to City; Last Car Produced Sept. 17, 1932." GM announced that its Janesville executives were being transferred to Detroit, Flint and other cities. It looked like the end of the line for GM in Janesville. And the future of the Blackhawk grocery must not have looked too bright either. Max Feingold and his partner sold groceries to their customers on credit when they needed a little help from paycheck to paycheck, or when there were temporary layoffs at Janesville's other factories. But a complete shutdown by the largest employer was different. And by now, Dina and Max had five children to feed.

After a bleak fourteen months, General Motors suddenly announced that the plant was reopening. To many in Janesville, it must have seemed like a miracle. Euphoria was sweeping through the city just in time for the start of the Christmas shopping season of 1933. Janesville's leaders organized the biggest celebration that had ever been seen in southeast Wisconsin. They called it the Janesville Jubilee Day, and it was held on Friday, November 24. The *Gazette* reported that "some 30,000 persons, young and old alike, took full advantage of the festivities." A free dance attracted five thousand people packing the Franklin Gardens. An estimated 23,000 flocked to free, all-day movies at the town's three movie theaters. At the Myers, the line waiting to see *Rafter Romance* starring Ginger Rogers and George Sidney "stretched for blocks on East Milwaukee Street down almost to Main, and around the corner onto South Buff." An evening banquet at the Monterey Hotel featured Wisconsin's governor, Albert Schmedeman, who was also at the front of the mammoth Jubilee parade that afternoon. Two miles long, it included virtually every civic and youth group in town; marching bands from the high school and the Salvation Army; a calliope; and Santa Claus and his reindeer.

But the highlight for many was the parade's Fourth Division, comprised of "several hundred Chevrolets dating from 1913 until the present." What a glorious sight that was! Most of the Chevys were driven by their owners—or in the case of Max Feingold, by his twenty-one-year-old son. As the *Gazette* reported: "Leon Feingold was the driver of a truck operated by the Blackhawk grocery, the firm which claims to be the first to buy a Chevrolet truck in Janesville." Indeed, back in 1923, Max Feingold did buy the first truck off the GM line. And eighty-four years later in 2007, the Janesville General Motors plant is the oldest in the country. In a certain sense, it can be said that it all started with Max Feingold. A framed photo of Max standing, smiling and looking hopeful in front of his Chevrolet truck is prominently displayed in his grandson's Senate office. Embedded in the scene is not only the history of a family, but also the story of a new, emerging middle-class America. It was the Feingolds' American Dream.

CHAPTER 2

"RENEGADE BY NATURE"

By the time Russell Dana Feingold was born on March 2, 1953, in Janesville, his parents had been married for thirteen years but were only beginning to enjoy a more comfortable middle-class life. It had taken the better part of twenty years before they had a real family vacation. Feingold's brother, David, recalls the first one, around 1956 or 1957, a driving trip along the Mississippi River to New Orleans. Well into the 1950s, the Feingolds' one-and-only family car was a 1938 Buick, a hand-me-down from Leon's father.

Leon Feingold started with virtually nothing after he graduated from the University of Wisconsin Law School in 1937. He immediately returned to Janesville, rented space in a small law office and started his own career as a solo practitioner. Among his first clients were members of the United Automobile Workers union at the General Motors plant; he prepared their income tax returns for a dollar each.

On a March day in 1939, Leon borrowed his father's car and drove forty miles to Madison for a date with a Jewish girl that had been arranged by his oldest sister, Volty. The young woman was Sylvia Binstock, a bright, charming senior at the University of

Wisconsin majoring in French and minoring in German. He picked her up at the French House, and they went out for dinner and dancing at the Chanticleer in Middleton, a popular place with college students. "We hit it off pretty well," Sylvia recalled, "but I didn't know if I'd hear from him again." But before a week passed, Leon phoned from Janesville, saying he had some business in Madison and asking for another date. Two months later, Leon asked Sylvia to marry him, and she quickly accepted. Since neither had much money, they waited more than a year before they were married in September of 1940. In the ensuing years, there was a consensus in the extended Feingold family that, as Volty put it, "one of the best things that ever happened to Leon was marrying Sylvia. She was a magnificent person."

Sylvia was born in 1919 in Memphis, Tennessee, where her immigrant parents, Isaac and Rachel, lived for a time before moving to Denver, joining other relatives. How and why the Binstocks started off in Memphis is not clear; one of Isaac's younger brothers, who preceded him to the United States, may have directed Isaac to a business opportunity in the Bluff City.

Before immigrating to Memphis around 1900, Isaac lived in a small town near Tarnow, in what is now Poland but what was then part of the Austro-Hungarian Empire. There the family name was Binenstock or Bienenstock. Isaac came from a large family—he may have had as many as fifteen siblings, although his relatives in the United States and Canada have not been able to account for all of them. Many remained in Europe—and Isaac's mother, Miriam Feige Binstock, even returned to Europe after her husband died in Memphis in 1918. In Europe during World War II, many Binstocks did not survive Hitler's evil. Miriam, who was Russ Feingold's great-grandmother, was killed in the Holocaust, as were at least nine other Binstock relatives, according to documents at Yad Vashem in Jerusalem. Most were shot and killed in a bunker in the final liquidation of the Tarnow ghetto in 1943.

Sylvia Binstock was a menopause baby, as people used to say, an unplanned second child arriving twenty-three years after the birth of her brother, Louis. And it was Louis who became the star of the Binstock family, a second father to Sylvia and a revered figure among Russ and his siblings. The fact that Sylvia's older brother was a rabbi, and a prominent one by the time Sylvia met Leon, had made a big impression on Volty, and on Leon as well. The Binstocks were still living in Memphis when Louis, a gifted student, graduated from high school. The Binstocks had little money—Isaac was probably more suited to be a Talmudic scholar than a businessman—and Louis assumed college was out of his reach until a wealthy benefactor stepped into the picture. Louis graduated from the University of Tennessee and then from its law school. But he soon found his true calling, inspired by a Reform rabbi's speech. After graduating from rabbinical school and postings with Reform congregations in Baltimore and Charleston, West Virginia, Louis became the senior rabbi at the new Temple Sinai in New Orleans in 1926. In New Orleans, he became well known for his eloquence, liberalism and civic work, and when he departed ten years later to lead one of the country's largest Reform congregations, Temple Shalom on Chicago's North Side, he was accorded a round of public tributes. One of the encomiums came from New Orleans's black community for Louis's civil rights work. Grateful black leaders presented him with an inscribed silver bowl.

Louis encouraged his sister Sylvia to attend college, even though their parents didn't have the money for her tuition. But when she graduated from high school in Denver, she recalled, "I had a scholarship to a two-year women's junior college in Denver. I could live at home. My brother said if I would take that, he would send me anywhere I wanted to go for the last two years. So I did that." After the two years, she wanted to go to the University of California in Berkeley, but her mother said that it was too far from home. Sylvia talked with a dean at the junior college who told her he knew someone at the University of Wisconsin and that maybe he could help her get a scholarship there. "That sounded pretty good," Sylvia remembered thinking. "When my mother heard that, she was thrilled. And that's how I got to Wisconsin."

After Sylvia and Leon were married in Denver and honeymooned in the Canadian Rockies and the American West, they moved into a small Janesville apartment. For Leon, there was never any doubt that he would come back to Janesville after law school; it was home and he loved it. Volty, on the other hand, couldn't wait to leave. She thought Janesville was confining and dull, a good place for farmers who liked to shop at J.C. Penney's on Main Street, but not a place for her. Going to the university in Madison had opened up a new, exciting world of possibilities for Volty, and when she graduated, she left Janesville for good. In retrospect, she realized that as close as she and her brother had been, "We saw things differently."

Adventurous and outspoken, Volty describes Leon as very deliberate, "the kind of person who had a plan and he would proceed with the plan." He also was serious and sober, honest and highly principled, even as a young man. Many years later, after a lifetime of practicing law and playing prominent leadership roles in Janesville's civic life, it was not unusual to hear somebody in Janesville say to Russ or to his brother, David, "Leon was the finest person I ever knew." Indeed, he was the kind of small-town lawyer reminiscent of Harper Lee's Atticus Finch.

Leon's lofty principles and love of politics led him to run as the Progressive Party candidate for Rock County district attorney in 1938. Like his parents, Leon had been inspired by the legacy of Fighting Bob La Follette. The Wisconsin Progressive Party, founded in 1934, recalled Fighting Bob's own Progressive Party and his presidential candidacy in 1924. Although unsuccessful, La Follette won 17 percent of the national vote, more than any third-party candidate for the remainder of the twentieth century until Ross Perot won 19 percent on the Reform Party ticket in 1992. But in 1938, the Wisconsin Progressive Party was losing its electoral steam in the face of opposition from a coalition of conservative or Stalwart Republicans and Democrats. Phil La Follette, Fighting Bob's younger son, was defeated decisively statewide in his bid for an unprecedented fourth term as governor—and he lost in Rock County by two to one, as did Leon Feingold. For Leon, fresh out of law school, his showing in Janesville, where he carried six of the town's fourteen wards, was at least respectable. And if he had to lose, losing to his good Republican friend John Matheson was not the worst possible outcome, either.

According to family members, Leon Feingold only ran for public office once more, a losing race for the Rock County Board, although there are no public accounts of it. But he became an active, occasionally influential participant in the rebirth of the Democratic Party in Wisconsin.

"The first time I ever saw Russ," recalled Tom Fairchild, was on a drive through Janesville when Fairchild stopped to say hello to his good friends Sylvia and Leon. "They said before you leave, you must see the new baby. And there was Russ in his crib." Not many months before in the 1952 election, Thomas Edward Fairchild was the Democratic candidate who ran against Wisconsin's Republican senator, Joseph McCarthy. The Feingolds were deeply involved in the grassroots, statewide "Joe Must Go" campaign. When he was growing up, Russ Feingold heard stories about anti-McCarthy strategy meetings that were held at his house. His father would tell him that right there, on that sofa, was where Ruth Jeffris sat. Jeffris was a member of the very Republican Janesville family that owned Parker Pen, the second largest employer in town. Like many Republicans in Wisconsin who might've been conservative on some issues but who were civic-minded, Ruth Jeffris despised McCarthy's divisive, mean-spirited tactics. She helped to fund *The McCarthy Record*, a nationally circulated booklet that documented McCarthy's transgressions.

The Feingolds campaigned hard for Fairchild, of course. But although the Fairchild-McCarthy race tightened in the closing weeks as more voters came to see McCarthy as a dangerous demagogue, Fairchild could not close the gap in a year when Republican presidential candidate Dwight Eisenhower took Wisconsin in a landslide. Still, even in a losing effort, Fairchild's exceptional intellect, decency and integrity won him the lasting respect of Democrats and many Republicans.

Tom Fairchild and Leon Feingold became friends when they were classmates at the University of Wisconsin Law School, although their personal backgrounds were quite different. Tom's father was a prominent Wisconsin lawyer and conservative Republican; he had been his party's nominee for Wisconsin governor in 1910. As late as 1932, his son Tom seemed to be following in his father's footsteps, campaigning for Herbert Hoover's reelection in Mercer County, New Jersey, while Tom was a student at Princeton. But the Great Depression, the New Deal and Tom Fairchild's return to Wisconsin and the university changed his political direction.

On the Madison campus, excitement about Roosevelt's New Deal was palpable. Wisconsinites played key roles in the Roosevelt administration; one, for example, was economics professor Edwin Witte, sometimes called "the father of Social Security." Fairchild took several of Witte's courses—and, along with Leon Feingold and other bright, politically engaged students, joined the campus

Progressive Club. The club became a meeting place for budding political leaders who, by the late 1940s, would be key players in the emergence of the state's revitalized Democratic Party.

Until the demise of the Wisconsin Progressive Party after World War II, leading Progressives resisted becoming Democrats, despite the fact that the vast majority had supported many of Roosevelt's New Deal policies. There were a variety of reasons, not the least of which was that running statewide as a Democrat in Wisconsin was almost always a losing proposition, just as running as a Republican in the Deep South was. Also, many Progressives identified strongly with the anti-slavery legacy of Lincoln's Republican Party and felt uncomfortable, to say the least, sharing a political home with Southern, segregationist Democrats.

Even as late as 1946, at an anguished meeting of Wisconsin Progressives in Portage, the Progressives were not quite ready to become Democrats. A majority voted to rejoin the Republican Party, following Young Bob La Follette's decision to run for reelection to the U.S. Senate as a Republican in 1946. But when La Follette lost to the then-little-known Joe McCarthy in the Republican primary months later, it was not long before younger Progressives began gravitating to the Democratic Party. And the first Democratic electoral successes came much sooner than anybody expected.

In 1948, some young Progressives were persuaded to run for various offices as Democrats. One of them was Tom Fairchild, who didn't even know if he was a Democrat when he received a pitch from his friend, Jim Doyle, the father of Wisconsin's current governor. "Jim assured me," Fairchild recalls with a laugh, "that nobody was going anywhere on the Democratic ticket that year. Everybody knew that Truman couldn't win"—and, of course, neither would anybody else on the Democratic ticket in Wisconsin.

But soon after Fairchild agreed to be the Democratic candidate for attorney general, newspapers began ridiculing the Republicans for slating highly unqualified candidates, including Fairchild's opponent. Fairchild began to think, "Well, maybe there's a chance here." And to test out his emerging optimism, Fairchild went to Janesville on a memorable Saturday to see his old friend. "The very first person I went to see was Leon Feingold," Fairchild remembers. At first, Leon was skeptical but then reconsidered and said, "Maybe you got something. I'm going to call some people." And Fairchild listened as Leon "called a whole bunch of Janesville Republicans and Rock County lawyers who were known as real staunch Republicans. And before he was through," Fairchild says with a big smile almost sixty years later, "he had gotten endorsements for me from several of those guys. And from there on, that was it. I won by sixty thousand votes."

In fact, Fairchild was the first Wisconsin Democrat to win a statewide race since 1932. Truman carried Wisconsin, too. And several young, progressive Democrats were elected for the first time to the state legislature—among them was Gaylord Nelson, who, twelve years later, would become only the second Democrat in the twentieth century to be elected governor.

After 1948, Tom Fairchild never won another election. After he lost to McCarthy in 1952, he went on to a distinguished career on the Wisconsin State Supreme Court and then as chief judge of the U.S. Court of Appeals for the Seventh Circuit. After his retirement from the bench, his law clerks established the annual Thomas E. Fairchild Lecture at the University of Wisconsin Law School. In 2005, Russ Feingold gave the Fairchild Lecture, an eloquent defense of one of the most controversial votes of his Senate career, a vote he cast in the impeachment trial of Bill Clinton.

The pent-up demand for goods and services following World War II brought prosperity to virtually every part of the country, surprising many economists who thought depression-like conditions would return when the war ended. The United States was about to become the world's first middle-class society—and the growing auto industry was the vehicle, as much as any, to a new way of life for millions of Americans that was unimaginable not many years before. One in six manufacturing jobs—in steel, rubber, road construction—would soon be tied to the auto industry. And little Janesville, with its big GM plant, epitomized the new prosperity of the 1950s.

For almost everybody in Janesville, the 1950s were very good years. The year Russ Feingold was born, GM's Fisher Body and Chevrolet plants added a second shift. By the end of 1953, production of Chevy cars hit 144,000, a 45 percent increase over the previous year. Soon the plants were producing sleek models with rear fins, such as the beautiful Bel Air, that are now prized classic cars selling for many times the original cost.

Starting in the 1950s, the United Automobile Workers union negotiated agreements with GM that provided Janesville workers for the first time with a pension at sixty-five years of age—it paid $1.50 per year of service to a maximum of $45 a month. For the first time, workers were also eligible for accident, hospital and life insurance. By the mid-1950s, a beginning assembler at the Chevy plant earned the magnificent sum of $2 an hour. There were other sizable companies in town—Parker Pen, where many young women fresh out of high school could find good jobs, Gilman Engineering and Gibbs Manufacturing. But GM was the largest employer. It defined the postwar promise and identity of Janesville more than any other, as it had from the day that Max Feingold bought the first Chevrolet truck.

General Motors was not only booming, but so, too, was business in Janesville's old downtown. Friday night was the big night for shopping. Unless you arrived early, it was hard to find a parking place on any of the streets near Bostwick's department store. Plans for new schools were on the drawing boards, and new houses and subdivisions were going up everywhere. The father of Russ Feingold's childhood friend Pete Duesterbeck taught himself carpentry after he returned from the war and was quickly in demand as a homebuilder. Many of his clients, Pete recalls, were GM executives who had been transferred to Janesville from other GM plants. "He was a custom-home builder," Pete says, "and a lot of times the executives wanted their houses reproduced" to look like the old houses they used to live in. Pete's father steered some of his real estate work to Leon and Sylvia Feingold, who started a title and abstract business that Sylvia managed for many years.

The Feingolds' house on Vista Avenue where Tom Fairchild saw Russ in his crib was not one of the new postwar houses. It had been built in 1931 by Russ's grandparents Max and Dina. They had purchased a vacant lot a few blocks from Max's Blackhawk grocery store and had the house built with the help of some bartering deals. Russ's aunt Volty recalls helping her mother decorate the new house, and it was home to Volty, Leon and the other three sisters throughout their school years. But in 1948, Dina, who was only fifty-eight, died of Hodgkin's disease. After her death, Max took a trip to Israel, fell in love with the new country and moved there permanently in 1950. Leon and Sylvia, who had been living in cramped quarters a few blocks away with their two children, Nancy and David, moved into the Vista Avenue house.

The Feingolds' two-story, white clapboard Dutch colonial with black shutters would not have been out of place in a New England town. It had four bedrooms upstairs, but it was not a large house, nothing like the grand Queen Anne Victorians built in the 1880s on Courthouse Hill about a mile away. The approximately 1,600-square-foot colonial, which somehow looked bigger from the outside than it was, was on a block of houses of similar size but varying designs. By Janesville standards of the 1950s, it was a nice, comfortable house, although Russ Feingold thought it had been designed for small people. "In the Feingold gene pool, Dave and I are giants in the Feingold trait category," he says. (As adults, the brothers, at approximately five feet, nine inches, were noticeably taller than their stocky father.) What added some charm to the property were the stately Dutch elms that lined Vista Avenue out front, and the large, fruit-tree-filled backyard that included a rock garden. The backyard at 1207 Vista was a favorite of Russ's. "When I was growing up, the backyard was like a grocer's yard," he says. "There were big cherry trees, apple trees, currant bushes, raspberries, strawberries. It was a little bit of a food wonderland." The lovely rock garden was created by Russ's grandmother Dina, and inherited by Sylvia.

On Russ's block, and in the immediate neighborhood, there was no shortage of kids to play with. A good many were Russ's friends from kindergarten through high school—and some have remained close friends to this day. And his sister, Dena, who was only two years younger than Russ, was part of the neighborhood group. Dena remembers that by the end of the summer, the grass around the Feingolds' house was worn down because so many of the hide-and-seek games were played there. Dena, Russ and the other kids could walk or bike to just about anyplace they wanted to go in Janesville. All the public schools Russ attended were within walking distance. Downtown, with its movie theaters, Woolworth's and the library, was only about a mile away. Nearly across the street from the Feingolds' was Vista Park, a square block of level, green grass where you could hang out, play sports and, in the summers, enjoy arts-and-crafts and other programs offered by the Janesville Department of Recreation. Vista Park also had a drinking fountain, and older boys would terrorize younger ones by "kidnapping" them, setting them on the fountain and turning on the water. That was about as violent as things got among Russ's circle of friends or, for that matter, among most of Janesville's kids growing up in the 1950s.

Russ's bedroom was in the back of his house, overlooking the fruit trees and bushes and a large willow tree. His room was also above the kitchen, and he recalls being awakened by the clanking of pots and pans as his mother made breakfast. "To this day, I am immune; I can wake up and go back to sleep seventeen times a night." Her children regarded Sylvia as a wonderful cook, although she wasn't so sure. But even she admitted that her pies were exceptional. Everybody thought her pumpkin pie was superb. But Dave's top choice was the apple or cherry, while Russ's favorite was lemon meringue.

On a typical evening when Feingold was growing up, his parents were home by five o'clock, and everybody was seated at the dinner table shortly thereafter. His mother did all the cooking, as well as everything else around the house, her children remember. By all accounts, Leon and Sylvia were a great match, two people with shared values and superior intellects. But Leon also was an old-fashioned traditionalist, the undisputed head of the house, who left the domestic duties to his wife. After dinner, he often disappeared downstairs to read. Gregarious and even jovial in public, he tended to be quiet, sober and reserved at home. Politics was often the dinnertime topic, but there were frequently others that reflected the range of Sylvia's and Leon's interests. Both loved the theater, art and music. Opera regularly filled the Feingold house, and they drove to Chicago periodically to attend performances by the Lyric Opera and the Chicago Symphony. The theater productions that the Feingolds took their growing children to see in Chicago or Madison often had political or social themes, such as *Sunrise at Campobello, Inherit the Wind* and *The Diary of Anne Frank*.

Another of Leon's passions was baseball, specifically the Chicago White Sox. On a summer night, you could find him on the front porch, sometimes with Russ or Dave, listening to a Sox game on the radio. Being a White Sox fan in Janesville was unusual; most locals who followed baseball in the 1950s became Milwaukee Braves fans after the team moved from Boston in 1953. In looking back on his Janesville childhood, Feingold jokes that he was different from most of his classmates in three ways: "I was one of the only Democrats, I was one of the only Jews, and I had some sports affiliations that were out of the mainstream." As a young kid, he says, "the most dangerous was being for any Chicago team." To another child, being something of a lone wolf on such important matters as politics, religion and sports might have felt uncomfortable. Russ Feingold, even as a very young child, reveled in it. "I have always been sort of a renegade by nature," he says.

And like his dad, he also relished being from Janesville and being connected to its people and history. His dad made the simple things seem special, even romantic. Feingold treasures the memories of his family buying fresh eggs every Wednesday from a friendly farmer; local milk from one of the dairies; vegetables from Ritter's farm. In the third grade at Roosevelt Elementary School, one of Feingold's favorite teachers, Clarice Bergerson, had a gift for making not only Janesville history but the discipline itself come alive. "She taught me to enjoy history," says Feingold, who recently visited Bergerson in Strum, Wisconsin, where she has retired. "She also made me believe that Janesville was possibly the most significant place in American history because Carrie Jacobs-Bond was born here, Chief Black Hawk used to hide out here, and the man who did the first open heart surgery was born in Janesville." Rusty was so inspired by his teacher, and so knowledgeable about local history, that when the Feingolds hosted out-of-town visitors, especially Leon's judicial and political friends, the eight-year-old narrated the historical car tours of his hometown.

Yes, life was sweet, simple and comfortable for the Feingolds and their Janesville neighbors as the 1950s came to a close. But the next decade—indeed, the sudden arrival of a new era—was going to provide a challenge even to families as cohesive, loving and committed to social justice as were the Feingolds.

CHAPTER 3

THE SIXTIES COME TO
1207 VISTA AVENUE

When the 1960s began, tranquillity still reigned in Janesville. To be sure, the turbulent 1960s were still a few years off for most Americans. In 1960, there were no signs of a divisive war halfway around the world, and few signs of a major social upheaval at home, although in February of 1960, in Greensboro, North Carolina, and Nashville, Tennessee, black college students launched lunch counter sit-ins to challenge white supremacy. But if you lived in Janesville, where there were even fewer blacks than Jews, those student protests seemed far away and hardly prophetic. In that respect, the view of the world from Janesville in 1960 was probably not much different than it was from the living rooms of most white Americans in the North.

When social change came to Janesville in the 1960s, it came slowly at first. One seemingly small yet telling incident involved Gilbert Carleton, the pastor of one of Janesville's four Catholic parishes, St. John Vianney.

Carleton was one of the youngest Catholic pastors when he came to town in the 1950s to lead the newest parish on the southeast side. The oldest Catholic church, St. Patrick's, on the west side of the Rock River, had been an Irish parish. Next came St. Mary's, a German parish, on the east side of the river. As in the Catholic parishes that had been organized in the late nineteenth century in big cities such as Milwaukee and Chicago, Janesville's early Catholic parishioners belonged to a parish based on their ethnicity, and that often shaped social relationships as much as religion.

In Janesville, there was also some social distance between the town's Catholics and Protestants. Janesville native Tim Cullen, who later served on the City Council and was one of Russ Feingold's first political mentors, recalls that there was still little interaction in the 1950s between Catholic clergy and their counterparts at the Congregational, Methodist and Lutheran churches. He also recalls how religious differences could show up in unexpected places. He was about ten years old—this would have been in the mid-1950s—and playing with his friends several blocks from where the Feingolds lived. Among his buddies, he recalls, "My brother and I were the only Catholics. I think the rest of them were Lutherans. And we had a great time growing up." But he remembers that on one summer day, "the kids in the neighborhood were having a meeting in this house, which was next door to us. And I can remember my brother and I staying outside [because] they said the meeting wasn't for Catholics. That had to have come from their parents, because we got along fine. I don't think it ruined my day, but it made an impression on me."

Some of Janesville's old religious divisions and attitudes started to change in the late 1950s and 1960s, around the time of Vatican II. It was then, Cullen recalls, that one day the extroverted, ecumenical Father Carleton joined Janesville's venerable YMCA. In some ways, Carleton was a man about town, hanging out with some of Janesville's well-to-do one day, and shooting craps at the Elks

Club with a different bunch the next day. But the Y, where many of Janesville's movers and shakers went to swim and kibitz, had been a place that many Catholics avoided. To them, the Y represented unfriendly, anti-Catholic history. On July 1, 1899, the evangelical Protestant Gideons held its first organizational meeting there. The Gideons' link to Janesville was a native son, John H. Nicholson, one of three Christian traveling salesmen whose vision would eventually result in Gideon Bibles—the King James version—being placed in hotel room nightstands from Janesville to Jakarta. But when Father Carleton joined the YMCA and jumped into its swimming pool, decades of taboo were washed away.

It was also about this time, in 1966, that Leon Feingold became president of the Janesville Rotary Club, the town's most prestigious civic organization. In the 1960s, the Rotary Club's meetings and its civic activities brought together the town's leading professionals and top businessmen at a time when many businesses were still locally owned. Russ Feingold recalls that his father enjoyed taking him to club meetings and that becoming president was "one of [his] biggest thrills ever, something he was terribly proud of, [because] he never thought they would make him president." After all, this was still a town where the local country club, one of the nation's oldest, did not admit Jewish members. Leon Feingold's emergence as the first Jewish president of the Rotary Club, and perhaps the first Democrat, was another sign that Janesville, like the rest of the country, was changing.

For Russ Feingold, growing up Jewish in Janesville in the 1960s was a positive experience, he says. From teachers and others, he often had the feeling that "I was honored because I was Jewish. It was an amazing way to be treated." And his Jewish friends in town also say they have fond memories of community and school life.

Jewish education was an important part of Feingold's upbringing, as it was for his siblings. Because he and his sister Dena were only two years apart, they were often in the family car together in the 1960s when their father drove them to Sunday school at Temple Beth El in Madison. "Dena and I were two peas in a pod," Feingold says about their closeness growing up. At Sunday school and in the Beth El congregation, the discussions and sermons were frequently about social and political issues related to civil rights, the Vietnam War and other contemporary topics. "I understood my religion as the pursuit of justice," Feingold says. That was a widely shared view in the Feingold family and included, of course, his uncle, the prominent Chicago rabbi Louis Binstock, who attended Feingold's bar mitzvah in Madison. Nobody could have guessed on that day that there would be another rabbi in the family—in fact, a historic one. For in 1982, Dena Feingold became the first woman rabbi in Wisconsin.

In Russ Feingold's formative years, as a boy and even into young adulthood, nobody outside of his parents was as influential in shaping his understanding of current issues and politics as his older brother, Dave. And as the 1960s unfolded, Dave was often *the* most influential.

Like all the Feingold children, David Binstock Feingold was very smart, studious and popular. Dave was born in 1945, three years after Nancy. Their mother often said there were two sets of children—the older ones, who grew up when the family's financial fortunes were often precarious, and then Russ and his sister Dena. Nancy, who went off to college when Russ started the second grade, was not only smart but a fair-skinned beauty. Some said she was the most beautiful girl at Janesville High School.

Dave was eight years older than Russ but, if anything, the difference in age made their relationship closer rather than more distant in the late 1950s and 1960s. Dave was the kind of sensitive, thoughtful older brother who was interested in mentoring Russ, and Russ was the kind of precocious little brother who was eager to be mentored.

As kids, they spent endless hours playing games around the Feingold house. One was basketball—at first there was a hoop in the backyard and then one above the garage door. The basketball games, whether one-on-one or H-O-R-S-E, were very competitive. Both Russ and Dave recall that when somebody was winning a lot, the other person escalated the stakes so he could claim a bigger victory. One of them would say, "Okay, let's play for Vista Avenue." And then the loser of that game would say, "Okay, let's play for Janesville." And the next game would be for the year or the entire decade. But a series of games would invariably end up, they remember, as the championship of "time and space" because, Dave explained, "there was no higher or further that we could go. And later we'd try to remember who was the champion of time and space, and I would often claim to be the champion when I wasn't."

Their razzing and sometimes witty repartee were part of the fun, at least for Dave. Russ recalls their Ping-Pong games when his older brother showed him no mercy. "I would get on a losing streak and start making excuses. I'd say, 'You know, Dave, I'm not doing very well because I have a headache.' And Dave, who wasn't wearing his glasses, would say, 'Well, gee, I can't even see your head.'" And then there was the time when Russ's brother delivered a heavy dose of deflating realism. In 1959, when Dave was fourteen, he went to Chicago with their dad to see a rarity in Major League Baseball: a Chicago White Sox World Series game. When they got back to Janesville, Russ, who was six, was all excited about going the next year. But his big brother, as big brothers sometimes will do, stuck a needle into his ballooning hopes. "Rusty, I hate to tell you this," Dave remembers saying, "but the last time the Sox won the pennant was 1919, and this is 1959. It will be forty years before the Sox win again. And he was just crushed." As it turned out, Dave's prediction was only off by six years, but when the White Sox finally made it back to the World Series in 2005, Russ and Dave saw a game together.

While they shared fun and games growing up, Russ remembers there was also serious interaction. "Dave took a huge interest in kind of bringing me along," Russ says. Around the time that Russ was in the fifth grade and Dave was starting college, Russ recalls that his brother began using the Socratic method to force him to think critically about his assumptions and propositions. And Dave pushed his younger brother intellectually—he had Russ reading and thinking about George Orwell's *Animal Farm* and *Burmese Days* before Russ graduated from elementary school. "I thought, why would he give [these kinds of books] to me if he didn't think I could handle it," Russ says. "I think he opened my mind to my potential at a much earlier age than would have happened normally."

By the time Dave graduated from Janesville High School in 1963, he had racked up a stellar record as a student and leader. As a senior, he was president of the Student Council. One day the principal called him into his office and ordered Dave to have the Student Council adopt a new, more restrictive student dress code. Dave dutifully consented, but only a few years later—and even to this day—Dave Feingold was chagrined by his unquestioning, obedient response to an authority figure's fiat. But that's the way it was, often enough, in the spring of 1963, before the 1960s really began. Not many years later at the same high school, when Russ Feingold was elected Student Council president, the dress code would be thoroughly debated, discussed and changed.

In college, Dave Feingold was inspired by the civil rights movement and its heroic young leaders. In 1966, he joined a YMCA program at the University of Wisconsin that sent Dave and about thirty others to Chicago for the summer. Dave lived with a black family on the West Side, worked on a tenant-union organizing project and, during those historic months, joined in Martin Luther King, Jr.'s., marches to protest housing discrimination in the city. That summer, the Chicago Freedom Movement, King's first civil rights campaign in the North, officially kicked off with an outdoor rally at cavernous Soldier Field on a brutally hot July day. Driving down from Janesville to be part of the big event with Dave were his parents and thirteen-year-old Russ and sister Dena.

King captivated Russ and, along with hearing Dave's many stories of his Chicago experiences that summer, Russ began learning about all the civil rights figures and thinking of them, he says, "like they were saints." Indeed, fighting housing discrimination in Chicago required a saintly resolve. Dave recalls marching with King on one of the frightening days when angry white mobs, violently opposed to blacks moving into their neighborhoods, threw rocks and bottles at the interracial marchers.

A remarkable woman from Chicago's West Side, Josephine McCord, and her husband, Leo, headed the family with whom Dave lived that summer. Not only was she an enthusiastic, charismatic figure in the Chicago civil rights movement, but she was also raising ten children. That summer, Dave invited some of the McCord children to stay with his family in Janesville. They all had a wonderful time, but Dave remembers that when his mother took five young McCords to the Toot 'n Tell, a little drive-in restaurant, the man in the next car just stared and gawked the whole time. In monochromatic Janesville, the McCord kids were an exotic sight.

Soon after Dave Feingold's civil rights summer, he recounted his Chicago experiences in a speech at the 75th anniversary meeting of the Janesville YMCA. He not only described the racial discrimination and its dehumanizing effects he witnessed in Chicago, but he also implored business and civic leaders sitting in front of him to do more about addressing Janesville's own racial short-comings. "We must take a look at Janesville, its industries and homes . . . to see if they are really open," he urged. But, of course, they weren't very open, especially when it came to housing opportunities. If you were black and worked at the GM plant in the late 1960s or '70s, you probably drove to work from your Beloit home about ten miles away. As far back as the 1920s, town leaders wanted no part of racial integration. As the *Gazette* reported on July 14, 1920: "To relieve Janesville of conditions such as are arising in Beloit and other rapidly expanding industrial cities of the north, the Janesville Realty Board . . . placed itself behind a movement to devise a plan to keep the colored man in his place."

As the 1960s unfolded, some of Janesville's leaders were struggling to overcome its exclusionary past. In 1966, guest speakers at the Chamber of Commerce's 50th anniversary dinner included a diverse group of women—two Jews, an African-American, a Protestant and a Catholic—who were traveling around the country promoting religious and racial equality. Combating racial discrimination was on the agenda of a new interfaith group called the Janesville Dialogue. By 1968, the Janesville City Council adopted an open housing ordinance after a push from the Janesville Area Human Rights Council and the League of Women Voters. But when it came to actually implementing racial integration, Janesville and Chicago and most other American towns and cities had much in common. Tim Cullen, who has lived in Janesville his entire life, regrets his hometown didn't do more to break down racial barriers years ago so that by now there would be a more sizable black middle class and a more diverse community. Janesville had a hard time fully embracing the interracial message that twenty-two-year-old Dave Feingold preached that evening at the YMCA.

Within the Feingold family, the civil rights movement was a

unifying force; it represented their most cherished values of fairness, opportunity and individual dignity, which stretched across at least three generations. To them, it embodied the highest ideals of the American democratic tradition and Reform Judaism. But the Vietnam War, the other momentous political event that shaped the 1960s in America, was another matter entirely. For the first and only time, the closely knit Feingold family was split, with Leon on one side and Dave and Russ on the other. The "Generation Gap" of the 1960s had come to 1207 Vista Avenue, and it was painful.

Overlapping Dave Feingold's civil rights work in the mid-1960s was his intensifying opposition to the Vietnam War. Like many young Americans, his growing anger was sparked by a sense of betrayal. In the 1964 presidential election, Lyndon Johnson defeated Barry Goldwater in a landslide, in part because of Goldwater's bellicose views on foreign affairs in general and on Vietnam in particular. Compared to Goldwater, Johnson sounded like the peace candidate. But privately, in the summer before the election, Johnson and his advisors were planning to expand the U.S. role in Vietnam. And before the presidential election, Johnson maneuvered Congress into giving him new war authority by misrepresenting a military encounter with the enemy in the Gulf of Tonkin off the Vietnam coast. Only two skeptical U.S. senators, Wayne Morse of Oregon and Ernest Gruening of Alaska, had the courage to vote against the Tonkin Gulf Resolution. The results were swift and dramatic: while there had been only 23,000 U.S. military "advisors" in Vietnam in 1964, the number of U.S. military personnel exploded to 184,000 by the end of 1965, and to 450,000 a year later. And as the number of American soldiers in Vietnam mushroomed, so, too, did American casualties, opposition to the military draft and the antiwar movement.

The University of Wisconsin's Madison campus would become

a hotbed of antiwar activity. Dave Feingold returned to the campus for his junior year in 1965, and soon organized and became president of one of the early campus antiwar groups, Americans for Reappraisal of Far Eastern Policy. The group was part of a national network created by activists such as Allard Lowenstein, who also became a key leader in the "Dump Johnson" movement that would seek to replace Lyndon Johnson as the Democratic Party nominee in 1968.

Russ Feingold recalls visiting Dave's Madison apartment and absorbing the atmosphere of student protest and social change. Bob Dylan's provocative poetry floated through the air; Russ can still hear it and can mimic Dylan's delivery. His brother also introduced Russ to the protest music of the legendary folk singer Phil Ochs, whose stirring stanzas of "I'm Gonna Say It Now" Russ can recite verbatim:

> *Oh I am just a student, sir, and only want to learn*
> *But it's hard to read through the risin' smoke of the books that you*
> *   like to burn*
> *So I'd like to make a promise and I'd like to make a vow*
> *That when I've got something to say, sir, I'm gonna say it now . . .*
>
> *I've read of other countries where the students take a stand*
> *Maybe even help to overthrow the leaders of the land*
> *Now I wouldn't go so far to say we're also learnin' how*
> *But when I've got something to say, sir, I'm gonna say it now*

In the spring of 1967, with the military draft looming, Dave Feingold made a decision: he was going to seek conscientious objector status with the Rock County draft board and perform alternative service. His father was very unhappy—in fact, extremely upset—with Dave's decision. The day of reckoning between father and son was played out in a tearful confrontation at home. And fourteen-year-old Russ was more than a mere bystander.

For Leon Feingold, his son Dave's decision was deeply disturbing, even threatening on more than one level. For starters, Leon Feingold was not an antiwar Democrat, and he did not agree with Dave's antiwar views. He was never in favor of dumping Johnson. Nor was he ever a fan of Eugene McCarthy or Robert Kennedy, the antiwar Democrats vying for the Democratic presidential nomination in the winter and spring of 1968. After Johnson announced he would not seek reelection, Leon supported Hubert Humphrey, Johnson's vice president. And he was not pleased that his other son, Russ, had become a big Bobby Kennedy backer, with Bobby's photo hanging on his bedroom wall. Among other things, Leon had never forgiven Bobby Kennedy for being one of Joe McCarthy's lawyers on his Senate committee.

Across the country, the political differences over the Vietnam War that fractured the Democratic Party also fractured friendships and families. But Russ recalls that the big drama in his house wasn't about "Lyndon Johnson versus Hubert Humphrey versus Robert Kennedy and Eugene McCarthy. For me it was about my dad versus my brother. [It was a] terribly tense situation." Indeed, in the spring of 1968, Leon's strong objections to Dave's very public opposition to the war and military service were not only about political differences; they were also about personal ramifications in Janesville and beyond. As Dave says, "For my father, especially, it was just scary to be out that far, you know, living in a small community." Janesville was not only a conservative community; it was also very patriotic. After World War II, more than ten thousand citizens turned out for the dedication of a downtown memorial to the Janesville 99, members of a tank company who were sent to the Philippines, where they "endured some of the war's worst conditions and tortures." Sixty-four did not survive.

The climactic conversation that day in the Feingolds' living room between Leon and Dave, with Russ sitting nearby on a couch, was difficult and heated. Leon was worried about the stigma Dave's decision might leave on his family and, especially, on his sons—and Leon made it very clear to Dave that he was talking about the impact of the decision on Russ's future, too.

When the confrontation between Dave and his dad ended in a tense stalemate, Dave embraced Russ on the couch. He knew that Russ supported him. Many years later, Feingold says that both his dad and brother were "two completely sincere people" who at the time were looking at the world from very different perspectives. "My dad believed in America and all the values that I still believe are possible, but Dave was talking about some of the problems." And the "problem" of an escalating war in Vietnam had intruded into the Feingolds' lives and couldn't be ignored. Dave, with no help from his father, successfully petitioned the draft board and then found an approved, alternative service site in Chicago with the Urban Training Center for Christian Mission. For the next two years, he worked in low-income neighborhoods with street gangs and other youths, fighting racial discrimination and learning new community organizing skills.

Leon and Dave's wounded relationship healed nicely and naturally not long after their showdown. In Janesville, there would be no negative community repercussions to Dave's stand against the war and draft. Maybe it was because opposition to the Vietnam War, even in a place like Janesville, became more familiar as the war dragged on. To be sure, a majority of the town probably continued to support it—as a rough gauge, Richard Nixon would carry Janesville in 1972 (as he had four years earlier). But by the late 1960s, increasingly visible signs of antiwar activity were appearing on the banks of the Rock River—and one of the antiwar demonstrations even featured a surviving member of the Janesville 99.

★ ★ ★

Russ Feingold went to bed early on a Tuesday night after studying for his math exam, his last exam before graduating from Marshall Junior High School. It was Tuesday, June 4, 1968, which was also the night of the all-important Democratic presidential primary in California. If Bobby Kennedy won, his chances were good of winning his party's nomination at the party's convention in Chicago that summer. In Chicago, the word was spreading that Dick Daley, the powerful mayor and political kingmaker, had told Bobby he was going to announce his support for him if he took California. Since it was going to be late in Wisconsin before the California votes were counted, Feingold would find out in the morning if his hero had won.

Feingold was barely awake when his mother delivered the horrifying news in his bedroom, and his immediate, agonized scream carried through the house. Now two of his heroes had been gunned down within two months. In April, he had watched Bobby Kennedy on television give an extemporaneous eulogy in a black neighborhood in Indianapolis, just after Martin Luther King, Jr., had been assassinated in Memphis. It was supposed to have been a political rally for Kennedy, and when he stood up to speak on a flatbed truck on a cold, windy night, the crowd had not yet heard about the Memphis shooting. "I have bad news for you, for all of our fellow citizens, and people who love peace all over the world," Kennedy began, "and that is that Martin Luther King was shot and killed tonight." The audience gasped in disbelief and horror. In the next ten minutes, Kennedy then gave one of the most moving, heartfelt speeches that a generation of Americans had ever heard.

"Martin Luther King dedicated his life to love and to justice for his fellow human beings, and he died because of that effort," Kennedy said. And after telling his audience that it appeared white people were responsible for King's death, Kennedy continued: "For those of you who are black and are tempted to be filled with hatred and distrust at the injustice of such an act, against all white people, I can only say that I feel in my own heart the same kind of feeling. I had a member of my family killed, but he was killed by a white man. . . . But the vast majority of white people, and the vast majority of black people in this country want to live together, want to improve the quality of our life, and want justice for all human beings who abide in our land. Let us dedicate ourselves to what the Greeks wrote so many years ago: to tame the savageness of man and to make gentle the life of this world. Let us dedicate ourselves to that, and say a prayer for our country and for our people."

At one of the nation's worst moments, millions of Americans had seen Bobby Kennedy at his best, speaking not only for himself but also expressing the grief and sorrow, fears and hopes of all Americans of goodwill. In a country of 200 million people, only Bobby Kennedy could have reached the hearts of so many of his fellow citizens that night in Indianapolis. Russ Feingold, barely a teenager, was among them. "I just loved the guy," he says. There was something about him—"he seemed too shy to be in politics," Russ says thinking about his memory of Kennedy. To Feingold, there was something unique about Bobby Kennedy that was at once calming and yet exciting, something that suggested America could yet live up to its democratic ideals. On that early June morning in his bedroom, Feingold "slammed my fist down on that trundle bed I had and said to myself, I'm not going to let these sons of bitches who killed King and Kennedy [stop their work]. I'm going to do this. I'm going to be the guy who goes out and tries to continue their work in some way. I had no idea it would ever be this."

CHAPTER 4

NOT TOO SERIOUSLY

Well before high school, Russ Feingold's friends noticed personal qualities that set him apart. Barbara Block, who lived across the street, recalls that it was Feingold who took the initiative and organized a stamp club when they were in the fourth or fifth grade, rounding up about a dozen Roosevelt Elementary School classmates and presiding over stamp-trading meetings at his house. Several years later, Feingold resuscitated a moribund B'nai B'rith Youth Organization chapter in southeastern Wisconsin, which soon won an award for best in the region. When he was twelve, he made a big, lasting impression on Barbara Wexler, whose family had just moved to Janesville from upstate New York. She didn't know anybody, and she was starting school in the middle of the year, scared to death about her first day at Marshall Junior High. When she arrived with a ton of butterflies in her stomach, a handful of Jewish students were there to greet her. But the one who stood out was Russ Feingold. He extended his hand and with the warmest, most reassuring smile said: "Welcome to Marshall, we've been expecting you."

When Feingold walked into Craig High School in September of 1968 for the first day of class as a tenth-grader, it was already familiar territory. It was the same building where his sister Nancy and brother, Dave, went to high school. Feingold says that when he started at Craig, it felt like he had already been there. But when his sister and brother attended, it was called Janesville High School and was the only high school in town. In February of 1968, a second, new high school was opened on the West Side to accommodate the burgeoning baby boomers. A flip of a coin decided the names of the two high schools. The new building became the home of Parker High School, named after George S. Parker, the founder of the Parker Pen Company, and the old Janesville High was renamed after Joseph A. Craig, who had brought General Motors to town. The local captains of industry ranked right up there with Teddy Roosevelt in Janesville's pantheon of notables.

Many Americans who attended public high schools in the 1950s and 1960s went to one that was a lot like Craig. A two-story, mid-century brick building, Craig housed some 1,500 students spread over three grades. The school day was divided into seven class periods, including mandatory study halls from which one could not leave to go to the bathroom without a hall pass. Tom Joynt, a young history teacher at the time, recalls that maintaining control of students was one of the school administration's highest priorities, if not the highest. Academically, students were rigidly divided—or tracked—into ability groupings. The highest, Level One, included an interdisciplinary humanities course and some of the best teachers. If a Level One student received an A in a course, it was worth more points than an A in a lower-level course, which puzzled some students. Tom Joynt also recalls that older, worn textbooks were given to lower-level students—and that when a student walked around school with an old, red-covered history text, it was a dead giveaway that he or she was not one of the smart kids.

If a student had some inspiration and gumption, like Chuck Arneson, he could break out of the academic caste system. A classmate of Feingold's, Chuck recalls he was only an average student at Marshall Junior High School, and was placed into lower-level courses when he came to Craig for the tenth grade. But he soon realized that most of his friends—Russ Feingold, Greg O'Hara, Tim Green, Greg MacDonald—were heading for college and were in higher-level courses, and that's the direction he wanted to take, too. "I marched into the guidance counselor's office and said, 'I need to get out of these three-credit classes.' And I did," Chuck says. As stratified as Craig—and Janesville— could be, Chuck Arneson, Russ Feingold and many of their classmates remember having friendships with students of different social and economic backgrounds. For Chuck, whose father was a foreman in the composing room at the *Gazette*, these friendships changed the course of his life.

When Russ Feingold says he had "a blast" in high school, and that they were among the best years of his life, some of those recollections are about the social scene. Sports were big at Craig—in Feingold's senior year, the Cougars' football and basketball teams won conference championships. Going to football games at old Monterey Stadium, with the GM plant visible beyond the south end zone, was great fun. He was not on a team but went to all the games and was an enthusiastic fan. After the games, "jams" or dances were held in Craig's J-Room or student commons, where Feingold would show up with his girlfriend, who became editor of the school paper. In Feingold's senior year, there was also a Christmas formal with Yuletide decorations and a "Look of Love" theme for the Valentine's Day dance. House parties were popular, and at one memorable party at Sue Wexler's house, somebody spiked the punch. Before the night was over, the guests were in a playful, prankish mood. Feingold hid a bag of Cheetos in Mrs. Wexler's clothes dryer. Much to her surprise, the next time she threw in a load of clothes, they came out Cheeto orange. To this day, when

Feingold visits Mrs. Wexler, he brings her a bag of Cheetos, for old times' sake.

For many Janesville teenagers, and sometimes for Russ Feingold, the big amusement on Friday and Saturday nights was "riding the circuit," as it was called. In a scene out of *American Graffiti*, scores of cars loaded with teenagers paraded through downtown, heading east on Court Street across the Rock River and up the hill, and then west on Milwaukee Street back over the river, and then up Court Street again. The coolest cars were 1969 Camaro Super Sports, or the Chevelles with the huge 454 engines, or Mustangs and GTOs. Riding the circuit went on for hours, with boys looking for girls, girls looking for boys and both playing silly games. One was the so-called Chinese fire drill: when a car packed with passengers stopped for a red light, everybody got out, ran around the car and tried to get back inside before the light changed to green. After a night of riding the circuit, if you still had time before you had to bring your parents' car home, you might drive out Milton Avenue to the Interstate and have a burger at the Oasis, an all-night truck stop with a giant fiberglass cow out front, and Kelly, the waitress with a heart of gold, inside.

Russ Feingold may or may not have been the smartest kid in Craig's senior class when school started in September of 1970. He doesn't think so, although there was talk among Craig teachers that his IQ was 160 or more. "I got extremely good grades," he says, "but I was never the top student. There were three or four people who were truly off-the-charts brilliant." Throughout Feingold's life, that is the way he often characterized his intellect, as at least a notch or two below the "truly brilliant." But what made him distinctive in his social world was a potent combination of intelligence, an extraordinary capacity for hard work, and a steely determination not only to succeed but to leave his personal mark. All of the Feingolds were smart and talented, but Russ was beginning to reveal a fifth gear that was all his own. And two experiences in his senior year were indicative and prophetic.

Following in his brother's footsteps, he had joined the debate team as a sophomore. "Russ was a debater from the time he was born," says his sister Nancy. When Nancy was home from college and Feingold was only about seven or eight years old, she remembers their verbal jousting in the family car. Russ more than held his own, sometimes provoking Nancy. At which point she remembers her mother saying, "Nancy, he's just a little boy." Dave Feingold had been an excellent high school debater and, by his senior year, the team was pretty good, too—not quite as good as the top teams in the state but one of the best in recent Janesville history. Now, eight years later and in the summer before his senior year, Russ Feingold wanted his last debate team to be something special—and he had a perfect mentor to help him, Bill O'Brien, the recently arrived debate coach. Thirty years old, enthusiastic and intense, Bill O'Brien—"Wild Bill" is what Feingold and the other debaters called him—grew up poor in Neenah, Wisconsin, where his father was a mill worker at a paper company. Bill attended the local Catholic schools, studied speech communication in college, and knew the state's college and high school debate world. He and Feingold hit it off, becoming lifelong friends. O'Brien told Feingold that if he wanted the team to be more than pretty good, then he should begin by attending a summer debate institute. And that's what he did, declining an invitation to the Badger Boys State conference on government and politics and instead enrolling in a rigorous three-week session for high school debaters at the University of Wisconsin in Eau Claire. It was led by a highly regarded college debate coach, Grace Walsh, a sharp, diminutive character known to her friends as Gracie. She was also known for nodding off while judging college debates but somehow recovering in time to make the right decision. Feingold loved her slyly combative style; he remembers her telling him and the others that she was going to teach them "how to slip the blade in nicely." Feingold also learned about research methods and how to organize information. From O'Brien, he learned how to frame an argument and speak persuasively, not in the stereotypical machine-gun style of many high school and college debaters who fire out facts as fast as they can.

O'Brien was awed by Feingold's dedication. "He was just a brilliant student," O'Brien says. "But you match that native intelligence with his work ethic, it was really something." Before the debate season started, Feingold and some of his teammates made weekly research trips to the University of Wisconsin Law Library in Madison, pulling out of Janesville at sunrise on Saturdays. Those trips, as well as debate itself, had a big influence on one of the juniors on the team, Jackie Kinnaman, who was inspired to be a lawyer. "Russ was the one who set the standards," she remembers, "for how much research we were going to do, what kind of cases we were going to develop, and how many hours we were going to spend working on debate." During the week, they practiced at Craig and then Feingold and a small group would gather on weeknights for more practice before a weekend debate tournament. They drilled each other on the information they had collected on 4 × 6 cards. Feingold memorized everything in his enormous card collection. When a teammate called out the name or source of information that was on one side of the card, he could recite verbatim the quotation that was on the other side.

In Feingold's junior year, Craig's four-person, first-team debaters were unranked in the state. But going into his senior year, Feingold recruited two new additions to the team, Tom Cain and Andy Muzi. Both had been his friends since kindergarten. Tom, whose house was directly behind Feingold's, was a bright Janesville kid. Andy was about as un-Janesville as a teenager could be. Apart from his superior intellect—Feingold says Andy was one of the truly brilliant students at Craig—Andy stood out because he was the school's bearded, most prominent hippie. Indeed, he may have been the only one that year in the world of Wisconsin high school debate.

Early in the season O'Brien tried to keep the team hidden from the Wisconsin competition by taking it to tournaments in Illinois and Minnesota. The four-person team of Russ, Tom, Andy and David Miller did not win every match at first, but they started clicking and peaking at the right time. All schools debated the same topic: whether the federal government should establish, finance and administer programs to control air and water pollution. O'Brien wanted his best debater, Russ Feingold, to argue the first or second negative because it was the most difficult, requiring an extemporaneous response to the opposing team's affirmative case.

The perennial powers in Wisconsin high school debate were favored to battle it out again in 1971. So it was even something of an upset when the unheralded Craig Cougars made the final four in Madison. And when Milwaukee Marquette lost in the semifinals, Russ Feingold and his team were ready to take advantage of an opening: in a Cinderella-like ending, they knocked off Monona Grove and became the first Janesville high school to win the state championship. That was big news in Janesville, where a photo of Feingold and his team appeared on the *Gazette*'s front page.

That was not the only story involving Russ Feingold that made the Janesville newspaper in February of 1971. A week before the debate championship, a headline read: "Craig High Classes Are Disrupted." And as Craig's Student Council president, Feingold was right in the thick of the controversy.

Traditionally, high school student councils tended to be bland, predictable institutions. Getting elected president was usually a popularity contest—and Feingold was a popular guy. His predecessor as council president, Mickey Crittenden, says "the source of Russ's popularity was his personality." Not only did he make friends easily, Crittenden recalls, but in a school with the usual cliques of jocks, nerds, hoods and hippies, Feingold had friends in all the groups. "He was this skinny dude everybody liked," Crittenden says.

Unlike the placid times when his brother was Student Council president, Russ Feingold took office when student protest, and cries of "student power," were sweeping America's university campuses and sometimes trickling down to high schools. By the late 1960s, many of the most visible campus-based protests were directed against the Vietnam War, and some of those had turned violent. On the University of Wisconsin–Madison campus in August of 1970, a bomb exploded in Sterling Hall, which housed the Army Mathematics Research Center, killing a young researcher. But the Vietnam War was by no means the only target of protest. On many campuses, students, inspired by both the civil rights and antiwar movements, also protested educational policies they believed were undemocratic and unjust. The issues varied from campus to campus, but often included admissions policies (especially the admission of more black students), curriculum reform and codes of student conduct. The thread that ran through these protests was the demand that students should have a voice in a school's decision-making process. At their most energetic and heated, the student power tactics included demonstrations, class boycotts and sit-ins.

Russ, of course, identified with the great protest movements of the 1960s, and his year as Student Council president had just begun when he and others on the council challenged the Craig administration to change their restrictive dress code, which was unpopular with the students. By mid-September, for the first time girls were permitted to wear slacks and boys could dress in jeans. Throughout the year, Feingold led campaigns for other precedent-setting changes aimed at democratizing the school and making it more inclusive. His classmate Pete Duesterbeck, who had known him since elementary school, says that "one of the strengths I saw in Russ was that he would pick the nontraditional students and get them involved. I saw that as a real strength because these were people who were castoffs or they weren't recognized as the in-crowd." By the end of the school year, Russ Feingold and his Student Council allies published a five-page, single-spaced list of school reforms and other work they had implemented. But it was the "open campus" issue that roiled the school and the Janesville community.

During the fall semester, a symbol of general student discontent at Craig was the prisonlike enforcement of rules that snared students who were in the hallways between classes or who wanted to leave the building during study hall periods. The students' festering resentments came to a head one day when a teacher grabbed a student in the hallway and roughed him up. A rumor spread that the teacher broke the student's jaw. The relatively new Craig principal, William McBay, thinking he would calm the tense atmosphere, told a school-wide pep rally that if anybody had comments or concerns about school policies they should come to his office. Taking him up on his offer faster than he expected, one hundred or more angry students soon marched down the hall and into McBay's office, where fighting words were exchanged. Some students started moving the principal's desk as if they were going to overturn it. McBay, in a panic, hollered, "Where's Feingold?"

McBay assumed Russ Feingold had organized the protest, although Feingold says that's not how it happened. He knew that some friends had been talking about a protest but that when it began, it was spontaneous. He went with others into the principal's office and was there when McBay said to him: "What do they want?" "Open campus," Feingold fired back, realizing they had the principal in a vulnerable place. An open campus policy would allow students to leave the building and use their non-class time as they wished. "Well, you get on the intercom," Feingold remembers McBay saying, "and calm the kids down." As the *Gazette* reported the next day, "It had been announced over the public address system by Russ Feingold . . . that 'progress is being made.'"

But tensions remained high. The principal was certain that some disloyal teachers must have been giving Feingold tactical advice—he suspected both Bill O'Brien and Tom Joynt. McBay told Joynt: "You had to know something about this." But Joynt, who was a Student Council advisor, didn't know anything about it. An exasperated McBay shouted: "What in God's name is happening to us? We've got to get control."

Days later, Leon Feingold received a phone call from the school. "We have a report here that your son Russ is thinking of blowing up the high school," the caller said. Leon Feingold rarely used profanity; strong language for him was calling somebody he found truly reprehensible, such as Richard Nixon, a "phony." But he blurted out "Bullshit!" when he heard the preposterous falsehood about his son.

To resolve the demand for an open campus, principal McBay appointed a committee including Russ Feingold, other students, teachers and members of the Janesville community. But Feingold saw immediately the committee was stacked against him. Two of the student appointees, Mike Smith and Blair Jackson, though Feingold's friends, were on the other side of the open campus issue. And one of the adults, perhaps the first among equals on the committee, was Jane Cullen. Jane Cullen, who was not related to Russ Feingold's eventual mentor Tim Cullen, came from one of the most prominent, wealthy Republican families in Janesville. These Cullens were at the top of Janesville's conservative social and political establishment. No doubt Jane Cullen would uphold traditional school rules and the authority of the principal to enforce them. But that's not what happened. In the committee meetings, Cullen listened to Russ Feingold's arguments—especially, that if students were given greater freedom, they would have to prove they could use the freedom responsibly, and that educating young people to be responsible citizens was a traditional value of public education. At some point, Cullen uttered the unthinkable: "You know, I think Rusty's right." That remains one of Russ Feingold's fondest high school memories, along with the pro–open campus presentation that Jane Cullen and Feingold made together to the Janesville school board. The "trial" period for a new open campus that the school board approved has now endured for more than thirty-five years—and the open campus protest of 1971, and Russ Feingold's leadership of it, have become something of a legend at Craig High School.

When Russ Feingold was about to graduate in June, he and another student were honored as "Boys of the Month" at a Rotary Club luncheon. They were introduced by Craig's principal and, with Leon Feingold in the audience, the unforgiving McBay said of Russ: "I can't wait until he graduates so I can get my school back." He wasn't smiling, and he wasn't kidding when he said it. Russ was surprised and a little hurt by McBay's unyielding resentment. But, of course, the principal had inadvertently delivered a high compliment. Russ Feingold had, indeed, made a difference—and not only at the high school. The student protest at Craig prompted the *Gazette* to publish a three-part series on Janesville's schools in which many teachers and administrators acknowledged the need for more reforms, both in the classroom and broader school environment. Some reforms already on the drawing board were intended to make classroom instruction less generic and more tailored to the learning needs of individual students—so that, for example, all students, not just the college-bound, would be well served and respected.

A small stream of democratic reforms was starting to flow through the Janesville school system, the current running a little faster thanks to Russ Feingold's leadership. That leadership reflected both his passion for the democratic ideals he had absorbed from his family, and his identification with the civil rights movement and its heroes who sought to turn those ideals into reality. To be sure, Craig High School was a small stage, but the issues Feingold and his allies raised were important because they addressed the quiet inequalities that affected the lives of many students and, ultimately, the integrity of the school itself.

Tom Joynt, who later became superintendent of the Green Bay public schools and a university professor, was struck not only by how effective Russ Feingold had been as a seventeen-year-old political leader, but also by his uncommon courage. There was talk at Craig that one day Russ Feingold would be a senator or even run for president. In the nineteenth century, he might have skipped college and proceeded directly into the world of public affairs and reading the law. But following in the Feingold family tradition, he was headed to one of the country's great public universities, one that traced its ascendancy to the early-twentieth-century leadership of Wisconsin's visionary governor, Fighting Bob La Follette.

"Toto," said Dorothy, "I have an idea this isn't Kansas." That was the caption on the front page of the *Daily Cardinal* that welcomed Russ Feingold and some eight thousand other freshmen to the University of Wisconsin in September of 1971. Above the caption was a full-page, 1960s-style psychedelic drawing evoking the campus culture and the turbulent, bittersweet times. In the foreground were Toto and an innocent-looking Dorothy, small suitcase in hand, trying to make sense of a scene that might have been fanta-sized by the Wizard on acid. Among other hipsters, the Cowardly Lion was in repose smoking a joint. But in the background was an arresting reminder of researcher Robert Fassnacht's tragic death in the Sterling Hall bombing a year earlier.

The Sterling Hall episode had shaken the campus community like none other. The University of Wisconsin, with its long his-tory of student activism and progressive politics, had seen many large anti–Vietnam War protests in the second half of the 1960s. Some antiwar rallies and marches led to confrontations with police, and sometimes students and police were injured. Tear gas was a familiar campus aroma and lingered in many buildings for years. But even in the tensest public confrontations, such as the Dow Chemical protest on campus in 1967, nobody was killed. Sterling Hall was different. Not only was there a death, but the attack was carried out surreptitiously (later three young men were apprehended for the crime). It had come only months after the deadly violence on the Kent State University campus where four students were shot to death by Ohio National Guard troops.

With perhaps more campus violence on the horizon, Russ Feingold's parents had been worried about sending him to Madi-son, as people referred to the University of Wisconsin campus. Feingold recalls "there was a dinner conversation right after the bombing of Sterling Hall. My dad was upset, even though he was the biggest UW backer in the world." Symbolically, the tragedy was brought a little closer to the Feingolds' world when their own rabbi, Manfred Swarsensky, delivered Robert Fassnacht's eulogy in Madison. "May we have the inner strength to transmute tragedy into triumph, despair into hope, and death into life," the rabbi said. "Life is still worth living. America is still worth saving. This country is still man's last hope on earth." When Russ Feingold's father suggested he apply to Harvard instead of going to Wisconsin, Feingold was adamant: "I said, 'No way,' I always wanted to go to Madison, that was the way we were brought up. I loved the campus and to me the biggest loss in the world would have been if I did not go. . . . I was always destined to be a Badger."

Russ Feingold's years at the University of Wisconsin were surprising in at least two respects. The first had to do with the campus itself, and the second with his choice between politics and academics. After Lyndon Johnson's escalation of the Vietnam War, the University of Wisconsin became one of the most prominent antiwar campuses in the country. And after the Sterling Hall bombing in August of 1970, the years ahead seemed likely to be filled with more, not less, antiwar movement fervor. But the 1970–71 school year—the year before he arrived on campus— turned out be, mostly, the year of "grave calm," as a student writer characterized it. By midyear, CBS News called the *Daily Cardinal* office and asked an editor if the antiwar movement was over. The irreverent student-journalist shouted to the office: "CBS News wants to know if the movement is dead. Someone stick their head out the window and see." The movement was not yet dead, but it was diminishing in numbers if not emotion. Yes, May Day in Madison of 1971 saw antiwar protests, tear gas and demonstrators fighting with police. And at a simultaneous antiwar protest in Washington, D.C., some Madison residents were arrested, including a *Daily Cardinal* photographer and reporter. On campus, there were still antiwar leaders but, gradually, fewer followers, and that trend continued during Russ Feingold's freshman year, when his big extracurricular activity was not protesting the war but jumping into presidential politics.

The Wisconsin presidential primary was an important event on the national political calendar. In 1960, John Kennedy narrowly defeated Hubert Humphrey in an acrimonious battle on the way to winning his party's nomination. In 1968, two days before the

Wisconsin primary and with public opinion polls forecasting a resounding defeat for President Johnson, the president shocked the nation by announcing he would not run for reelection. The antiwar candidate Eugene McCarthy won the primary with 56 percent of the vote, setting the stage for the intraparty fight among him, Humphrey and Russ Feingold's hero, Robert Kennedy.

Now, nearly four years later, his sister Nancy gave him a book by Jerry Bruno, who had been a Bobby Kennedy advance man. Bruno's enthusiastic endorsement of John Lindsay as the man who could best bring Bobby's ideals into the White House immediately registered with Feingold. Lindsay, a former Republican congressman and New York City mayor turned Democrat, was indeed running for president as a Kennedy-like figure. His identification with civil rights and racial justice especially appealed to Feingold. Tall, handsome and urbane, Lindsay was also a vociferous critic of Richard Nixon's Vietnam War policies. "I thought Lindsay had charisma and style," Feingold says. "I thought he would be a great candidate."

Among Wisconsin antiwar Democrats, South Dakota senator George McGovern appeared to have the most support in the upcoming April primary, although other Democrats favored Edmund Muskie. But in the winter of 1972, Russ Feingold threw himself into the Lindsay for President campaign. He went down to Lindsay headquarters and said: "I want to organize the university." Over the next few months, he recruited some 150 Lindsay volunteers, he recalls. He worked side by side with his old high school classmate Pete Duesterbeck, who was also a freshman. And Russ recruited other old friends on campus, such as Ron Luskin, who was from Kenosha and had met Feingold when they belonged to Jewish youth groups. Luskin was surprised when Feingold started talking about running himself as a Lindsay delegate to the Democratic National Convention and recalls scratching his head and thinking: "We're going to ride to Kenosha on a Saturday to do what?" But sure enough, Feingold organized about twenty-five university students who lived in the First Congressional District, which included Kenosha as well as Janesville. "We showed up at the district convention and all of a sudden we elected Russ as a Lindsay delegate," remembers Luskin, still impressed that somehow his nineteen-year-old friend had pulled it off. Russ was also proud of the work he had done for the Lindsay campaign on the Madison campus. "I created this great organization. The plan was that Lindsay would do well by the time he came to Wisconsin [for the primary]. But the whole thing went to hell because he got creamed in Florida."

That was the end of John Lindsay's presidential career and also the end of Russ Feingold's political career on campus. His intense few months working for Lindsay, Feingold says, was the "only time in my academic career I stopped studying." He had two main goals: he wanted to be a top student, maybe Phi Beta Kappa, and he wanted to go to Harvard Law School.

The people who knew Russ Feingold best during his undergraduate years marveled not only at his herculean capacity for studying. His extraordinary personal discipline that allowed him to be much more than a nerdy bookworm also amazed them. Russ Feingold was the only student on campus in the early 1970s that Ron Luskin knew of who diligently carried a calendar book to organize his daily life. His college friend Enid Brenner teases Feingold now about how he even scheduled the precise amount of time he allotted for showering. He denies that, but doesn't quibble about being exceptionally well organized and disciplined.

Russ Feingold's daily routine didn't change much during his four years at the university. After his freshman year living in Sellery Hall, a university dormitory, he shared a second-floor, three-bedroom

West Dayton Street apartment near the campus with various room-mates over the next three years. The roommates typically included old friends, such as Luskin and Duesterbeck. Russ Feingold was on a noon-to-midnight academic schedule, avoiding morning classes if he could. When he was not in class in the afternoon, he was study-ing on the third floor of the new Helen C. White library near the Memorial Union. After a dinner break at his apartment, back he went to the library until midnight. "Russ had a pathway to that building," recalls Luskin, who cooked dinner every night during their junior year while Feingold and another roommate washed the dishes. On Saturdays and Sundays, Pete Duesterbeck remembers that Feingold would get up late in the morning and spend most of the day at Helen C. White, as everybody called it. Sometimes when he returned to his apartment, Feingold asked Pete to quiz him on what he had read. As he had done for high school debate, Feingold took notes on file cards. "He'd have this big stack," Pete remembers, "and he'd say, 'Hey, can you sit with me for a little while and drill me on some of this stuff.'"

Although Helen C. White and Russ Feingold were nearly inseparable, he had other relationships in his life, even when he was studying. The evenings at the library were group affairs. Fein-gold's girlfriend, Sue Levine, whom he met as a freshman, was usu-ally with him and sometimes his younger sister, Dena, who arrived on campus when he was a junior. A new friend was Mike Hughes, whom he got to know at the library.

Mike and Russ both grew up in southeastern Wisconsin, but otherwise they came from different backgrounds. Hughes was an athlete from Kenosha, where he was a star high school quarter-back. His father, who worked for more than thirty years at the American Motors automobile plant, passed along his love for fish-ing and hunting to his son. At Russ Feingold's house in Janesville, his parents didn't allow any of the children to have even a toy gun.

"Russ was inquisitive about everything," Hughes says. He wanted to hear Mike's stories about deer hunting or getting up with his dad at four in the morning to go salmon fishing on Lake Michigan. "He was fascinated with those kinds of stories." And Hughes was fascinated by Russ Feingold's academic dedication. Hughes gave up football after his freshman year and became a serious student. Feingold's study habits were a model for him. And although Hughes thought Feingold was "an academic machine," that was not all he admired and liked about him. "He was such a dichotomy," Hughes says, meaning that there was also a big, fun-loving side to Feingold that would kick in when studying was over. After a night at the library, Feingold says, "we'd stay out until four in the morning," drinking beer and talking about politics and sports at the Kollege Klub or the Stone Hearth. On weekend nights, there were small parties and, in the fall, football games at Camp Randall Stadium, which Feingold loved. Madison was a "much better place for me than a small private school, which would not have fit my personality," he says.

But it was not only the multitude of people and possibilities of a large, 35,000-student campus that suited him. Surprisingly for such a smart, seemingly self-confident, verbal young man, Russ Feingold much preferred the anonymity of the university's large lecture classrooms where he was intentionally invisible. "I did not want to spend a lot of time with the professors," he recalls. "I was the guy who sat in the back of the room. I never spoke in class. I was afraid to even be called on." Instead, he was going to show his stuff on exams, he says, an approach that worked perfectly until the end of his junior year.

Feingold, who had just completed the second semester of Joel Grossman's two-semester constitutional law course, made an appointment to talk with him about his final grade, an "A/B," which at the university was the equivalent of an A-minus/B-plus.

About two hundred students took the course, and teaching assistants did much of the grading. Grossman had never spoken to Feingold until he walked into the political science professor's office to complain about his grade, or so Grossman assumed. But Feingold came in not to complain, the professor soon discovered to his amazement, but to apologize for earning only an A/B. "That's not me," Grossman recalls him saying, explaining that he had received straight As since he came to Madison. Russ Feingold's visit was something of a confessional, Grossman thought, because Feingold felt he had betrayed his own standards. Grossman recalls Feingold telling him: "I don't know what happened, but it will not happen again."

Later, Grossman agreed to serve as Feingold's senior thesis advisor. In several respects, it was no ordinary senior thesis. First, it was extraordinarily well researched and insightful; it was one of the best theses Grossman had ever seen. Second, the provocative topic he selected and the way he approached it revealed his inclination for independent, against-conventional-wisdom thinking. Third, the conclusion he reached about the topic, the history and modern significance of the Second Amendment, would shape his views as a legislator when he dealt with the politically tricky issue of gun control.

Twentieth-century scholars had paid little attention to the Second Amendment and, by the 1960s and 1970s, it sounded like an anachronism: "A well regulated Militia, being necessary to the security of a free State, the right of the people to keep and bear Arms, shall not be infringed." While the Second Amendment had not attracted mainstream attention, the issue of gun violence in the 1960s moved onto the national political agenda. Congress passed the Gun Control Act of 1968, the first new, albeit limited, restriction on firearms since the days of Al Capone and Prohibition. In the aftermath of this modest measure, an emerging gun control movement pushed for stronger local and state gun restrictions. In May of 1974, one of those jurisdictions considering a handgun ban was the city of Madison.

The timing of Madison's proposed ordinance and Feingold's interest in the Second Amendment was only a coincidence, he writes in the preface to his thesis. "Nor was my decision to study the Second Amendment based on any special personal interest in the gun control movement. Rather, my objective . . . was to select a constitutional provision that had been either neglected or largely discredited while such provisions as the First, Fourth and Fifth Amendments were reaching central or even 'saintly' status in American law." Many years later, reflecting on all of this, Feingold recalls the mostly liberal students in Grossman's constitutional law class in the spring of 1974. "Everybody is wearing jeans and nobody is questioning anything. And finally I thought to myself, why is the Second Amendment not taken seriously? Why isn't it considered intellectually in the same breath as the rest of the Bill of Rights that all the liberals and progressives were saying should be expanded indefinitely?" The prevailing opinion at the time, at least among pro–gun control liberals, was that the Second Amendment did not confer an individual right but only a collective right of a militia or National Guard to bear arms. Feingold says: "I thought to myself, I bet that is not true. So I went and studied the origins of the Second Amendment."

He examined constitutional history, gun-related court cases, and, in the summer of 1974, with the help of a small research grant, traveled to Washington, D.C., where he interviewed a broad range of experts on various sides of the gun control debate. Back in Madison for his senior year, Feingold spent months developing his analysis and argument, the late-night sound of his typing echoing down a floor to Enid Brenner and her roommates.

Essentially, what Feingold concluded was that the Second

Amendment was, indeed, relevant to contemporary American society because it conferred an individual right to bear arms. The Bill of Rights, he argued, which was intended to restrict government power, was concerned with protecting individual, not collective rights. That included the right to a firearm, he was convinced. And nearly fifteen years after he wrote his thesis, some leading liberal scholars, such as Sanford Levinson and Laurence Tribe, came to similar conclusions regarding the Second Amendment debate over collective versus individual rights. "Basically," Feingold says now, "the assumption is someone should be able to have a weapon unless there is some overriding reason not to." (In practice, that has meant that although Senator Feingold has voted for some gun control measures, he has opposed others and is sensitive to restrictions that might overreach.)

After Joel Grossman read Russ Feingold's 315-page manuscript, he told Feingold that he should think about turning it into a book. Grossman also says that he would have given Feingold an A plus if the university had had a grade higher than A. Grossman, who is now a professor at Johns Hopkins University, says that Russ Feingold is one of the top five students he has taught in a forty-three-year career.

Feingold's senior thesis in political science, which he dedicated to his brother, Dave, and Robert Kennedy, might have been the ideal way to cap off a stellar undergraduate career. As a freshman, he had started in Integrated Liberal Studies, an interdisciplinary program that his sister Nancy and brother, Dave, had also taken. It ranged from the classics to physical science to contemporary literature. Eventually, he decided on a double major in political science and history. In retrospect, he thought he had received a great education—and except for that lone A/B in Grossman's class, he was a straight-A student. His only regret was not taking foreign languages. "The courses were early in the morning and I thought, nah, I don't want to do that." But he also thinks it was his little rebellion because foreign languages were so important to his mother. She had majored in French and spoke five languages fluently—and late in her life, she learned some Norwegian before taking a trip to Scandinavia. She picked it up so quickly that others in her Norwegian class asked her where in Norway her ancestors lived. Nonetheless, before his senior year was over, Russ Feingold achieved his two major academic goals: he made Phi Beta Kappa and was admitted to Harvard Law School.

During the fall of his senior year at Madison, Russ Feingold and his parents were attending Yom Kippur services at Temple Beth El in Madison when, during a break, Feingold jokingly mentioned to his father that he had received a letter inviting him to apply for a Rhodes Scholarship. He hadn't taken it seriously because he thought he was ineligible. Although he didn't know much about a Rhodes, he assumed the scholarship for study at Oxford University was only for athletes, and mainly Ivy League athletes. When his father asked him if he was going to apply, Russ said he had thrown out the application. Leon led them on a short walk down the hill to the Lake Wingra shoreline and said, "Why wouldn't you try for that?" He told Russ that being an athlete was not a prerequisite—and he recalled that one of his University of Wisconsin classmates who won a Rhodes was such an unathletic weakling that "he couldn't even lift a book." When Russ told his dad that he was eager to start law school, his dad told him that law school, even Harvard, could wait if he won a Rhodes.

Since Russ was certain he was not going to win, he was relaxed for the first round of Rhodes interviews, which went well. He advanced to the second round, which was also on the Madison campus, and that went well, too. Rather suddenly, he found himself in the third and final round of interviews in Chicago. And now he was facing Ivy Leaguers who lived in the Midwest. "I don't think any of us thought I was going to win this thing," Feingold says, referring to his family. His parents, and girlfriend, Sue, had come to Chicago with him. The night before the final interviews, Russ shared a room with his dad, who kept him awake much of the night, firing hypothetical questions at him. "He was driving me nuts," Russ remembers. In the morning, as he was about to leave the hotel, he became sick in the hotel lobby, but his mother put the little embarrassing episode into a more uplifting perspective: "Just like a racehorse before a big race," she told him reassuringly.

The final interviews were at the University Club at the University of Chicago and, for Russ Feingold, the way in which he handled the situation "was a major event in my life" because he learned on this memorable occasion that he could feel "confident in just trying to be myself." The Rhodes interview committee consisted of about a half-dozen men, and the first question came from a lawyer from a big Cleveland firm whom Russ had met the night before at a reception. He wanted to know why "you've spent all year writing a thesis on one of the most insignificant provisions in the Bill of Rights." And Russ quickly responded: "With all due respect, sir, I think you're wrong. The Bill of Rights is about limiting government power. I come from a state where gun ownership is a very important part of people's freedom and their way of life." And as Russ continued, in passionate command of his subject and with a nicely calibrated touch of aggressiveness, he detected by the lawyer's knowing nod that he had just won over one of the judges. Russ also noticed that the chairman of the committee, Barry Bingham, Jr., the publisher of the *Louisville Courier-Journal*, had smiled when "I had come back strong" in response to the lawyer's question. Now Bingham asked in a soft Kentucky drawl: "Mr. Feingold, you expressed an interest in the state of Israel and you wrote this paper about American attitudes toward Israel. Do you know what the Law of Return is?"

"Yes, I do, Mr. Bingham," Russ said. "It's the law that if you have a Jewish mother, that you have a presumptive right to be an Israeli citizen."

"Is that true in all cases?" Bingham asked.

"Well," Russ began, as he cleverly trumped Bingham's sly query, "there is the case of Meyer Lansky, the organized crime figure . . . ," and everybody laughed.

The committee's overall reaction to him had been so positive that suddenly Russ thought he couldn't lose, although he just as quickly tried to suppress his optimistic feelings. But a little later, when the twelve candidates were brought back into the room, they called out his name as one of the new Rhodes Scholars.

Russ's father was almost speechless when Russ told him the good news. "Wow!" was the first and only word he could summon. Later, in a newspaper story about Russ and his family, Leon said Russ was "just a plain kid who doesn't take himself too seriously." It was the quote that Russ most appreciated from his dad because it captured how he felt about himself, and how he hoped others would view him, regardless of his lofty academic achievements. His dad knew, Russ says, that "I wasn't Mr. Smarty Pants. He knew I wasn't a National Merit Scholar." All the more reason that Russ remembers being "really happy with myself because it was so far beyond anything I even thought [was possible]. It's not the direction that I expected my life to go."

In late September of 1975, Russ Feingold and the other Rhodes Scholars left New York on the *Queen Elizabeth 2*, sailing at sunset past the Statue of Liberty. "It was unbelievable," Feingold says, which captures his feelings not only about the glorious New York Harbor scene but also about actually standing there on the ship's thirteenth floor with his Rhodes companions.

When Feingold was a college sophomore, his parents had taken him and his sister Dena to Israel for ten days, but that was the only time he had traveled abroad. His geographical frame of reference was Wisconsin and on his first drive through the English countryside to Oxford University, he thought that "this looks like Wisconsin only kind of older." At Oxford, he was assigned to one of the colleges, Magdalen. "Each young man was given two huge rooms," he recalls. "One was a bedroom with its own sink and everything. The other was a sitting room overlooking the deer park at Magdalen College, with overstuffed couches and bookcases. Every morning the scout, or servant, comes and wakes you up. You think, 'Oh, this is great. She will bring you tea.' But the purpose was to get your butt out of bed. In other words, you could not put a 'Do Not Disturb' sign out. She would come in and yell, 'Russ.' She had a Welsh accent. 'Can I get you your tea?' It was like, get up and get to work."

The heart of the Oxford experience was the weekly tutorials. There were also voluntary lectures, which Feingold frequently attended, in part out of habit from his University of Wisconsin experience. For the tutorials, a student discussed a reading or essay he had written with his don. "In the tutorials," Feingold says, "you would come in with what was called a half-gown. That was required. You would wear your half-gown, and [the don] would wear his full gown." The meetings were either at the don's residence or in his college office. "You would trudge in and they would say, 'Good morning, Russ. How are you?' You would respond, 'Sir, good to see you.' They would say, 'Would you like a spot of sherry?' They would pour you a glass of sherry. They would ask, 'Would you like to read out your essay?' You would read out your essay. They would listen quietly. This is the test of whether you have done your work and if you are doing well."

At Oxford, friendships with other Rhodes as well as Marshall

Scholars were also an important part of the experience. Feingold played racquetball with Tom Friedman, the future *New York Times* columnist, and enjoyed the company of Mike Sandel, who became a Harvard University professor, and Scott Matheson, who lived below Feingold and whose father was the governor of Utah. But perhaps the most exhilarating part of the two-year Rhodes experience for Feingold was the travel. "The academics were great, and I loved being part of history," he says. "In my college, C. S. Lewis and J. R. R. Tolkien used to talk together along the paths. *The Decline and Fall of the Roman Empire* was written by Gibbon, maybe in the room where I stayed. I never got tired of that." But each Rhodes Scholar received a travel stipend, and after eight weeks of classes, the schedule called for a six-week break, plus four months off in the summer and plenty of time for exploring the world. He traveled widely—to Russia, the Middle East and throughout Europe. It was a classic broadening experience for a bright but insular young man for whom almost all of his first twenty-two years had been confined to the forty-five-mile ribbon of cornfields and dairy farms from Janesville to Madison.

Final exams were the culmination of the two years at Oxford and, for Feingold, they would be his only exams. He had skipped the practice exams that one could take at the end of each quarter. He had started one, but walked out because he didn't think he could do it. Indeed, he had begun to wonder if maybe he had spent too much time traveling or that he wasn't cut out for the law, which is what he was studying at Oxford. Final exam grades were scored as firsts, seconds, thirds and fail. Feingold says that his professors had him down for a third or maybe a second. After a year and a half of relative pleasure, "the last few months are just a terror because you know you're going to take forty hours of exams in a gown in one week," he says. "Then you do not find out the results for five weeks." When the day of reckoning arrives, the grades are posted for everybody to see. "You all walk in," Feingold recalls, "and I'm standing there with other people, and I am pushed forward. I look up and go, 'Oh, my God, I did not get a second.' I looked at the third. I am not there. I looked at the failed. By then, people are slapping me on the back. I had gotten a first. I was stunned." Not only that, but Russ Feingold won the award for the best examination in jurisprudence, which came with a £100 prize. "I could not believe it," he says.

Before starting Harvard Law School, Russ Feingold and his college girlfriend, Sue Levine, were married in Milwaukee, where her family lived. The wedding ceremony was held at the Levine family's conservative synagogue, Beth Israel. The ceremony, however, was conducted jointly by Beth Israel's rabbi, Herbert Panitch, and the Feingolds' Reform rabbi, Manfred Swarsensky, an unusual Conservative-Reform pairing. Perhaps one hundred or so people attended. After the wedding, Sue and Russ, who had traveled in Europe and elsewhere when he was studying in England, drove a few hours north and stayed in a lovely bucolic setting in Wild Rose, Wisconsin, not far from where his old friend Pete Duesterbeck lived.

Sue had received her master's degree from Columbia University, specializing in teaching the visually impaired. She worked at the Newton School for the Blind while Russ attended law school for two years (his law studies at Oxford had counted toward one of the three years at Harvard).

Feingold felt less like a typical Harvard Law student because he was newly married and because he was partially in the first-year class and partially in the second. He was in the same graduating class as future chief justice John Roberts, but didn't know him. His closest friends tended to be a few he knew at Oxford—one was Pete Carfagna, who was from Cleveland. Feingold recalls they played on "one of the worst intramural basketball teams in the history of Harvard Law School." As for his classes, he had some of Harvard's most prominent professors: Arthur Miller for civil procedure, Alan Dershowitz for criminal law, and Duncan Kennedy for American legal history. The truth was, however, that Russ Feingold was not only sick of studying; he couldn't wait to get back to Wisconsin.

CHAPTER 5

THE F.L.

Russ Feingold returned to Wisconsin to practice law and run for office but even some of his closest friends didn't understand just how eager he was to pursue his childhood dream. And many didn't fully appreciate that even though Feingold was a young man of modest means, material success paled in comparison with the appeal of public service.

Both Russ and Sue liked the Madison area and, after Russ graduated from Harvard Law School in 1979, that's where they looked for a place to live. Apartment hunting one day, they were driving down a hill on Madison's West Side and, at first, Russ didn't realize they had crossed the boundary line into Middleton. That's where they found an apartment they liked. By the time they signed the lease, Feingold knew exactly which State Senate district they would be living in—it included not only Middleton but Janesville, too. He remembers thinking: "Oh, my God, Janesville and Middleton. It was *the* perfect district." At the time, it was represented by one of the founders of the modern Wisconsin Democratic Party, Carl Thompson. But Thompson was old—"very old," Feingold thought—and perhaps ready to retire. Democrats who were more established than Feingold would undoubtedly be interested in succeeding Thompson, but that didn't stop a confident if not cocky Russ Feingold from feeling that "I could pull this off."

But at first, his new job occupied much of his time. He weighed offers from two Wisconsin law firms before deciding on the larger, Milwaukee-based Foley & Lardner. Being able to work on litigation was the main attraction, but Foley & Lardner also offered the higher starting salary, $21,000, an almost unbelievable amount, he thought, especially for somebody who had hardly a dime to his name. And then he received a call from Foley & Lardner, and remembers somebody saying: "We're sorry, Russell, but we're going to pay you $27,000." The Milwaukee firm wanted to keep pace with the new salaries in New York.

Russ Feingold was the seventh lawyer hired for Foley & Lardner's expanding Madison office. Several others arrived at about the same time—Harvey Temkin, David Harth and Steve Shimshak among them. They were all young, smart and energetic, and tended to see themselves as something of a departure from Foley & Lardner's image as an old-guard-Republican, corporate law firm. Harth, whose office was next to Feingold's, recalls that because it was a small, new branch office, "we didn't have a seasoned partner overseeing our work so we kind of made it up as we went along." They all worked hard, but Temkin recalls nobody worked harder than Russ Feingold—he would come into the office in the morning with legal briefs he had dictated at home that were ready for his young assistant, Nancy Mitchell, to transcribe. "Poor Nancy," Harvey often thought. Feingold was soon billing two thousand hours a year. "People liked him and he was very focused," Harth recalls. "It wasn't like he was just a dilettante spending a couple of years in a law office until he could pursue his real calling. He was a real grinder. He was committed to his cases."

Feingold was enjoying the legal work and his new cadre of

friends. His cases ranged from First Amendment issues for the *Milwaukee Journal* to pro bono work on behalf of an inmate at the Waupun state prison. Also, in 1981, he volunteered and successfully handled a political case, the attempted recall of a Democratic state senator, Tom Harnisch—and in the process, started developing political friendships that would prove helpful. Socially, Feingold, Harth and the others were a close-knit group; they hung out together and periodically convened at the old Salad Bar where they would hoist a few after work. It may have been at one of these bull sessions when they started joking about which one of them would stay the longest at the law firm. Harth, Shimshak and Feingold made a bet: the one who stayed the longest would get $25 from the other two. "I thought Russ would win the bet," Harth remembers thinking.

But less than three years after Russ Feingold started at Foley & Lardner, David Harth and everyone else was shocked when Feingold announced he was quitting the firm to run for the State Legislature. And just about everybody thought it was a bad idea. His peers and the senior partners at the firm essentially laughed at him, not taking him seriously at first. Nobody could believe that a man with Russ Feingold's potential as a lawyer would walk away from a brilliant legal career, not to mention the kind of money he would be making, to run for a lowly state office. "The firm loved him," Harth says. "He was the golden boy there." Steve Shimshak told him bluntly: "You're out of your mind." A senior partner called Feingold in for fatherly advice, laying out a seemingly irresistible future of riches and glory that would be his if he stayed with the firm—and warning that he would be making a *terrible* mistake if he left to run for office. Even his old college friend, Mike Hughes, was dumbfounded by Russ Feingold's choice of politics over a law career. When Feingold returned from Harvard to Madison, he and Mike resumed their friendship. They played racquetball during the lunch hour, Mike leaving his little gray cubicle at the state budget office and walking to meet Feingold at the Foley & Lardner offices, where everything was gleaming and plush. This is where Russ should be, he deserves this, Hughes would say to himself, remembering Russ's endless hours studying at the Helen C. White library. Hughes felt not a trace of envy but only admiration for his friend. But when Feingold told him what he had now decided to do, Hughes says: "I remember looking at him and saying, 'Are you nuts?'"

Leaving a lucrative career wasn't the only thing that seemed nutty to Hughes and almost everybody else. Due to a reapportionment ruling, "the perfect district" that Russ Feingold had envisioned was gone. And other legislative districts and candidates were affected, too. In June of 1982, only a month before the filing deadline for candidates running in the fall election, a federal judge's reapportionment decision dramatically altered the legislative map for Dave Travis, a Democratic State Assembly incumbent from Madison. Travis was in a quandary, not knowing whether to run in his greatly reconfigured assembly district or for the State Senate. He was taking a lot of time to decide, and a rumor spread that he was not going to run for the Assembly seat. Feingold seized the opening and tried to beat others to the punch by announcing at a morning news conference that he was running for the Assembly seat. The rumor, however, was not true—and Feingold discovered just how untrue it was when he bumped into Travis in an elevator in the state capitol. "Hi," Feingold said, "I just announced for the Assembly." Travis was furious; he wouldn't even shake Feingold's hand. In short order, a meeting was convened with Feingold, Travis and the speaker of the assembly, Tom Loftus, and the Senate majority leader, Tim Cullen, Feingold's friend and would-be mentor from Janesville. Glaring at Feingold, Travis said: "What are you doing running in my district? It's my seat." Feingold was immediately apologetic, explaining there had been a misunderstanding. "I wouldn't run against you, Dave."

As the meeting continued, Feingold finally said to his friend Cullen: "All right, Tim, I'll run against Bidwell." Everett (Cy) Bidwell was an elderly but very respected and entrenched State Senate Republican. He had been in the legislature for almost three decades. Nobody at the meeting thought that Feingold running against Bidwell sounded like a winning idea. In fact, Feingold recalls Cullen saying to him: "You're telling me a Jew is going to beat an eighty-three-year-old man in that district?" Feingold didn't hesitate. "I'll win it for you," he said. And then Feingold told Travis that all along he had wanted to run for the State Senate. Nobody at the meeting had any reason to know that "all along" really meant from the time Feingold was a seven-year-old at the Rock County 4-H Fair, when his father introduced him to a state senator. But before he could publicly declare his candidacy for the Senate seat, Feingold had to announce he was withdrawing from the Assembly race. Before his roller-coaster day ended, his first "campaign" for public office had lasted a grand total of six or seven hours. Around the state capitol, many political insiders had a good laugh at Russ Feingold's expense.

Almost certainly, Leon Feingold would have tried to stop Russ's foolhardy quest. Leon had come to believe that running for elective office and becoming a full-time politician was not only a hard way to make a living, but it was also hard on family life. Moreover, he wanted to push his son in the direction of a distinguished legal career. Of course that was something of a contradiction, because throughout Leon's life he had remained passionate about politics, vigorously working to elect good, honest, progressive candidates.

Leon Feingold did not have a chance to change his son's mind.

Not long after Russ Feingold returned to Wisconsin and started practicing law, Leon was diagnosed with colon cancer and died less than a year later, on December 4, 1980. He was sixty-eight. He was known widely and highly respected in Wisconsin legal circles and beyond—he had been president of the Seventh Circuit Bar Association, among other such professional roles. In Janesville, he had been a leader of numerous civic groups and had served for twenty-four years as an influential member of the city's Planning Commission, an important agency that shaped Janesville's rapid growth after World War II. But ultimately, it was not only Leon's legal ability and deep involvement in the civic life of his town that set him apart and made him a distinguished figure. In Janesville, Leon was the personification of integrity, a person of "undeviating commitment to high principle," in the words of a *Janesville Gazette* editorial after his death. Whoever chose those words had, indeed, captured the distinctive, defining ethical dimension of Leon Feingold's life.

"A long shot" was the term frequently used to sum up Russ Feingold's chances of defeating Cy Bidwell, meaning that they were somewhere between highly unlikely and hopeless. Bidwell's Twenty-seventh District, which had also been altered by reapportionment, was nevertheless solidly Republican and largely rural, extending north and west from Middleton and into a five-county area of small farming communities. When Harvey Temkin, who was among Feingold's more religiously observant Jewish friends, heard where he would be campaigning, he roared: "They're going to kill you!" It was not entirely a joking observation. And when Feingold told his assistant, Nancy Mitchell, where he was running, she laughed and said: "But, Russ, nobody knows who you are." That was almost literally true. And Feingold was not going to have a lot of money to spend on campaign advertising, certainly not from his own modest bank account. Although he had a nice salary during his short tenure at the law firm, he and Sue had bought a house in Middleton and started a family. Jessica Feingold was two years old when Feingold began his campaign, and another child was on the way.

Although Feingold was a novice at campaigning, he had more than a rudimentary understanding of how it was supposed to be done. For most of his life, he had observed his father either managing political campaigns or playing some other prominent role. Leon's specialty was helping his lawyer friends who were running to become Rock County circuit court judges. He did it with gusto, tirelessly working the phones and recruiting his "willing workers," as he called his campaign volunteers. During the campaign season, the Feingold family garage had a supply of a candidate's car tops and yard signs ready for distribution.

Russ Feingold also learned a thing or two about effective campaigning—and politics in general—from Les Aspin and his staff. Aspin, who earned a Ph.D. in economics from the Massachusetts Institute of Technology, was among the first Democrats in the southeast corner of Wisconsin to break the Republican stranglehold when he was elected to Congress in 1970. (He later became the secretary of defense in the Clinton administration.) Janesville was in Aspin's district, and Feingold volunteered in Aspin's 1970 campaign. In the summer after his freshman year in college, Feingold received a paid internship in Aspin's Janesville office, where he worked closely with Tim Cullen, who was Aspin's ombudsman. An exceptionally talented politician in his own right, before joining Aspin's staff Cullen had also been a trailblazer, becoming the first Democrat elected to the Janesville City Council (although the council elections were ostensibly nonpartisan). Aspin created highly detailed, elaborate campaign plans. Little was left to chance, including the design and specific location of every yard sign. If somebody walked into Aspin's campaign office asking for a bumper sticker, a well-trained Aspin worker never merely handed it over. He would walk outside with the Aspin supporter and put the sticker on the car bumper himself.

The heart of Russ Feingold's campaign was going door-to-door, introducing himself to strangers in places like Black Earth, Richland Center, Portage and Baraboo. Over and over again, he would begin: "Hi, I'm Russ Feingold. I grew up in Janesville and live in Middleton with my family." He said that more than 15,000 times, he estimates, between June and the November election. His campaign literature highlighted his personal background: Rhodes Scholar, honors graduate of the University of Wisconsin, homeowner and father. Often alone, he went from town to town behind the wheel of his old, decrepit Chevrolet Nova, its broken trunk lid held in place with masking tape. On one unusually hot summer day when the thermometer soared to triple digits, he became disoriented walking from one farmhouse to another and ended up lost in a cornfield.

When he wasn't alone, a new friend, John Sylvester—known to everybody as Sly—volunteered to drive him on these rural odysseys. His 1972 Impala junker was not much of an improvement over Feingold's Nova, and as traveling companions they must have made quite an impression on the local dairy farmers and shop-keepers. There was Feingold, still skinny and wearing his wiry black hair in "an Afro out to here," as Sylvester recalls the style, and Sly, his blond hair spiked on top and long in the back, looking like "a twenty-one-year-old punk." Apparently more than one of Feingold's friends told him that he was enough of a shock to rural sensibilities without having Sly by his side adding to the assault.

But from the start, they liked each other and had things in common. They both loved politics, which they discovered when Feingold saw Sly reading a book about the 1980 presidential election in a Foley & Lardner conference room. Sly, the son of a German Lutheran Milwaukee family, was a messenger at the firm—a "really stuffy law firm," he thought—and was already impressed with Feingold's friendliness before he got to know him better. "I thought he was cool. He was nicer than the other attorneys; he spent more time visiting with the secretaries and messengers." But their first political conversation turned into a little debate about the 1980 presidential election—Sly believed that Ted Kennedy had cost Democrats a victory because he had run against Jimmy Carter in the primary, while Feingold thought Carter was the reason Ronald Reagan won. As they continued talking, they discovered that both had volunteered in John Lindsay's presidential campaign, Feingold organizing University of Wisconsin students, and the eleven-year-old Sly going door-to-door for Lindsay on Madison's West Side.

On the small-town campaign trail, Sylvester marveled at how Feingold connected with people who were so different than he was. "He knew nothing about farming when he first started," Sylvester says. "Here you had a Jewish Rhodes Scholar knocking on the doors of these German farm families. He was such a good listener and so polite and made such a good impression . . . that it cut through all the other things that were kind of hurdles for him." Sylvester sensed that Feingold's childhood background had prepared him for this. "I think it's because he grew up with blue-collar kids and rich kids, and . . . if you were a Jew in Janesville you had to get along with everybody."

Unlike Sylvester, Republicans were not privy to the inroads Feingold was making in Bidwell's base. As one Republican observer had said: "What is a young Madison lawyer going to tell a farmer in Richland County?" In fact, Feingold geared a portion of his campaign message to farmers, proposing a low-interest loan program for younger farmers and a change in the state inheritance tax, making it easier for children to inherit their parents' farm. He also emphasized property tax relief and a reduction in the sales tax, senior citizen programs and a jobs credit to encourage employment. But it was not only the issues he highlighted that defined his campaign. He would win praise for the ethical way he campaigned, and especially for not attacking Bidwell personally and refusing to make Bidwell's age a campaign issue. Perhaps the closest he came to even implying Bidwell was not up to the job was when Feingold tried to counter the charge that he lacked Bidwell's experience. "I've had experiences Senator Bidwell never had. I've had the experiences of campaigning for five months, talking to voters. That's something Senator Bidwell hasn't done. I've rarely found anyone who has seen him campaigning."

As election day drew near, Feingold's feelings about his prospects ran from hot to cold. The political signs pointed to a pretty good year for Democrats, both in Wisconsin and nationally. In his own campaign, he was encouraged by the reception he received in a place like Reedsburg, a very conservative town. "I knocked on every door three times. Everybody was so nice," he remembers. Feingold-for-Senate signs were on display everywhere, many campaign signs having been built from 2×4's and hand-painted by his friend Mike Hughes. But when Feingold knocked on more doors late in the campaign in Baraboo, the old Ringling Brothers circus town, and in Portage, the reactions worried him. "I had this feeling that people were just shunning me." By Halloween, two days before the election, he says, "I didn't really know if I was going to win or not." That night, a group of neighborhood little boys rang Russ Feingold's doorbell. "Trick or treat," they said when he opened the door. He gave them candy and then one of them said sweetly from behind his Halloween mask: "Good luck, Mr. Feingold." That almost brought him to tears. It was not only the kindness of a small child that so affected him. It was also the sudden realization that his intense five months of campaigning were over and that he had thrown every ounce of energy into it.

On election night, the results rolled in slowly (about 90 percent of the votes were on paper ballots). There were some surprises for Feingold, both bad and good. The town of Reedsburg, where he had been warmly received, went about three to one against him. He had misinterpreted Wisconsinites' penchant for politeness as a sign of support. But Reedsburg aside, he was running surprisingly well in rural areas that Bidwell was expected to sweep, especially in Columbia County. That, together with his strong showing in Middleton and a portion of Dane County, had turned the election into a cliffhanger by midnight. But finally, when the last votes were tallied, Russ Feingold had come up short. At four in the morning, he made a little impromptu concession speech to a small band of friends that preceded by only hours the sad headline in the Madison *Capital Times*: "Bidwell Wins by 19-Vote Margin."

Bidwell was a gracious winner. "I didn't think it would be this close," he said. "You've got to give the kid credit, he conducted a terrific campaign. It was a clean campaign, one of the cleanest for me." Bidwell said he expected a recount.

The recount or canvass started the day after the election and continued for three weeks. Two days after the election, Feingold suddenly thought he had become the winner when the Sauk County canvass uncovered sixty-four votes for him that had not been counted on election night. But his euphoria was short-lived. As the canvass continued throughout the district, the lead seesawed. With Thanksgiving approaching, Feingold was ahead by fourteen votes only to see Bidwell pull ahead by four. Finally, it all came down to the recount in Columbia County, where Bidwell lived. The *Capital Times* called it a "high stakes drama." Not only was Russ Feingold's future about to be decided but so, too, was control of the State Senate. If Feingold won, the Democrats would be assured of a controlling majority.

The last four thousand votes of the 1982 election were

counted north of Madison in Portage, in the office of the Columbia County board chairman. Three county canvassers sitting at a long Formica-topped table called out the name of Bidwell or Feingold after examining each paper ballot. Russ Feingold, wearing a knit sweater under a sport coat, sat in one corner keeping his own tally. Other Democrats were watching, too, and the official Republican observers included a tough-minded state representative, Tommy Thompson (later to become governor and the first Secretary of Health and Human Services in the administration of George W. Bush). When Bidwell made an appearance, "he smiled at Feingold," a newspaper reporter noted, and "Feingold smiled back." And then, finally, deep into November, with the last sugar maple leaf long on the ground, the last white plastic bag of ballots was cut open, and the last ballots counted—the last ballots of the 46,651 that had been cast in the Twenty-seventh District for either Bidwell or Feingold. The result: by a grand total of thirty-one votes, Russ Feingold was Wisconsin's newest and second youngest state senator.

Feingold was thrilled, but it was going to take a little while before the victory felt real. Pulling out of Portage, Russ and Sue drove back to Middleton, but he realized they would not get home in time to see the glorious news on television. So they pulled into a shopping center and rushed to the television department of a Gimbel's department store where he was able to see confirmation of his victory on multiple TV sets. Soon there was a long-delayed victory party at the Park Motor Inn across from the state capitol. In the coming months, the Republicans would challenge the election results and try to block Feingold from being sworn in as a senator, to no avail. At the swearing-in party when Russ Feingold finally assumed his Senate seat, Bidwell's homey compliment was immortalized in the icing on top of a big white cake: "You've got to give the kid credit."

★ ★ ★

Russ Feingold's first race for public office was against the same kind of high-minded Republican that Leon Feingold ran against in 1938. Leon and John Matheson became lifelong friends, a relationship that had served as a vivid lesson to young Russ that good, honorable people could respect each other despite their political differences. In a post-election editorial, the *Capital Times* praised both Feingold and Bidwell while lamenting the increase in negative campaigning that was already on the rise by the early 1980s: "It was an exemplary campaign. At a time when the mud was flying fast and furious in other races, both candidates in this contest stuck to the issues and eschewed personal attacks. Though politically poles apart, they spoke admiringly of each other. . . . If the antagonists in more campaigns behaved so well, we might recover the civility that has all but gone out of electoral politics." Not only was Feingold proud of the editorial's high praise, but he knew Leon would have appreciated it, too. "He certainly would have enjoyed my race," Feingold said after the election. "I think at first he would have shaken his head over my quitting a good law firm, but I think he would have enjoyed it."

Rather than soliciting special interest contributions, Feingold relied on Wisconsin's partial public financing system in which small individual contributions to his campaign were matched by money from the Wisconsin Election Campaign Fund. The fund was supported by voluntary one-dollar checkoffs on individual income taxes. In total, Feingold raised a little more than $35,000 in his big upset victory.

In addition to his emerging public image as a principled politician, behind the scenes in state political circles he had earned respect for his hard work and risk-taking that ensured a Democratic Senate majority. But there was a little more to his victory story. As it turned out, 1982 was a fortuitous time for the twenty-nine-year-old Democrat to take his plunge into politics. Almost certainly, the strong showing of Wisconsin's newly elected Democratic governor, Anthony Earl, had helped pull Feingold across the finish line a winner. For his first time out, Russ had been lucky as well as good—and he knew it. In the future, when he faced impossibly long political odds, he and his friends would wonder when the old "F.L."—the Feingold Luck—would reappear.

CHAPTER 6

A TRUE PROGRESSIVE

In politics, it's good to have friends in high places, and Senate majority leader Tim Cullen liked and respected his young Janesville friend Russ Feingold so much that he offered him a seat on the most prestigious, politically powerful committee in the Wisconsin legislature, the Joint Finance Committee. The state budget and appropriations went through the Finance Committee. Cullen's invitation was a high compliment because there was an informal Senate rule that a senator had to serve at least one term before he or she could hope to get on Finance. In offering the plum assignment to Russ, Cullen would inevitably incur the wrath of more senior, envious Democrats who had been passed over. But Cullen says, "I knew him, I liked him, I trusted him and I wanted to put the best people, the best brains, in that committee because they did most of the legislature's work." As for Feingold, this was obviously one of those godfather-like offers that he couldn't refuse. So Tim Cullen was surprised when Russ Feingold said no.

Cullen understood that people ran for the State Legislature for a variety of reasons: some wanted to make it a career, some wanted to serve for a while and then cash in and become a lobbyist, and some had their eyes on higher office. Cullen and many others had no doubts about Feingold's intentions. What Feingold's approach might be to reach the next level was not something Cullen had given much thought to when he offered him the seat on Senate Finance. But when Feingold turned him down and told Cullen what he preferred, Cullen understood instantly that Russ had, indeed, given it a lot of thought. Feingold's plan, Cullen understood, was, first, not to get embroiled in the rough-and-tumble political horse-trading that goes on in the Finance Committee, where sometimes unsavory deals are struck to grease the legislative machinery and where budget battles are highly partisan. Rather, he told Cullen, what he did want were committee assignments that dealt with aging, agriculture and labor issues—important public policy issues to be sure, but also issues that appealed to three important constituencies in Democratic primaries. Moreover, Russ Feingold wanted to play the role of an advocate rather than the role of an insider—and that was okay with Cullen, who appreciated that both roles were useful in the legislative process. "I said, 'Fine. You can have it.' And he ran with it."

Feingold became chairman of the Committee on Aging and recalls one of his first public appearances. "I got up before this huge group of seniors and said, 'Hi, I'm twenty-nine years old and I'm the chairman of the Aging Committee.' And they kind of groaned and I said, 'But I plan to get where you guys are someday,' and everybody laughed." In May of 1984, the first proposal he pushed through the legislature ended the state's mandatory retirement age, which had been seventy. Only a few kinds of jobs were exempted, such as for police and firefighters, the governor calling the new law "one of the broadest of its kind in the nation." Forced retirement, Feingold said, was a "basic human rights issue," but University of Wisconsin administrators didn't see it that way. Many were furious with him because they thought his law would make it much more difficult to replace veteran professors. For a time, Feingold says, "whenever there would be a professor walking around who was disoriented or senile, they were known as Feingold professors."

But in the area of aging and senior citizen issues, Feingold made his biggest mark helping Alzheimer's disease families. Early in his first State Senate term, he became interested in the problem almost by accident. "No lobbyist came to me. I basically started at ground zero. It first came to my attention in an article about Rita Hayworth," the actress who was afflicted with it. He discovered that the state of Wisconsin, like most others, was doing very little to help Alzheimer's victims and their families. But by 1985, working with senior citizen organizations and others, he got the legislature to provide almost $3 million for a range of support services for Alzheimer's families, including an early commitment to respite care. It was a big breakthrough. "Sometimes, if you ask me what's the most important thing I ever did," Feingold says now, "it might be that vote, when I helped create the idea of respite care for older people." Throughout the 1980s and in every state budget, Feingold used his perch as chair of the Committee on Aging to push for more community-based and home-health alternatives to institutionalization, not only for Alzheimer's patients but also for other elderly, disabled and mentally ill people. After he left the State Legislature, the Coalition of Wisconsin Aging Groups created the annual "Russ Feingold Award for Service to the Elderly."

In one sense, the politics of Feingold's Alzheimer's and other senior citizen initiatives was pretty simple. As one frustrated Republican senator who opposed state funding of the Alzheimer's legislation had complained: "There were a lot of people on the Finance Committee who didn't like putting it in the budget, but how can you vote against the elderly?" For Feingold, his Alzheimer's work represented the perfect intersection between good politics and good government. He had wanted to be a legislator because he believed government should do things to help people. And before the effects of Ronald Reagan and the conservative tide spread to Wisconsin, "that's what I thought I would be doing as a Democrat [when we were] in the majority," Feingold says.

But then an issue arose that had nothing to do with his work on aging, and Feingold soon discovered, firsthand, that money and political power blurred liberal and conservative positions. It was an issue that pitted the big banks against the small, community banks, and the way he responded to it gave Feingold a public identity not merely as an up-and-coming liberal politician but, more accurately, as the emerging heir to one of the giants of the Progressive Era, Robert M. La Follette. Had Tim Cullen understood Russ Feingold's identification with Fighting Bob's politics and legacy, he would not have been taken off guard when Feingold turned down the Finance Committee offer. Apart from the influence of family, no other person is more important to understanding Russ Feingold's political worldview and style than La Follette, a larger-than-life figure that young Russ not only encountered through his dad's stories but also through La Follette's remarkable autobiography, which Feingold read as an impressionable teenager.

For millions of Americans, Robert M. La Follette, more than Theodore Roosevelt or Woodrow Wilson, was the most inspirational leader and personification of the Progressive Era in the first two decades of the twentieth century. Muckraking journalists such as Lincoln Steffens portrayed and promoted La Follette as nothing less than the savior of American democracy. After La Follette's first two historic terms as governor, the title of a Steffens article in 1904 captured the adoring attitude: "Enemies of the Republic:

Wisconsin: A State Where the People Have Restored Representative Government." Indeed, Wisconsin under the gubernatorial leadership of La Follette and his successor, Francis McGovern, helped make Wisconsin arguably the most progressive state in the country by 1911.

La Follette's progressive Republicans wrestled control of state government away from the conservative or Stalwart Republicans who were led by wealthy individuals and corporations, especially in the lumber and railroad industries. The progressives opened up the political process by abolishing the special-interest-dominated party caucus system of nominating candidates and instituting the direct primary. Clean government reforms also included regulating lobbying practices and banning gifts to legislators. In other policy areas, sweeping tax reforms "placed Wisconsin in the vanguard of states promoting the Progressive Era's 'revolution in taxation,'" writes historian John D. Buenker. "The equalization of property taxes, the establishment of a permanent tax commission, the enactment of an inheritance tax, and . . . the adoption of the nation's first successful state income tax" became a model for reformers in other states. "In addition to going a long way towards tax equity," Buenker observes, "Wisconsin's new tax structure also provided the potential for raising the amount of revenue necessary to finance a modern state government and a new service state." In fact, the "Wisconsin Idea" became widely known as shorthand for new, enlightened rational government that would rein in laissez-faire capitalism, invest in vastly expanded educational opportunities and infrastructure, and use the expertise at the University of Wisconsin to create pioneering programs to promote the health, safety and economic interests of ordinary workers and farmers alike.

The progressive reforms and activist government did not come without ferocious political battles, and *La Follette's Autobi-*

ography is his often gripping narrative of the struggle between the public interest and big-money private interests and, in his view, between what was morally right and wrong. Among all the political stories La Follette tells, none is more memorable than his account of a meeting in a Milwaukee hotel room. There, a Wisconsin lumber baron and Stalwart Republican U.S. Senator, Philetus Sawyer, offered him a bribe to fix an important court case presided over by La Follette's brother-in-law. La Follette, who was then practicing law and had not yet been elected governor, was outraged. Although he was already inclined toward reform politics, the episode at the Plankinton House served as a life-changing epiphany. "Nothing else ever came into my life that exerted such a powerful influence upon me as that affair," La Follette wrote in 1911, twenty years after it took place. "It was the turning point, in a way, of my career. Sooner or later I probably would have done what I did in Wisconsin. But it would have been later. It would have been a matter of much slower evolution. But it shocked me into a complete realization of the extremes to which this power that Sawyer represented would go to secure the results it was after."

The alleged bribe of La Follette remains one of Wisconsin's most famous political stories. Sawyer denied it, and some historians have questioned the accuracy of La Follette's version—that perhaps it was "the truth imagined." But in any event, La Follette used the story to enhance his image as a man of uncommon courage and honesty who believed, first and foremost, that wealthy interests left unchecked would corrupt not only American politics but justice itself. If big money was not the root of all political evil, it was the source of much of it. And if Sawyer and wealthy interests generally would go to any "extremes" to preserve their power, then La Follette was prepared to be even more tenacious, creative and dedicated in challenging that power.

He fought for a decade until Wisconsin voters approved the direct primary, which was largely intended to diminish the importance of big money in the electoral process. As governor and later as a U.S. senator, he campaigned furiously throughout Wisconsin and elsewhere for one progressive cause or another, sometimes to the point of exhaustion and hospitalization. In one typical Wisconsin battle, he writes in his autobiography, he traveled and "spoke forty-eight days in succession, never missing one single day, excepting Sunday. I averaged eight-and-one-quarter hours a day on the platform. We had two automobiles so that if one broke down . . . I could transfer to the other. . . . I took only one meal a day at the table during those forty-eight days. My noon luncheon consisted of a bottle of good rich milk and two slices of the crust of bread buttered."

When he drove into a legislative district in which the legislator, Republican or Democrat, had opposed a La Follette reform bill, La Follette would read the "roll call" to the legislator's constituents. The roll call or calling the roll was a highly controversial tactic designed to embarrass and pressure a La Follette opponent by informing the locals of the offending legislator's roll call vote. La Follette was not reluctant to endorse Democratic candidates over anti–La Follette Republicans when a Democrat pledged to support his reform agenda.

It was this kind of political independence that was not appreciated by conservative Republican leaders in Washington when La Follette arrived to take his Senate seat in 1906. His reputation had clearly preceded him; although his Republican Party controlled the Senate, La Follette was given the worst committee assignments. One was the Committee to Investigate the Potomac River Front, which, La Follette discovered, had never held a meeting nor had a bill referred to it. That La Follette started out as a distrusted outsider in his own party and ended up one of the great senators of the twentieth century is, in some respects, the best part of his stirring story. And it's one that captured the imagination of a young Russ Feingold.

★ ★ ★

In 1985, Lee Swanson was the president of the State Bank of Cross Plains, a small community bank located in Dane County, not far from Russ Feingold's Middleton home. Swanson and many other Wisconsin community bankers had a problem: a regional interstate banking bill supported by big banks was making its way through the state legislature. Many of the small bankers felt threatened; they saw interstate banking as akin to a giant steamroller that was going to come into Wisconsin and flatten them into oblivion.

At one point as the legislative saga unfolded in Madison, Swanson and other community bankers were in Washington and paid a visit to one of Wisconsin's U.S. senators, Robert Kasten, a Republican. Almost all of the community bankers were Republicans, too, but that didn't matter in this instance. "We went in as a lobbying group to visit with him," Swanson recalls years later. "And in his office he said to us you guys haven't stepped up to the plate like this [other] group of people had." Swanson knew what that meant because the small bankers had been badly outspent by the big banks. They hadn't contributed as much to political campaigns and "we never could spend the kind of money they do or have the lobbyists that they do," Swanson says. When they came home, Swanson and the others went to see Russ Feingold.

Swanson had met Feingold only once and that was when Feingold was going door-to-door in his 1982 campaign and showed up on Swanson's front porch in Cross Plains. Now Swanson was calling on Feingold because, first, he chaired the Senate committee with jurisdiction on the interstate banking bill (his Committee on Aging was shorthand for the Committee on Aging, Banking,

Commercial Credit and Taxation). Second, Swanson hoped Feingold might be sympathetic to the small bankers' concerns. And he was, passionately, because the small bankers, who were largely from small towns, reminded him of Janesville, his father and his father's business and civic friends and the healthy social fabric they had fashioned. "That was a very, very important part of my analysis," Feingold says about why he came down on the side of the small bankers. It was "based on my upbringing in Janesville. Based on having gone to the Rotary Club with my father, and seeing the lawyers, bankers and farmers—everybody sitting in the same room and knowing each other and caring about each other. When the decision-maker about loans is sitting in Cleveland, Ohio, it's not the same."

By the mid-1980s, banking regulations that had been in place since the Great Depression were under attack by the banking industry. The proponents of relaxed regulation argued that banking would be more efficient in a more free market environment. In Wisconsin, the proposed regional interstate banking legislation, similar to legislation already passed in more than twenty states, allowed banks and other financial institutions in seven Midwestern states to acquire and be purchased by other banks in those states. The states stretched from Ohio to Minnesota. Since even Wisconsin's biggest banks were smaller than their counterparts elsewhere in the region, it was reasonable to assume, as Feingold did, that the ownership of many Wisconsin banks would shift to places such as Cleveland and Minneapolis if interstate banking was approved.

Feingold says that it was the importance of local ownership, and not the size of the banks per se, that led him to champion the small bankers' cause. Lee Swanson recalls that "Russ was always for more diversity, less concentration." As a general proposition, Feingold placed a high value on diversity. "Goes back to my first paper in college," he says, in which he analyzed the demise of Janesville's stately Dutch elm trees. "The nickname of Janesville was the 'Bower City.' And the reason it was the Bower City—my street in Janesville was an example of this—we had these beautiful elm trees . . . on each side of the street. . . . They came together to create a bower over the street. Well, that's all we had in Janesville, elm trees. A little old bug comes over from Holland, and because we did not have diversity, because we only had one kind of tree, Janesville was denuded of the very symbol of the city." For him, the analogy to the banking issue was that a community, or a state such as Wisconsin, was likely to benefit from the distinctive resources of both large and not-so-large banks. "I think that an economy dominated by big corporations that does not have middle-size and new start-up businesses challenging them and pushing them and competing with them is weaker, less efficient and more likely to collapse."

Whatever qualifications Feingold might have held about banking and bigness dropped out of the high-profile public debate on the banking bill that came to a head in the spring of 1986. The debate turned into a David and Goliath struggle between Feingold's small bankers, consumer groups and farmers, including many in Feingold's Senate district, and the big banks and big businesses that could benefit from having access to more capital. Feingold made his sentiments clear: "The bankers always win, and the farmers never win," he said, "I'm tired of it." In a hearing on the legislation in Feingold's committee, proponents argued that Wisconsin could not afford to be an island surrounded by a sea of change. But a small banker from the state of Maine, where the first interstate banking law had been enacted, testified that the majority of commercial deposits were now controlled by out-of-state interests. "The question is whether or not the concentration of power in the hands of fewer and fewer people is healthy," the Maine banker said, adding that "bigness doesn't mean better." And a Wisconsin dairy farmer warned that the bill would allow "legal financial extortion as a way of life. It is a vile and loathsome bill. Ignore the big bucks lobbyists," he urged. Feingold himself raised the issue of how the big banks were muscling the bill through the legislature. "There is too much damn money involved," he said about the big banks' lobbying tactics.

In fact, the lobbying had been smoothly, even spectacularly effective, one of the biggest banking industry lobbying campaigns in many years. In the fall legislative session, the banking bill sailed through the Democratic-controlled Assembly 75–22. The Democratic governor, Anthony Earl, supported it. In the State Senate, a head count showed that most members of both parties were on board, including the Democratic majority leader, Tim Cullen. Much of the lobbying campaign had been led by the Wisconsin Bankers Association and by lobbyists working for the Marine Corporation in Milwaukee. The Marine, as the bank was called, was one of three large banks in the state and its president, George Slater, was a driving force behind the legislation.

With just a week to go before the legislature adjourned, the only person standing in the way of final victory for the banking lobby was Russ Feingold. Russ recalls that many months earlier, "Tim Cullen came up to me. I don't think he knew what he was doing, because he didn't realize how stubborn I could be until he knew me [better]. He said, 'I want you to take this banking bill in your committee and give it a good look.' Which meant, you know, sort of make them come to you. But he did not want me to bottle it up in committee."

But now many Senate Democrats were furious because Feingold had slowed the process to a near-halt in his committee. And even after his committee finally voted 6–4 in favor of sending the bill to the Senate floor, Feingold nevertheless announced that he, as chairman, was thinking about not allowing the bill to be reported out. The progressive *Capital Times* cheered him on in an editorial titled, "Feingold Takes a Courageous Stand." It said that "Sen. Russell Feingold . . . had made some powerful enemies this week: the big banks, the powers-that-be in the Senate, even the governor of his own party. What makes Feingold such an able foil for all the big money folks is his intellectual ability combined with a legislative style that is tough yet not abrasive. Feingold may lose this fight before the Legislature goes home next week, but perhaps his courageous stand . . . will give some of his colleagues pause."

Traditionally, a Senate committee chairman had absolute authority to hold a bill in committee, regardless of how the committee voted. It was as close to an absolute if unwritten rule as there was in the Senate. So, when Russ Feingold officially announced that he was going to do just that, sit on the bill until the legislature adjourned some days later, Lee Swanson and his community bank colleagues were ecstatic. They had just beaten the big boys! Feingold's public rationale for killing the legislation was that "the only reason this bill has all the steam it has is that legislators have been pursued by lobbyists so relentlessly that they just want to pass it and get it off their backs." Even though it was largely true, the observation probably didn't sit well with some of his colleagues. He added that the legislation was "a raw deal" for just about everybody in the state, including the larger Wisconsin banks, which would be swallowed up by bigger out-of-state banks.

The great victory that Swanson, Feingold and many others enjoyed lasted for not quite a week, because on Thursday, March 20, 1986, Feingold's Democratic Senate colleagues, led by his Janesville friend Tim Cullen, took unprecedented action and engineered an end run around him. The opening paragraph in a newspaper story about the incident captures some of the flavor: "Senate Democrats designed a laughable Rube Goldberg machine to slip a new regional interstate banking bill onto the Senate floor after failing to convince Sen. Russell Feingold to release the bill he is holding lifeless in his committee." Essentially, the "machine" or vehicle was a virtually identical interstate banking bill drafted by Cullen and other Democratic leaders, which was assigned to another committee, where it was approved and sent to the Senate floor. The parliamentary maneuvering was done in such a way as to maintain the appearance, flimsy as it was, that the sacrosanct principle of a committee chairman's absolute power had not been violated. But of course it had been—and for the first time in anybody's memory, maybe in the history of the Senate. Feingold called it a sham, and said: "It just shows that if people want a bill badly enough, just about any action will be taken to pass it." The interstate banking legislation was headed to the governor, who was waiting to sign it into law.

Two decades later, Tim Cullen, Feingold's friend and mentor, reflected on the climax to the interstate banking episode. "I cared about Russ and his future—and I handled [the banking legislation] in a way that I thought he was going to end up being a winner. [But] I thought on the merits he was just wrong. He was looking backward rather than forward." It wasn't, however, only about "the merits"; it was also about political power. The banking lobby had captured the governor's support as well as overwhelming support in both houses of the legislature. Ultimately, Cullen and other Democratic leaders just couldn't ignore the political calculus.

So, Cullen tried to orchestrate a win-win resolution to the morality play that had unfolded. Cullen says that he never talked to Feingold about the tactics he used to get a bill to the floor, but that he, Cullen, had given it much thought. He believed that the dramatic ending he created was only going to help Feingold politically. "Because here was the lone voice, the state senator standing up for the little banks and getting crushed by the power of the majority party and the majority leader," Cullen says. "I thought Russ was going to come out of it absolutely intact with his base. The worst thing that could have happened to him would have been for him to report the bill out . . . and [then] he goes against it on the floor but it passes, and he tries to go back to all these bankers and say, 'I stuck with you all the way.' But they'll say, 'Well, you did but you reported the bill out. You allowed it to happen even though you voted against it.' But the way it happened, he never did a single act [that helped] the passage, so he remained true to what he believed in and who he was trying to help. I always thought it helped him politically and I never worried a bit that I'd hurt him."

Cullen was right about the political consequences. The small-town community bankers felt that Feingold had done his best against tough odds. Lee Swanson thought he had been coura-geous. And years later, Swanson recalls that the entire legislative experience had produced some positive results, not the least of which, he felt, was a better public understanding of the important role small banks played in their communities.

Russ Feingold had made many new friends, even Republican friends, by leading the charge against the interstate banking bill. And two newspaper articles were especially flattering. Feingold's favorite appeared in the *Milwaukee Journal* with the headline: "Feingold the Bold: He Fought the Tide." For him, "Feingold the Bold" captured perfectly the public image he sought. But it was a newspaper column by the editor of the *Capital Times* that was per-haps the biggest prize of all.

The *Capital Times* was founded in 1917 by one of La Follette's disciples, young William J. Evjue. In the 1960s, Evjue's Sunday morning radio commentary filled the Feingolds' family car when Leon drove Russ and Dena home from religious school in Madi-son. Some twenty years after those Sunday morning political ser-mons, Russ Feingold was anointed as the new progressive torchbearer by none other than the esteemed editor of the *Capital*

Times, Dave Zweifel. "State Senator Russell Feingold has been in office less than three years," Zweifel began, "but already he has demonstrated the kind of dedication to the progressive tradition of this state that sets him apart." And what set Feingold apart, Zweifel saw, was the same combination of political values and personality traits that had set La Follette apart: an affinity for the underdog, for smallness over bigness, for community over anonymity—and all supported by a sometimes "stubborn determination" to go against conventional thinking, majority opinion and to stand up, alone if necessary, for a worthy cause.

Feingold was only thirty-two years old when Zweifel's column appeared, and it provided him with a new, lasting public identity in Wisconsin political circles, one that was captured in the headline over the column: "Russell Feingold: A True Progressive."

In retrospect, for Feingold two other things stood out about the interstate banking battle. He began to see firsthand, he says, that the legislature was "changing into a very negative, money-dominated, special-interest place in a way that seemed inconsistent with Wisconsin tradition. It sort of was the beginning of my enormous resentment of the power of money to corrupt the political process . . . that experience of seeing the raw power of these special interests over both parties. I remember thinking [that] this is really corrupting my state." And in Washington, where the Democratic Party leadership was losing its self-confidence as the so-called Reagan Revolution unfolded, the new, influential, corporate-backed Democratic Leadership Council symbolized a new era of pragmatic capitulation.

The interstate banking experience also reinforced Feingold's strong feelings about the importance of preserving community institutions. He thought it was dangerous to disturb the web of personal relationships. "I realized this was part and parcel of my belief that this is a foundation of community in America. And that these bills dressed up in the name of 'progress' . . . could be very destructive of what Republicans like to call 'values.'"

The ink was barely dry on Wisconsin's new interstate banking law when the Marine bank and George Slater sold out to the much larger, Ohio-based Banc One. It was a conspicuous sign of things to come in Wisconsin (and throughout the country in the late 1980s and 1990s). Only one of the three largest Wisconsin-based banks survived the bank consolidation movement. As for community banks, Lee Swanson's State Bank of Cross Plains survived, but hundreds of community banks across the country did not. When you drive around America's smaller towns today, you see many former bank buildings that have been turned into restaurants and bed-and-breakfasts.

Lee Swanson laments that small towns have frequently been written off by the large bank holding companies simply because smaller markets don't yield big enough profits. To be sure, new banks have sometimes sprouted in small towns to take advantage of the new opportunities. But remote, absentee bank ownership also has affected larger cities. For example, when a bank holding company in Charlotte, North Carolina, bought a bank in, say, New Orleans, it typically sent in top managers from corporate headquarters to run it. The managers knew little about key local players and politics and generally stayed for only a few years before they were transferred to another bank in another city. This was not the way it used to be, as policy analyst Otis White explained in a *New York Times* article: "From the 1950's to the 1980's, bank chiefs were the capi di tutti capi of civic leaders in most cities, the bosses of all bosses. They ran important companies, but that wasn't why they were powerful. Their power came from continual involvement in civic work, an intimate knowledge of their communities and their occasional boldness." And in a place such as New Orleans after the devastation of Hurricane Katrina in 2005, White believes the rebuilding process is going to be more difficult, maybe much more difficult, than it would have been years ago because so much of the local banking leadership and community relationships are missing.

Walk into a twenty-first-century American supermarket, and you are likely to see three kinds of milk in the dairy case: conventional, organic and hormone-free. An early chapter in the high-stakes, hormone-free milk story began unexpectedly in Russ Feingold's State Senate office not long after he had been elected to his second term.

His reelection in 1986 had been easier than his first race, thanks in part to another reapportionment that gave him a more Democratic district. After four years in office, his aggressive work on a cluster of issues—and his "smarts and savvy" in the view of many around the state capitol—had helped raise his political profile. Some political handicappers were already mentioning him as a possible candidate for the U.S. Senate.

Unfortunately, Feingold's marriage did not survive beyond his first State Senate term. In 1986, Russ and Sue divorced after nine years of marriage. They now had two daughters, Jessica, six, and Ellen, three. Following the divorce, Russ and Sue, who lived minutes from each other, shared raising their daughters.

The fight over the interstate banking bill had helped raise Feingold's profile, but it was not really an issue that generated mass interest. He also was identified with other issues, such as health care and the elderly, small business and the environment, and his work on these issues attracted the support of a number of activist organizations. And, because he chaired a committee that had jurisdiction on taxes, he was in the middle of several well-publicized debates on tax reform. After the Republican Tommy Thompson was elected governor in 1986, for example, Feingold offered a major tax reform alternative to the new governor's proposal. His included property tax relief rather than a cut in income tax rates. "The property tax is the real sore thumb in Wisconsin's tax system," Feingold said. He had held hearings around the state and knocked on thousands of doors during his reelection campaign, "and I know that the income tax is not the burning issue. It's property taxes."

But no single issue in Russ Feingold's State Senate career provided him with as much visibility beyond Madison as a new, emerging controversy involving, of all things, milk. For most of the twentieth century, Wisconsin produced more milk and cheese than any other state. Dairy farming was not only a way of life for tens of thousands of Wisconsin families, but the state's identity was synonymous with the wholesomeness of its dairy products. For as long as anybody could remember, the motto on Wisconsin license plates was "America's Dairyland." (In the 1990s, when there was a public debate about changing the motto to something more zippy or edgy, a hard-nosed Wisconsinite proposed "Eat Cheese or Die.") Maybe some Chicagoans thought the country's most famous cow was Mrs. O'Leary's, but in much of Wisconsin no animal enjoyed a loftier, loved status than a top-producing Holstein or Jersey that gave ten golden gallons on an average day.

But now, one of America's biggest chemical companies had a new vision: they wanted Wisconsin's dairy farmers to stick a hypodermic needle in the rear ends of those cows and fill them with a new synthetic growth hormone so they would produce even more milk. And that was the ominous news that a delegation of small dairy farmers brought to Feingold's office not long after he had been reelected to a second term.

The St. Louis–based Monsanto Company had spent millions, probably hundreds of millions, developing a bovine growth hormone (BGH), which was the chemical industry's first big agricultural biotechnology product. Three other companies were also working on this genetically engineered product, which was also sometimes referred to as bST for bovine somatotropin, but it was Monsanto that surveyed the Wisconsin landscape and envisioned cash cows as far as their corporate eyes could see. Monsanto's BGH would boost a cow's milk production by 15 percent or more. But what looked like a financial bonanza to Monsanto looked like a doomsday disaster to the small dairy farmers, who shared their concerns with Russ. The country was already swimming if not drowning in the overproduction of milk, cheese and butter. Federal government warehouses were nearly bursting with the excess, but even government programs had not been able to keep milk prices from falling for farmers. Overproduction was one big reason that more and more Wisconsin dairy farmers had thrown in the towel and given up a way of life that had been passed down from one generation to another.

Russ Feingold had become acquainted with the farmers who came to see him about BGH because he had worked with them on a few other farm issues. They farmed in his district or nearby and were all small dairy farmers—the approximate definition of "small" being a farm worked largely by the family owners themselves and that provided the majority of their income. Many of the small operations had herds of fewer than fifty cows. One of the small dairy farmers, John Kinsman, had a somewhat typical farm family background but an uncommonly well-developed sense of social justice and civic responsibility.

Kinsman was born in Lime Ridge, northwest of Madison in Sauk County, where his great-grandparents had arrived in an ox-drawn covered wagon from Vermont in the mid-nineteenth century. They were dairy farmers, as were Kinsman's grandparents and father. When Kinsman was eighteen years old, he was drafted into the Navy during World War II. It was 1944 and the beginning of his "gradual awakening" that the world was often a far different place than the one he had read about in his high school history textbooks. An important, life-changing experience, part of his awakening, was the racial segregation he witnessed when the Navy assigned him to radio school in Gulfport, Mississippi. "I saw the terrible discrimination against black people. And as I left the Navy, it was just beginning to be integrated. A young black man was in my company, and he was very lonely." Later, Kinsman and other Wisconsin farmers began an exchange program with black Mississippi farmers that has continued for some forty years. Now eighty-one years old, Kinsman also credits the influence of his mother and his religious beliefs with shaping his social consciousness and sense of justice. A Roman Catholic who attends St. Boniface church in Lime Ridge, Kinsman says he has a "faith perspective . . . as far as justice goes, and I believed in it."

Kinsman recalls that small farmers were often treated condescendingly by policymakers, but when he and his friends shared their BGH fears with Feingold, "he immediately took it seriously." Soon Feingold introduced legislation requiring that BGH-produced milk be labeled so that consumers would know what they were buying. "To me it was just going to be a little bill," he recalls. But when Monsanto got wind of it, the company reacted like a dangerous tornado was heading their way, a storm that could wreak havoc on a potential worldwide BGH market that some estimated to be worth as much as $1 billion in annual sales. Feingold recalls that he and the group of dairy farmers "obtained an internal [Monsanto] memo—I don't know how—where there was a description of what I was going to propose. There was a handwritten note by a Monsanto executive which said, 'We need to step on this and smash it hard,' or something to that effect. And that's what they did." Or more precisely, that's what they attempted to do.

An army of Monsanto lobbyists descended on the state capitol. Feingold remembers holding a news conference with three farmers and "there would be twenty guys in suits standing there," Monsanto lobbyists tracking his every move. "It was hilarious," he says. One of the lobbyists Monsanto hired was former state senator Tom Harnisch, who had survived a recall in 1981 thanks in part to Feingold's legal work. As the BGH issue grew more heated, Harnisch told Feingold to keep it up because Feingold was putting his children through college. Harnisch started calling the munificent Monsanto "Ma Santo," or Mother Monsanto. Another Wisconsin-based lobbyist, Jeffrey Remsik, remembers how deadly serious Monsanto was about the threat Feingold and the small dairy farmers posed. He worked for Monsanto for seven or eight years and went to regular corporate strategy meetings in St. Louis, in addition to being part of the weekly telephone conferences. "It consumed a lot of people," Remsik says, thinking about how much Monsanto invested in the Wisconsin campaign. At its peak, Monsanto had a team of forty to fifty people working on the BGH problem, he says. And Feingold had heard from other Monsanto lobbyists that he was an item on the agenda of Monsanto board meetings. "What are we going to do about this guy?" they were asking.

The explicit issue that Feingold and the farmers highlighted was the harmful, even devastating, economic impact of BGH on dairy farmers. But an implicit question raised by Feingold's labeling bill was far more politically potent: was BGH-produced milk safe for consumers? Because the early research about the safety of BGH to humans or animals had not raised red flags, Feingold explained that labeling would simply be a "vehicle to allow consumers to show their support for our family farmers." But that's not how many others interpreted the rationale for labeling. If there was absolutely no question about health and safety issues, then why the need to alert consumers with a label? And that, of course, is what worried Monsanto about Feingold's labeling bill, the implicit suggestion that there might be something risky about drinking BGH milk. Monsanto's claims that tests revealed no health concerns fell well short of persuading Dairyland skeptics. By 1989, the conservative *Milwaukee Sentinel* not only endorsed Feingold's bill but said there was "little question that [BGH] research . . . should continue." And the *Milwaukee Journal,* in an editorial titled "Why Rush? Cows Can Wait," asked "if BGH is so worry-free as proponents suggest," why were they against the labeling bill?

The Wisconsin BGH controversy had leaked into the national, mainstream media, too. In a long feature story in the *New York Times* in 1988, BGH and agricultural biotechnology were placed on a larger canvas of the growing debate over the social, economic and health costs of so-called technological progress. "Small towns are picking up the pieces after a long farm depression caused by overproduction and deflated prices," the article noted. "State and federal agencies are cataloguing the damage to the environment from industrial farm practices—the ground water in 40 states, for example, has been found to be contaminated with 60 different pesticides. Health groups are gaining more understanding of the threats from other toxic substances in food, including those from various animal drugs. . . . Perhaps not since the abolitionist movement led to the destruction of slavery have so many economic, political and cultural issues converged around the production practices on American farms."

In the late 1980s, the BGH controversy raged. Kinsman and other small dairy farmers picketed in front of the University of Wisconsin Memorial Union, protesting the BGH research at the university's Arlington Experimental Farm that was funded by one of the chemical companies. At a hearing in the state capitol that Feingold organized, one of the witnesses was a member of the

European Parliament, the governing body of the twelve-nation European Economic Community. The EEC had recently banned BGH, a ban that continues to this day in Europe, Canada and other countries.

In Wisconsin, Monsanto was losing the public relations war, although not without a fight. A Monsanto-friendly dairy farmer wrote an op ed in the *Milwaukee Journal* saying that "Feingold has been orchestrating an effort that should be awarded 'the biggest political hoax of the century.'" And some of the University of Wisconsin agricultural deans were probably none too happy with him because of the bad press they were receiving from newspaper coverage about their school's "secret BGH research." Through all of the controversy, Kinsman says that "Russ never backed down." The small dairy farmers thought they finally had a champion who cared about preserving not only their economic well-being but a cherished way of life.

Although Feingold didn't back down from his support of the small dairy farmers, they all agreed to something of a compromise, at least for the time being, when in May of 1990 Governor Tommy Thompson announced his support for a moratorium on the sale of BGH in Wisconsin. The Wisconsin politics of BGH had become a little complicated. Some of the larger dairy operations, including large cheese-makers, were opposed to labeling of any kind. And while Thompson appeared to be on Monsanto's side—he had threatened to veto Feingold's labeling bill—he was up for reelection and couldn't ignore the numerous small dairy farmers strongly opposed to BGH.

But when Thompson announced his support of a BGH moratorium, the news reports declared it an important victory for the anti-BGH forces. The headline in the *New York Times* read: "Wisconsin Temporarily Banning Gene-Engineered Drug for Cows." And the opening paragraph probably sent a chill through Monsanto's boardroom: "In a decision that could spell enormous trouble for the fledgling agricultural biotechnology industry, Gov. Tommy G. Thompson of Wisconsin yesterday approved legislation that temporarily bars the sale or use of a genetically engineered drug for use in dairy cows." It was the first ban in the country, the *New York Times* noted, even though the Food and Drug Administration was likely to approve BGH the following year. The story identified Russ Feingold as the one who led the battle in the legislature. Feingold told the *Times*: "Although the Governor has tried to dodge the issue, he did in fact finally agree with our point that Wisconsin is not ready for bovine growth hormone. It's a milestone. We've served notice on Monsanto and the others that money alone does not control Wisconsin."

At least for now, there was indeed reason to cheer, even gloat a little. But the BGH issue was not over, nor would it be for years to come. Almost certainly, however, the issues raised in the BGH controversy in Wisconsin would have a lasting effect on American consumer attitudes about the health and safety of the nation's food supply.

Russ Feingold's appearance in that April 1990 article may have been the first time he was quoted in the *New York Times*. The media coverage of the BGH issue in Wisconsin over the previous four years had been extensive. And most of the BGH stories, or at least many, not only included Russ Feingold's name but also something about his fight to defend the purity of Wisconsin's milk. To be sure, he had helped the cause of dairy farmers and even consumers, but whether he had helped his own cause enough to get elected to the U.S. Senate—well, not many Wisconsin pols thought so. By 1990, the line of Democratic Senate hopefuls was forming and most observers placed Russ Feingold at the end of that line.

Max Feingold, Russ's grandfather, in front of his Blackhawk grocery store and his 1923 Chevrolet truck, the first to be manufactured at the General Motors plant in Janesville, Wisconsin, ca. 1923.

Sylvia and Leon Feingold with their children: Dena, sitting in her mother's lap; Russ in front of his older siblings, Dave and Nancy, 1956.

Feingold in his senior year at Janesville Craig High School, where he was the reform-minded president of the student council, 1971.

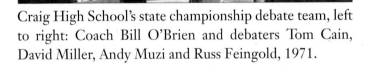

Craig High School's state championship debate team, left to right: Coach Bill O'Brien and debaters Tom Cain, David Miller, Andy Muzi and Russ Feingold, 1971.

Feingold in his first year as a Rhodes Scholar, Magdalen College, Oxford University, 1975.

6

Feingold, his first wife, Sue, and daughter Jessica, 1982.

7

Meeting with voters in rural western Dane County during his first campaign for the Wisconsin state senate, 1982.

8

After a recount, Feingold won his first election to the state senate by 31 votes; the oath of office was administered by the Chief Justice of the Wisconsin Supreme Court, Bruce Beilfuss, 1983.

In Dubuque, Iowa, campaigning in the 1988 Democratic presidential primary for Illinois senator Paul Simon; Feingold with his friends, John (Sly) Sylvester, left, and Sumner Slichter. Slichter has also been Russ's top legislative aide for twenty-five years.

At Dena Feingold's ordination in Cincinnati, where she attended the Hebrew Union College-Jewish Institute of Religion. She became the first woman rabbi in Wisconsin, 1982.

Feingold and his brother, Dave, early 1990s.

In November 1991, Feingold announced his candidacy for the U.S. Senate in the front yard of his house. Feingold and his second wife, Mary, with her two sons from a previous marriage, Sam and Ted, and Feingold's daughters, Ellen and Jessica, are standing in front of one of the garage doors on which Feingold painted his promises to Wisconsin voters.

13

Election night celebration in Middleton, Wisconsin, November 1992; Feingold defeated incumbent Republican Bob Kasten. On the left is Mary Feingold. On the right is Russ's sister Nancy and her late husband, Sterling Fishman.

14

Ellen and Jessica with their father, late 1980s.

15

THE JOHN F. KENNEDY
PROFILE IN COURAGE AWARD
The John F. Kennedy Library

In Boston, Feingold and his Republican colleague John McCain receive the John F. Kennedy Profile in Courage Award for the political risks they took fighting to reform the campaign finance laws, 1999. From left to right, front row: Ted Kennedy, Caroline Kennedy, McCain, Feingold and John F. Kennedy Jr.; top row: Victoria Reggie Kennedy, Cindy McCain, Mary Feingold, Edwin Schlossberg and Jean Kennedy Smith.

During the seven years it took before they won a historic victory in Congress, Feingold and McCain appeared at public events around the country to build support for campaign finance reform. At this rally in front of Boston's Faneuil Hall, appearing with Feingold are McCain and the two campaign finance reform leaders in the House of Representatives, Marty Meehan and Chris Shays, 1999.

As chairman of the African Affairs Subcommittee, Feingold has traveled widely in Africa, focusing on a range of issues such as human rights and anti-terrorism strategies. Here in 2006 he met with Ethiopian officials in Dire Dawa on a trip that included a stop in Kenya.

In Kabul on an Afghanistan and Iraq War fact-finding trip in 2005, Feingold traveled with Senate colleagues, left to right, John McCain, Hillary Clinton, Lindsey Graham, and Susan Collins.

Feingold introduced a resolution in the Senate to censure President George W. Bush after it was revealed the president authorized secret wiretaps of American citizens in violation of the law. While many rank-and-file Democrats cheered Feingold, most of his Democratic colleagues ran for cover.

After a series of Republican lobbying scandals outraged the public and helped the Democrats win control of the House and Senate in the 2006 elections, Feingold joined forces with Barack Obama, at right, in early 2007 to announce a major overhaul of the lobbying and ethics laws. Appearing with them at a news conference was Democratic majority leader Harry Reid.

CHAPTER 7

HOME MOVIES

From start to finish, Russ Feingold's audacious run for the U.S. Senate was an improbable mix of high ideals and low comedy, a quest as earnest as a peanut-butter-and-jelly sandwich and as hard-headed as a shot and a beer.

Officially, it all began on a windy, frigid, just plain nasty November morning in his front yard on Donna Drive, exactly one year before the 1992 general election. In the presence of about a hundred freezing friends, Russ Feingold kicked off his campaign standing in front of his two-car garage door. Painted on the doors was Feingold's simple, three-item "contract" with the people of Wisconsin:

1. I will rely on Wisconsin citizens for most of my campaign contributions.
2. I will live here in Middleton, Wisconsin. My children will go to school here, and I will spend most of my time here in Wisconsin.
3. I will accept no pay raise during my six-year term in office.

The garage door contract was a distinctive, amusing gimmick, the style, spirit and message a reflection of Feingold's personality and values. But it also served as a double-duty dig at one of his primary opponents and the Republican incumbent, who had accepted congressional pay raises and had not spent many of their waking hours in Wisconsin, or so many believed. At first, however, the garage door contract attracted only modest attention because Russ Feingold's candidacy was hardly front-page news. Indeed, on that November morning, nobody could have predicted that his homespun candidacy would turn into a rarely seen, jaw-dropping political miracle. Nobody, that is, except Russ Feingold and his new wife, Mary.

Like Russ, Mary Erpenbach Speerschneider had been divorced and had two children; her boys, Sam and Ted, were close in age to Feingold's daughters—in fact, two of them shared a birthday. Mary's family lived in Middleton; her mother, Liz, was an early volunteer in Feingold's first State Senate campaign. Mary was dark-haired, pretty and interested in being a writer. But unlike her mother, Mary was not drawn to politics and didn't envision living the rest of her life with a practicing politician. Before they were married, Feingold asked her about whether he should run for the Senate. "He had to bring it up three or four times before I took it seriously," Mary said. "Then I kind of panicked because I knew if he ran, he'd win. I didn't really want to marry someone who had such a compelling career." In a sense, Feingold sweet-talked Mary into it. "He would say, 'You know, I probably won't win,'" she recalled. "And I'd say, 'Let's talk about it as if we know you'll win.' But he'd kind of convince me to act as if he probably wouldn't. He knew if we talked as if he'd win, I wouldn't want to marry him." Russ and Mary dated for a few years before they were married in early 1991.

★ ★ ★

Russ Feingold's quest for a seat in the U.S. Senate passed through three surprising phases, each revealing in different ways a clash between troubling trends in contemporary politics and more hopeful alternatives. The first phase started long before the official announcement in front of his house.

Back on election night in November of 1986, the jubilation among Democrats in Washington, D.C., was not fully shared by Democrats in Madison, Wisconsin, Russ Feingold among them. Nationally, despite President Reagan's personal popularity, the Democrats won eight Senate seats, gaining control of the Senate while adding to their sizable House majority. But in Wisconsin, the news was not good at the top of the ticket: the incumbent Democratic governor, Anthony Earl, was defeated by Tommy Thompson, and the Democratic U.S. Senate candidate, Ed Garvey, lost a close, bitter race to the Republican Bob Kasten. Six years earlier, Kasten, riding Reagan's coattails, ended the distinguished Senate career of Gaylord Nelson, the father of Earth Day, an early opponent of the Vietnam War, and a highly respected, even beloved figure among Wisconsin progressives, including the Feingold family. Now Russ Feingold was staring at a television set at his victory party, thinking less about his reelection to the State Senate than about the man giving the televised victory speech, Kasten. "I want him," Feingold said, and his six-year campaign for the U.S. Senate had begun.

Just four years earlier, in 1982, when Russ Feingold took a gamble and ran against Cy Bidwell, the odds against him winning were long and most people discouraged him from trying. This time, however, the odds were much, much longer and the discouraging words stretched out over nearly six years, trailing him from Wisconsin to Washington. Soon after the 1986 election, Feingold started making periodic trips to Washington to meet potential allies and supporters—"potential" was indeed an apt word because he knew almost nobody and had only been to the nation's capital on a few brief visits.

Among his small number of Washington friends were Al Madison and his wife, Maryanne Sandretti. Feingold sometimes stayed with Al and Maryanne, bedding down in their unfinished basement on a sleeper sofa. In the late 1980s and early 1990s, Al introduced him to a slice of political Washington—labor leaders, pollsters, journalists and Democratic campaign contributors. Al remembers that although Feingold made a good personal impression, the Washington consensus about his political prospects never changed during this period: it was always, Al says, that "Russ didn't have a snowball's chance in hell." This is the kind of message that Feingold received over and over, either delivered to his face or more indirectly when his phone calls were not returned. "What amazed me," Sly Sylvester recalls about his friend's mostly dry runs to Washington, "is that he could take the amount of rejection you get in Washington when you are a little-known state senator without any money, but still keep coming back and impressing just enough people to keep himself in the game." But even in Wisconsin among seasoned political observers, Feingold's prospects were never bright. Dave Zweifel, the editor of the *Capital Times* who had written so approvingly about Feingold's progressive leadership in the State Senate, was a conspicuous example. When the 1992 Senate primary contest was in its early stage, Zweifel remembers Feingold coming into his office, sitting in front of him and saying confidently: "I'm going to win this thing." Zweifel was not persuaded.

Feingold's candidacy was given short shrift not only because he was a lowly state senator but also because political observers assumed other Democrats with more stature and money would run against Kasten. A case in point was the 1988 Wisconsin Democratic primary to nominate a successor to retiring Senator Bill Proxmire. No less than the former governor, Anthony Earl, was one of the candidates, but he was defeated by Herb Kohl, a multi-millionaire businessman who financed a lavish media campaign. And then Kohl won the general election, becoming one of the wealthiest members of the U.S. Senate. Had Russ Feingold been a candidate in that primary, the conventional wisdom would have given him no chance whatsoever. And now, just a few years later and with another U.S. Senate contest on the horizon, history was about to be repeated, or so it seemed. Another wealthy Democratic businessman, Joe Checota, inspired by Kohl's success, was planning to run for the Senate nomination, and his main opponent would be a well-regarded, five-term Democratic congressman, Jim Moody. When all of this ultimately materialized, the conventional wisdom was that Russ Feingold was the third man in a two-man race.

In the meantime, however, Feingold had plowed ahead, practicing an old-fashioned politics of citizen participation. With the help of a tiny cadre of friends and volunteers, he started organizing a grassroots network around the state. Not long after the 1986 election, Sly Sylvester remembers that he and Feingold pored over maps at Feingold's house, dividing the state into areas where they would eventually recruit regional and county coordinators for the Feingold for Senate campaign. In an age when successful candidates for high office relied on television to get elected, very few invested a lot of time and effort building personal relationships and a campaign organization. That exercise had become a quaint relic. And as Sly traveled the rural roads again helping Feingold in the early days of this long campaign, he knew that "a lot of people thought I was crazy." But the more time he spent with Feingold, and the more he learned about the Feingold family's attachment to Wisconsin's progressive history, the more Sly understood that Feingold's old-style approach to politics was an essential ingredient of who he was. "Russ wasn't just a hungry young guy who was inspired by maybe the Watergate generation or some things he'd picked up in college," Sly says. "His roots ran much deeper and his sense of obligation was much deeper. . . . He really had a vision for what he wanted to do," and that included engaging ordinary people in his campaign.

By 1990, a University of Wisconsin student, Mike Wittenwyler, had volunteered for the campaign, and Feingold put him in charge of the county contact system that he and Sly had gotten off the ground. Even though it was still early, more than two years before the primary, Wittenwyler remembers that they had at least one contact person in each of the state's seventy-two counties. Feingold expected detailed reports on all of them from Wittenwyler. "I had to call people once a month [and ask them], 'Hey, what's going on,' or the Tip O'Neill line, 'Tell me something new.'" Wittenwyler made sure that he talked to everybody and finished the reports when they were due because Feingold took them very seriously.

In fact, few details escaped Feingold's attention, even the placement of campaign signs around the state. Wittenwyler recalls Feingold coming into the small, cramped campaign office and debating with him about exactly where the "Feingold for Senate" barn signs should be posted. "We argued over whether a certain highway was a good place [for a sign]," Wittenwyler recalls with some amusement, or "whether there were enough cars to justify putting up a four-by-eight sign." On more occasions than Wittenwyler cares to remember, he and one or two other volunteers would get up at 6 A.M. on a Saturday, load a station wagon with Feingold signs, wooden posts, hammers and nails, and drive seven or eight hours north to, say, Superior. Then they would start driving back, stopping along the way to put up Feingold signs at the best locations. "I was supposed to show him a map once a month because he wanted to see progress," Wittenwyler recalls.

The twenty-year-old Wittenwyler was too young and too inexperienced to know how preposterous a Feingold victory was. At one point, however, the possible futility of the endeavor had briefly crossed his mind. "Yeah, maybe it's stupid," he had said to himself, "but I'm meeting a bunch of great people, having fun and getting experiences that I probably wouldn't get on somebody's campaign that had more money." He also had an innate love of the underdog and, even more important, there was Feingold's determined optimism. To Wittenwyler, it was not only that Feingold "was working as hard as I was," but also that "he believed in it, so we believed in it," Wittenwyler says, referring to himself and the other young, idealistic campaign workers.

"I always thought I could win," Feingold says many years later. "I don't do anything without thinking I can win. . . . I just kept plugging away and, regardless of who the potential Democrats were, I just thought, 'I'm going to find a way to win this primary and then I can beat Bob Kasten.' Of course, I didn't think [every day], 'I'm going to win. What's it going to be like to be a senator?' I focus on the task in front of me. So, I always assumed that I had a way to win. And I was excited about watching it unfold. For us to win in 1992, a hundred out of a hundred things had to go right."

Feingold's campaign manager, Bob Decheine, recalls that as the primary election drew closer, he had been encouraged by Paul Wellstone's upset Senate victory in Minnesota in 1990—and, in March of 1992 in Illinois, by Carol Moseley Braun's unexpected win over an incumbent in the three-way Democratic Senate primary.

After more than five years of campaigning, perhaps the first more visible, public sign that Feingold's hard work had borne a little fruit was the winning reception he received at the state Democratic convention in June of 1992, three months before the primary election. Feingold and his two opponents addressed some four hundred delegates, and it was Feingold who elicited "the warmest reception of the three," wrote Craig Gilbert, the *Milwaukee Journal*'s astute political reporter. "Some Democrats said that reflected his status as the favorite of party activists. Others said it simply showed he had worked this group longer and harder than anyone else." It was probably a combination of both. Not only were Feingold's county contact people at the convention, but so, too, were many others who had worked with him on some of his key state legislative issues, especially on aging and the bovine growth hormone controversy. In those statewide networks of senior citizens, small dairy farmers and consumer advocates, Russ Feingold was the people's passionate choice. Indeed, one senior citizen activist from Minocqua was so committed that he had taken it upon himself to place oval, white and blue "Feingold for Senate" stickers on paper towel dispensers and mirrors in public bathrooms across northern Wisconsin. Whenever somebody stared into a bathroom mirror in northern Wisconsin, he wanted them to see Russ Feingold, too!

Despite the Democratic delegates' enthusiasm for Feingold, the *Milwaukee Journal's* Gilbert was cautious about making too much of it, writing that "state conventions are iffy barometers of success in a primary."

But of course Gilbert's caution—his strong skepticism no doubt—was also influenced by the lopsided money advantage Feingold's opponents had, the hundreds of TV ads both had run while the Feingold campaign had not even produced one, and, finally, the polls that documented the mismatch. In fact, shortly before the state convention in June, the Feingold campaign's first and only poll was released, showing he had the support of a mere 11 percent of likely Democratic primary voters. Feingold's pollsters, Geoff Garin and Fred Yang of Peter D. Hart Research Associates, tried to put the best light on the results, pointing to the large number of undecided voters. The race was "wide open," Garin claimed.

Garin and Yang, two rising stars at the time among Washington's political pollsters, were working on the Feingold campaign because they had been impressed with Feingold when Al Madison introduced them in 1991. He was obviously smart, and they liked him and his idealism, so they took him on as a client even though they didn't think he had a chance to win. Even worse, he had no money and probably was not going to raise very much. Russ Feingold was not exactly their charity case, but he was an indulgence. One of Garin's first bits of advice to Feingold was not to waste his time finding a big-time Washington media consultant because none would be interested in his shoestring campaign. Coincidentally, back in Milwaukee, Feingold's old college roommate, Ron Luskin, suggested he talk with Steve Eichenbaum, a partner in a small advertising agency. Eichenbaum had never done political advertising, but he had an offbeat, creative touch that Luskin thought Feingold might appreciate. And he was right. The six-foot, five-inch Eichenbaum towered over Feingold, but they saw the world in a similar way, sharing a sharp-edged, sardonic sense of humor that Feingold rarely displayed publicly but that was an important part of his closest friendships.

In the summer of 1992, with July winding down and only six weeks to go until the primary election, the Feingold campaign desperately needed more visibility. Earlier, from his State Senate perch, Feingold had found ways to make some news on the BGH issue and on tax and budget battles with the Republican governor. But as far as the campaign itself was concerned, his PR plan had flopped. His campaign sent out a daily press release on one issue or another, but they were largely ignored. Feingold's news conferences didn't fare any better; often not a single reporter showed up. To many voters, if a candidate did not appear on television, he didn't exist. And even to some sympathetic, potential Feingold voters, his invisibility on television might have raised questions about whether a vote for

Feingold was a wasted one. Feingold's supporters were nervous, asking when his TV ads would start running.

With the election calendar rapidly disappearing and Feingold still around 10 percent in the polls, he and Bob Decheine went to see Steve Eichenbaum and delivered the bad news: rather than the $750,000 TV advertising budget that Eichenbaum had counted on when he was hired, the campaign could only afford about $185,000. When Eichenbaum heard that number, he was dumbfounded. His suddenly funereal face somehow caused Feingold to laugh. Eichenbaum turned to Decheine and growled: "What the fuck is he laughing at? He's going to get his ass kicked." And that made Feingold laugh some more before he turned serious and, as Eichenbaum remembers, said: "I've spent every free moment of my time on the phone trying to get money. I've done the best job I could. I wanted to see whether some regular guy that wasn't rich or connected had a shot at doing this. I've done the best I can and if that's what it is, that's what it is." And then Feingold stepped out of the room and Eichenbaum thought, "You know, it was long odds to begin with, but now he's dead. There's just no way."

After Eichenbaum recovered from the bad news, he began playing around with his limited possibilities. Feingold's opponents were spending a lot of money on well-crafted, professionally filmed TV spots, which the Feingold campaign couldn't afford. So Eichenbaum thought, "Let's just shoot [our spots] on a regular Hi8, just a consumer camera. And that's exactly what we did. We shot the whole campaign on a Canon Hi8. It was all video." And then Eichenbaum realized that "we're basically going to be shooting home movies," and he thought about that phrase—home movies—and began to think about the contrast between Feingold's modest Middleton house and Checota's Milwaukee mansion overlooking Lake Michigan. "I used to tease Russ about the way [his house] was furnished," Eichenbaum says. "'What the hell did you do, did you steal all the shit from the dormitory just before you left school?'" He also needled him about the "crap all over your garage doors," meaning Feingold's campaign promises. But now, in a creative burst, he told him, "If all of that doesn't make you a man of the people, I don't know what does." Inspired, Eichenbaum began producing a hilarious, two-minute TV ad that would introduce Feingold to primary voters by providing a sharp contrast between him and his two primary opponents, Checota and Moody. Although Feingold and Eichenbaum knew that Paul Wellstone had successfully used humorous TV ads in his Senate campaign, the spots Eichenbaum produced were highly original.

But even before Feingold's "Home Movies" hit the airwaves, something else happened that radically changed the dynamics of the campaign. In early August, a vicious advertising war broke out between Moody and Checota, one that Russ Feingold had anticipated. Shortly before it started in early August, an opinion poll showed that Checota, thanks to his massive TV ad campaign, was running neck and neck with Moody, the early favorite. When the poll was published, Feingold was, at first, depressed because he was still mired in third place. But by the next day, Sly Sylvester remembers, he had brightened considerably, telling Sly that Moody was going to "blow up" Checota, and while the two were preoccupied with slamming each other on television, he would have an opportunity to stand out as the alternative. And, by the third week in August, that's exactly what had happened.

The frequency and ferocity of the negative TV exchanges between Moody and Checota stunned even the professional politicians. Moody blasted Checota's business dealings and personal ethics, while Checota retaliated by ripping Moody about his income taxes and congressional votes. Since both men had sizable campaign bankrolls—Checota spent about $4 million of his own fortune in the primary—the huge flood of negative ads in a two-week period irritated the sensibilities of prospective voters. Even the chairman of the state Democratic Party called the unrelenting Moody-Checota attacks and counterattacks "repulsive." George Reedy, professor emeritus of journalism at Marquette University in Milwaukee, and President Lyndon Johnson's former press secretary, observed: "I think that both Moody and Checota lost their heads. You know, you can get into something like that without realizing what you're doing. Every step takes you further down the road, and those Checota-Moody commercials had reached the point where it was almost a burlesque of the dirty politician."

After nearly two weeks of Moody and Checota's grim feud, Feingold's lighthearted, funny introductory ad was not only a perfect contrast but a welcome relief no doubt to thousands of television viewers. The buzz about the ad started even before it ran. "The ad probably will make you chuckle," wrote a reporter for the *Wisconsin State Journal* who had previewed it two days before it appeared. "The boyish, handsome Feingold mugs for the camera, speaks well-delivered comic lines and tries to get across . . . his message—it's time for a Wisconsin fellow of average means to sit in the U.S. Senate."

The "Home Movies" ad opened with Feingold standing outdoors in shirtsleeves and loosened tie. "Hi, I'm Russ Feingold, the underdog who's running for the United States Senate. Underdog—that's the story of my life."

Over a photo of an Oxford University diploma, he said: "They said a kid from Janesville would never win a Rhodes Scholarship, but I did. They said I couldn't beat an incumbent state senator, but I did."

Holding a newspaper article, Feingold continued: "Now they say I won't be your next United States senator. That I don't have a fortune to spend on expensive TV commercials like my opponents. But I don't think wild spending is what people want in a senator anyway. I think people want a senator who's in touch with the problems of ordinary families. I believe that's me. I think these home movies will prove it."

The next scene showed Feingold outside Checota's Milwaukee mansion, where a driveway sign read, "Private. Dead End." With the camera rolling, Feingold walked up the driveway saying, "Our first home belongs to millionaire Joe Checota—he's one of my opponents. Let's see if he's around. Wow, look at these iron gates." When he rang the doorbell, the unexpected sound of a menacing, barking dog startled Feingold, which was captured on tape, much to Eichenbaum's delight. Finally, Feingold said to the camera, "I guess there's nobody here. Nice spread, huh? It's enough to make anyone feel like an underdog."

Then an image of Moody's house filled the screen, with Feingold saying: "Congressman Jim Moody, my other opponent, this is his home in Washington, D.C. He's lived there for years, but he does visit Wisconsin. . . . The congressman has another house in Jamaica, but we don't have the budget to fly there, so this brochure is going to have to do." Feingold held up a travel brochure that Eichenbaum created, showing an attractive woman relaxing in a luxurious Jamaican swimming pool. The scene shifted back to Feingold standing outside his small, Middleton ranch-style house, where he said: "I'm just the opposite. I've visited D.C., but I live right here in Middleton, Wisconsin. And if you elect me, I'll continue to live right here." The camera caught Feingold's garage door contract and followed him inside, where he showed the kitchen and the hallway and, as he opened a closet door, said in mock surprise: "Look—no skeletons!" He then delivered a low-key peroration from the family room: "My wife and I work hard to pay for this. And we don't have a lot of money to throw around. But money isn't what I need. What I need is your vote. And you can't buy votes in Wisconsin anyway. Time after time, good people without a lot of money have won elections here. Why? Because Wisconsin loves underdogs."

The two-minute "Home Movies" ad aired just once in every Wisconsin TV market beginning August 20. It provoked a large, overwhelmingly favorable public reaction and, when a new poll was released on August 27, Russ Feingold had leapt into a virtual tie with Checota and Moody. Much of the political reporting attributed the dramatic change of events to public reaction against Checota's and Moody's negative campaigning. Although they finally called a truce to the ad war, their tarnished images were beyond repair, magnified by the sharply contrasting Feingold ad and the favorable commentary it generated. Other humorous, attention-getting Feingold ads followed—one that was particularly funny and attracted national media coverage ended with Feingold holding a *National Enquirer*-like tabloid with the headline, "Elvis Endorses Feingold." Slyly, Feingold added, "You can't believe everything you read," a jab at his opponents for allegedly making things up. Amid the fun and media attention, Feingold was finally viewed as a serious contender for the Senate nomination after nearly six years of campaigning.

Now, the second phase of his quest for the Senate had become a two-week sprint to the primary election on September 8. Feingold thought the poll showing he was in a dead heat with his opponents had been a decisive "turning point." But still, the experts were skeptical. "What he seems to have going for him now is that he's not Moody and he's not Checota, and it may take more than that," said John F. Bibby, political science professor at the University of Wisconsin–Milwaukee. And his counterpart at the University of Wisconsin–Madison, Charles O. Jones, said Feingold faced the monumental task of increasing his name recognition and giving voters positive reasons to vote for him. "There just isn't that much time," Jones said. "He's late into the game." And Professor

Bibby added: "I'd still be very surprised if in the end he ran very close to the other two candidates."

But in these last days, when more voters were paying attention to the candidates, they saw important differences on key issues between Feingold and his opponents. For months, Feingold had pressed Moody and Checota to join him in three-man debates—and finally, in the home stretch of the campaign, debates were held. To this point, newspaper stories often described the three candidates as liberals who had few substantive disagreements. All were strongly pro-environment and supported universal health insurance, for example.

But on tax and budget issues, the distinctions were sharp, and Feingold's positions were reflective of the Wisconsin progressive tradition in which efficient, fiscally responsible government was a core value. While Moody and Checota favored supposedly popular middle-class tax cuts, Feingold opposed them. The highest priority, he argued, was attacking the growing national debt and budget deficits. In June, he had proposed an eighty-two-point budget deficit plan that his aide Sumner Slichter helped produce. Drawing on the work of the Congressional Budget Office, Feingold's plan featured large cuts in federal spending and tax increases on large corporations and wealthy Americans.

While his emphasis on fiscal responsibility was reminiscent of the La Follette progressives, it also played nicely on the contemporary political landscape that was being shaped by Ross Perot. The feisty Texan's own attack on soaring federal budget deficits was a centerpiece of his third-party presidential campaign and a major reason for his surprising popularity. Back in June, when Feingold unveiled his own deficit reduction plan, Perot was in first place in national presidential polls, ahead of George H. W. Bush and Bill Clinton.

The first debate, apart from giving Feingold badly needed

exposure, helped him in two other ways: he was immediately cast in a favorable light when much attention was given to a rehash of Moody's and Checota's negative campaigning, and he also stood out as a man of principle because, unlike his opponents, he opposed not only middle-income tax cuts but two trendy issues—term limits for Congress and a balanced budget amendment. He suggested both were ineffective and insincere schemes to "pander" to angry voters, a characterization that apparently many voters found credible coming from a man who sounded serious about reducing the federal deficit.

On the weekend before the election, the *Milwaukee Journal* published a poll that, if accurate, suggested an upset was in the making: Feingold was leading with 40 percent, followed by Moody with 26 percent and Checota at 23 percent. The surprising numbers hung over the last debate, which was televised live in Madison. When the candidates gave their closing remarks, Joe Checota said: "The blunt fact is that I want very much to be a United States senator and I've worked very hard for that privilege. But if it can't be me, I believe that Russ Feingold would better represent the people of Wisconsin." It was a stunning statement that caught Russ off guard and virtually everybody else, including Checota's campaign managers. Checota had delivered a strange combination of an honest admission about his dreams, an endorsement of Feingold and a final knee to the groin of Jim Moody.

Checota's quasi-endorsement was welcome news to be sure, but the endorsement Feingold was proudest of came earlier from Gaylord Nelson. On one of Feingold's exploratory trips to Washington, this one with daughter Jessica in tow, he went to see Nelson, who had a new career in his post-Senate years as chairman of the Wilderness Society. Feingold had a vivid childhood memory of Nelson. When Feingold was in the seventh grade and a newly elected member of the Marshall Junior High Student Council, the first "legislation" that he ever proposed was to have the council purchase a Wisconsin state flag. At the flag dedication, Nelson, then a U.S. senator, was the featured speaker, and Feingold introduced him. Nelson's appearance had been arranged by his old friend Leon Feingold. Now, more than twenty-five years later, Russ Feingold didn't think Nelson would endorse him because it was a contested primary and Nelson probably didn't want to take sides. But he asked anyway, and Nelson said: "Your father would never forgive me if I didn't." Feingold was thrilled and said years later: "That's the progressives sticking together through the generations, even after death."

On the Sunday before the election, the *Wisconsin State Journal* weighed in with its own unexpected endorsement. Reminding readers that it rarely voiced preferences in party primaries, the conservative-leaning paper said this race was different because of "what it could mean to the future of politics in Wisconsin. To paraphrase Winston Churchill, never have so many dollars been spent so cynically to influence so few voters." The size of Moody's and Checota's bankrolls did not trouble the newspaper, but the millions they spent polluting the public discourse did. In endorsing Russ Feingold, the paper pointed to his "intelligence, integrity and political instinct" that made him a worthy opponent for the Republican incumbent. Although the paper saw some flaws in his eighty-two-point program for cutting the federal deficit, it lauded him for "boldly attempt[ing] to slaughter some of Washington's sacred cows," and for not being stampeded into supporting ill-timed tax cuts. In short, Feingold was emerging from a long campaign with a public image that might have broad political appeal.

By election day, a landslide for any of the three candidates was about the last thing the experts expected. But that is what happened—and it wasn't merely a landslide, it was a huge avalanche. When all the votes were counted, Feingold had won a phenomenal 70 percent of the vote. At his victory celebration at a Middleton bowling alley, Feingold emphasized the themes that had most defined him, asserting that his campaign showed "that people do count more than money does, and that folks without a private fortune or top Washington connections can still run and win." In fact, Feingold's primary opponents had outspent him by about ten to one, and, in a sense, it was the abundance of their money that cost them the election. A *Milwaukee Journal* editorial celebrated the larger civic significance of his triumph. "What did Joe Checota and Jim Moody get for all their expensive nastiness? Tattered reputations and humiliating defeat. Russ Feingold's stunning, come-from-behind triumph in the Democratic race for the U.S. Senate nomination was a heartening rebuff to pit-bull politics and the power of money."

But it was also his extraordinary political skills that had allowed him to gain the maximum strategic advantage over his opponents. Most observers did not seem to appreciate just how politically creative Feingold had been. Among the few was a wry editorialist at the *Wisconsin State Journal*, who wrote: "In a jujitsu match, Japanese-style wrestlers rely on their knowledge of anatomy and leverage to use an opponent's strength and weight against him. . . . [The] 152-pound Russ Feingold has shown himself to be more adroit in the art of political jujitsu than either 'heavyweight' he encountered in the Democratic ring." And there was an insightful analysis by the *New York Times*'s Francis X. Clines, who had the good fortune after the election to observe Russ in action in Eau Claire, where a prominent member of the audience was Feingold's proud, high-school-era debate tutor, the irrepressible Gracie Walsh:

She offered a Mom-swallows-apple-pie-grin, as Russell D. Feingold, the conquering underdog, stepped up at a claque-laced news conference and recalled Ms. Walsh's summary of the fine art of competitive oratory: "Slip them the blade nicely, Russell." Oh he did, nicely, nicely. . . . Mr. Feingold made a stunning virtue . . . of mocking the major clichés of modern American politicking: all the negative attacks on opponents as agents of the Devil, monkish vows of no new taxes and temperance pledges to wrestle that unbalanced budget demon back into the bottle. Mr. Feingold would have none of that; instead he ran as the aberrant candidate with a practical sense of humor about politics, a risky course that culminated in his being endorsed by Elvis Presley . . . that his opponents could criticize as a fake attention-grabber only at the risk of seeming mirthless.

Feingold had produced, directed and starred in both a risky *and* virtuoso campaign performance; you could not have one without the other and be true to the grand tradition of Fighting Bob La Follette. La Follette's progressives mostly thought of themselves as perpetual underdogs against the big-money interests—and underdogs often had no choice but to gamble on unconventional, untested, sometimes unlikely strategies. Even winning elections now and then did not disturb the old progressives' basic mind-set. To be sure, the progressives who ran for office and won—the most successful—also knew when to assume the role of the practical politician, folding their cards when necessary. But over the generations, taking political risks for a worthy cause or principle became both central to the Wisconsin progressives' self-concept and their story line. Fighting Bob wore his proclivity for that kind of political risk-taking as a badge of honor, the same badge that Feingold wore in his rocketlike rise from obscurity to the political heights of a 70 percent primary victory.

After the primary win, the last phase—the general election contest between Feingold and Kasten—seemed like it might be a dull anti-climax. A *Milwaukee Journal* poll showed him leading the Republican incumbent 57 to 34 percent. Moreover, Kasten was not a popular politician in Wisconsin, nor did he have much of a presence in the state. Even worse, he was up for reelection in a year when voters seemed to be in one of their periodic moods to throw the bums out.

But Feingold knew he had his own vulnerabilities. The *Milwaukee Journal* poll, for example, showed that many likely voters did not know much about him or his policy positions. Although he received much media attention when he won the primary, earlier coverage had focused on his opponents and their TV ad war. And then there was the question of money: How badly would Feingold be outspent by Kasten? Would Kasten's inevitable attack ads painting Feingold as a rabid liberal overwhelm his capacity to respond effectively?

Kasten's campaign bankroll came from traditional Republican sources, plus "Jewish money," as the pros called it. (Although Jews voted overwhelmingly for Democrats, the pro-Israel lobby's bipartisan strategy included support for pro-Israel Republican incumbents like Kasten—support that resulted in an embarrassing incident involving Jim Moody in the spring in Washington, D.C. Like most congressional Democrats, Moody was also a staunch supporter of Israel and had been invited to address a pro-Israel political action committee meeting. But when its leaders belatedly discovered that Moody was a possible Kasten opponent, they refused to let him speak.)

As for Feingold, he began fantasizing how the next round of fund-raising was going to be unusually satisfying. Steve Eichen-baum remembers him saying: "You know what my fondest day is going to be? It's going to be the day after the primary. I don't care how long we party [on primary night]. I'm going to get up early in the morning, and I am going to go around to all of these Democrats who wouldn't give me any money because they told me I had no chance of winning. I'm not going to be cocky or condescending. I'm just going to walk in, smile and say: 'Hi, now I need your help.'" And Feingold added: "*That* is going to make me feel terrific."

The campaign staff began to funnel the most urgent fundraising calls that needed to be made through David Harth, who took a leave of absence from his law firm and became the campaign's chief of staff and Feingold's frequent traveling companion around the state. "Russ, you gotta get on the phone," Harth would say. "I don't want to," Feingold would occasionally reply. Generally, however, Feingold did not shrink from making the calls. After breakfast, for example, when he wasn't out campaigning, he'd sit at his dining room table and methodically make fund-raising calls from a list of prospects.

With Feingold, Harth crisscrossed the state in one of the campaign's symbols, a scruffy 1984 Ford Econoline van with over 100,000 miles on the odometer. Harth was not a political guy; one of his main roles was to manage the staff and, occasionally, to fire people. At least as important, though, was that he was Feingold's friend and part of his extended campaign family. "Russ relies on the people around him," Harth says, "so it was a very communal experience."

On a typical travel day, they'd gather in Feingold's living room early in the morning, drive to as many campaign events as possible, and end up back in Middleton late at night. "A lot of times we had pretty shoddy advance work," Harth recalls, "so a lot of times the crowds weren't there, but he was always positive. It didn't matter if there were two or three people at a stop. He'd do his thing, and search for more people to talk to and just go on to the next place." Harth marveled at his stamina and even-tempered disposition. Occasionally, there would be a short nap in the back of the van, but generally "he'd wear people out," Harth remembers. And "every day there was crisis, crisis, crisis, but he remained calm." Yelling or snapping at staffers was not Feingold's style.

Feingold and Kasten had their first joint appearance on a thirty-minute TV program less than a week after the primary. With much bravado, Kasten tore into Feingold for supporting tax increases, "looking like a cat about to eat a canary," as a newspaper story described him. He accused Feingold of casting his first vote in the State Senate for the largest tax increase in Wisconsin history. Calmly, Feingold replied: "The senator correctly and accurately portrayed my first vote." He went on to explain, however, that the tax increase was necessary to offset a large budget deficit left by the outgoing Republican governor.

Although Kasten agreed with Feingold that the budget deficit was the country's biggest problem, he wanted to make absolutely certain that voters knew Feingold wanted to increase taxes as part of his eighty-two-point deficit reduction plan. Russ was unapologetic. "Senator, you don't need to be quite so emphatic because you're telling the truth. I do support a higher tax bracket for those who make $150,000. Not everything we do is going to be pleasant."

They also disagreed on other issues in the first debate: term limits, a balanced budget amendment and the controversial nomination of Clarence Thomas to the U.S. Supreme Court, all of which Feingold opposed. When the debate turned to the subject of campaign tactics, Feingold pledged that "I'm not going to run a dirty campaign or negative ads about Senator Kasten under any circumstances even if he does them about me." Kasten, while saying he intended to focus on the issues, did not embrace Feingold's unambiguous pledge. And for good reason. The Republican formula for defeating candidates like Feingold was to bash and then bury them in a suffocating caricature of tax-and-spend, soft-on-crime liberals. Kasten himself had been a beneficiary of the approach. He had hired one of the masters of the low blow, Roger Ailes, as his media guru in his reelection campaign in 1986. That campaign had been especially nasty. When it was over, Kasten was forced to apologize publicly to his defeated opponent about indefensible, scurrilous personal attacks that his campaign made. But by then, Kasten had been reelected, proving that bare-knuckle negative campaigning can work when winning is all that matters.

This time around, however, the political environment in Wisconsin was a little trickier; voter backlash to the Checota-Moody TV wars forced Kasten strategists to avoid negative campaigning for as long as they could. The first Kasten TV ad was a clever, humorous attempt to beat Feingold at his own game. It featured an Elvis impersonator sitting in a Cadillac in the clouds next to a cardboard cutout of Feingold, who was holding up a tabloid with the headline "Elvis Endorses Feingold." The impersonator said: "I don't make many appearances, but when I heard that State Senator Russ Feingold was tellin' tales how I endorsed him, I had to come forward." Noting that Feingold would raise taxes by $300 billion, Elvis drawled: "Well, the King would never support that. And Feingold is even opposed to a constitutional amendment to balance the budget. Something y'all are for. Take it from the King . . . This Russ Feingold record got me all shook up."

Feingold continued to use humorous TV ads that helped define his image while highlighting Kasten's weaknesses. The most memorable drew attention to Feingold's claim that he was more in touch with Wisconsin voters because he had been traveling around the state listening to them for the past five years while Kasten was mainly in Washington. At the end of each ad in the series, Feingold held up his left hand, the back of it facing the TV camera. Wisconsin natives were well aware even before Feingold's commercial that the back of one's left hand was shaped like a map of Wisconsin, the thumb representing the Door County peninsula. While holding up his left hand, Feingold would say, "Next stop La Crosse," pointing to a spot on his hand near the pinkie joint where La Crosse is located. The series of ads became so familiar and popular that strangers who spotted Feingold on the campaign trail would get his attention by holding up their left hand and mimicking his TV performance.

Occasionally, Feingold's humor would also come through in the formal debates he had with Kasten. When Kasten charged that lawsuits were driving up the cost of health care and that Feingold was "in bed with the trial lawyers," Feingold got a big laugh with his deadpan reply: "I have no personal recollection of being in bed with a trial lawyer." Typically, however, the debates were serious affairs, with Feingold more likely to use ridicule than joke-telling as a rhetorical weapon. At the end of one early debate, he told the audience:

> You've been treated to a show here today. It's something I'm going to be calling the Kasten two-step. It's a new dance step. Step No. 1: If an issue is too difficult, ignore it. Don't talk about the deficit. Don't talk about the fact 38 million Americans don't have health insurance. Maybe it will go away! Step No. 2: If your opponent starts talking about the issues and has a solution, start labeling the guy. Call him a tax-and-spender. Say he's out of step. Say he's out in left field. God forbid you should talk about the actual proposal or tell the truth about it. That's the two-step dance that this whole campaign is about, Senator, because you don't have a leg to stand on when it comes to your proposals.

The candidates mainly debated domestic issues, although Kasten tried to cast doubt on Feingold's patriotism by attacking his opposition to the 1991 Persian Gulf War. On the eve of the war,

Feingold had signed a resolution calling for the withdrawal of U.S. troops. His unyielding response to Kasten was that the military action "could have been avoided," adding: "I, along with twenty-five other members of the Wisconsin Legislature, signed that resolution. We were appalled to learn that this country financed Saddam Hussein, that the Bush-Kasten administration had given him military aid, had given him our hard-earned dollars, to create that regime in the first place. That's reckless spending. That's reckless foreign policy."

By mid-October, Kasten was closing the gap but still trailing in the polls when his campaign zeroed in on one of the Republican Party's favorite hot-button issues: violent crime. In the 1988 presidential campaign, Democrat Michael Dukakis's prospects were badly hurt by a TV ad—and by related Republican attacks—connecting him and his policies to convicted murderer Willie Horton, who raped a woman while on a state-approved weekend furlough from prison. For many Democrats, the Willie Horton ad was yet another reminder of how vulnerable their party remained on the issue of crime—in large part because the Republicans were often shamelessly unrestrained in appealing to the public's darkest fears for maximum political advantage.

Many Democratic leaders, running scared for a generation or more, decided their best political strategy was to give in on criminal justice issues—to embrace Republican positions. That was essentially Bill Clinton's motivation in the 1992 presidential primary campaign when he went out of his way, literally, to dramatize his robust support for the death penalty. Then-governor Clinton was in New Hampshire when he announced that he was suspending campaigning and traveling home to Arkansas so he could preside over the execution of one Ricky Lee Rector. Rector, a young black man, had been convicted for murder. But he was now so mentally impaired from a bullet to his brain that when his last meal arrived before it was time for his lethal injection, Rector said he would save the dessert for "later." Clinton, who earlier in his career opposed the death penalty, could have intervened and stopped the execution, but he didn't.

Feingold was passionately opposed to the death penalty, saying it was "morally offensive," "barbaric" and not a deterrent of violent crime—the historic position that enlightened Democratic leaders, including presidential candidates, used to espouse. Kasten, however, repeatedly cited Feingold's death penalty opposition as proof—a definitive symbol—that he was soft on crime and out of step with Wisconsin voters.

But that was only the beginning. In shades of the Willie Horton episode, the Kasten campaign tried to connect Feingold to the recent parole of a child rapist-killer from the state prison. Kasten distorted Feingold's State Senate voting record so that, in Kasten's version, it sounded as if Feingold favored early parole for the most dangerous criminals. The Kasten campaign also used the old, sleazy "push poll" technique: in phone calls to thousands of Wisconsin homes, a Kasten-retained political consulting company asked, in effect, whether voters were more or less likely to vote for Feingold if they knew that he favored legislation that would make the state's convicted mass murderer, Jeffrey Dahmer, eligible for parole. After newspaper reporters learned about the push poll, and after Feingold angrily said to Kasten, "Is there no limit to what you will do?" the Kasten campaign announced it was dropping the Dahmer question. But perhaps the damage had been done, as the Kasten campaign intended. Who could say that news coverage of the push poll, for example, hadn't planted seeds of doubt among some voters about where Feingold really stood on the crime issue?

By the last weekend of the campaign, everybody knew the race was close—according to a *Milwaukee Journal* poll, Kasten had taken a small lead. He had outspent Feingold by about three to one, and his TV ads relentlessly attacked Feingold's positions not only on taxes and crime, but also on Feingold's opposition to key elements of Tommy Thompson's state welfare reform plan. But Feingold's TV ads mostly ignored Kasten's attacks. His advertising dollars were mainly spent as they had been in the primary, portraying him as a refreshingly honest, good-guy underdog and emphasizing his plans for national health insurance and, especially, for cutting federal spending and the budget deficit. Democratic strategists, however, were not sanguine about Feingold's unwillingness to fight fire with fire in his TV ads. That was risky if not self-defeating, they believed. But Feingold would not budge.

On election night, Feingold and his wife, their children, his mother and his siblings gathered in a suite at the Holiday Inn West in Middleton to watch the election returns. The polls closed at 8 P.M., and less than two hours later a local TV station reported that the Associated Press was calling Russ Feingold the winner. The Feingold suite erupted in joyous shouts, hugs and kisses. But at least for the first moment or two after the great news, Feingold was subdued, nodding his head as if to say, yes, this is what I thought would happen. That's not how the next day's newspaper stories characterized his victory, using adjectives such as "surprisingly strong," a reference to Feingold's comfortable 53 to 47 percent winning margin. When Feingold appeared in the hotel ballroom to speak to his ecstatic supporters at around 10 P.M., Kasten had not yet called to concede. Unlike his first Republican opponent, Cy Bidwell, Feingold had little respect for Kasten and couldn't resist delivering a public reprimand. "There's something seriously wrong with the way you campaign," he told Kasten in absentia. "Senator, what's wrong with the truth?" And then directing his remarks to his supporters, Feingold added: "I didn't appreciate the things he said. It wasn't very nice. But guess what? It didn't work."

Similar sentiments were expressed in a post-election *Milwaukee*

Journal editorial. The newspaper had not endorsed Feingold in the primary, but it had come to appreciate the larger significance of his campaign.

> The conventional wisdom says that negative campaigning and big money are a winning ticket. Russ Feingold proved the conventional wisdom wrong Tuesday. His 53%–47% trouncing of incumbent U.S. Sen. Bob Kasten, a mudslinger par excellence, was as sweet as it was instructive. Sweet because few people initially thought Feingold, a spunky but relatively unknown Democratic state senator, had a chance of toppling a well-funded, 12-year Republican incumbent. Instructive because Feingold ran the kind of race that cynics would consider hopeless: clean and issue-oriented, long on grass-roots energy, short on cash. May that kind of hopelessness thrive. Yes, there were times when the cuteness factor grated; how many more of those "next stop: La Crosse" ads did TV viewers have to watch? But Feingold's humor was appealing. So were his maverick ways—for example, his gutsy refusal to support a middle-class tax cut or term limits. . . . Kasten's unremitting nastiness also played a role. His squalid distortion of Feingold's record clearly turned off a lot of voters. Serves Kasten right. Maybe other dirt-throwers will now think twice.

Russ Feingold was one of only two Democratic Senate candidates to defeat a Republican incumbent in 1992. Clinton, who won only 43 percent of the presidential vote, had no coattails. Voter turnout was up significantly in many states—in Wisconsin it was the highest since 1964—and that was due mainly to the political interest generated by Ross Perot's historic candidacy. Nationally, Perot's 19 percent of the popular vote was the best showing of a third-party candidate since Theodore Roosevelt ran on the Bull Moose ticket in 1912. In Wisconsin, Perot did even better, capturing 22 percent of the vote. Exit polls showed that Perot voters favored Russ Feingold over his opponent by 56 to 44 percent, perhaps attracted by Feingold's Perot-like emphasis on reducing the budget deficit and his emerging image as a political independent who was also a Democrat.

For much of the twentieth century, Wisconsin voters had a reputation for being attracted to independent-minded politicians and mavericks—and, therefore, for a long time, Wisconsin was regarded among political professionals as different from other states. But nationwide over the last several decades, increasingly more voters saw themselves as independents, as allegiance to political parties declined. To be sure, Wisconsin may still have been ahead of the political curve when it came to the prominence of independent voters in 1992, but its ticket-splitting tradition was no longer unique. Indeed, the larger significance of Russ Feingold's stunning upsets in the primary and general elections was that his kind of bold, progressive and anti–political establishment politics almost certainly had broad appeal beyond Wisconsin. But whether that included Washington, D.C., where the political culture was adept at reeducating hinterland idealists, remained to be seen.

One of political Washington's time-honored rules was that new members of Congress were expected to defer to their elders. In Feingold's case, that meant deference to just about everybody, since at thirty-nine years old, he was about to become the Senate's youngest member.

CHAPTER 8

MR. FEINGOLD GOES TO WASHINGTON

Russ Feingold was not only the youngest senator when the new Congress convened in January 1993; he was also probably the poorest. That's what his bank account showed—but it wasn't puny because he had splurged on furniture for his Washington apartment where he would live during the week, when the Senate was in session.

Sly Sylvester and Mike Wittenwyler volunteered to move some of Feingold's personal belongings from Middleton. They swung by his house in a Ryder rental truck that contained some of Mike's things; he was also heading east to work in Russ's Washington office. A stickler for neatness and order, Mike had carefully packed and labeled his boxes, stacking them in a roped-off section of the truck. When he saw Feingold's load, Mike was appalled. Feingold's boxes, overflowing with books and papers, were an unstackable mess. And his secondhand furniture looked like it came from a Salvation Army thrift shop. "The furniture was junk," was Sly's blunt appraisal. Some was donated for Feingold's Washington apartment by a few friends and family members—Sly contributed his parents' old orange sofa bed from the 1960s, plus mattresses from a friend whose parents had died. Sly could only imagine what some of Feingold's new neighbors would think when they hauled his belongings up to his apartment near the Capitol. Feingold, on the other hand, didn't much care what they thought.

Russ Feingold's lack of personal wealth and his attitude about making money—it wasn't a high priority—immediately set him apart from many of his Senate colleagues and Washington's political culture. During his time in the Senate, about half of his colleagues have been millionaires. Historically, senators tended to be wealthier than House members and the general population.

Perhaps the peak of Senate wealth occurred in the late nineteenth and early twentieth centuries, followed by one of the democratizing landmarks of the Progressive Era, the ratification of the Seventeenth Amendment in 1913. The reform provided for the direct election of senators and was motivated in part by the corrupting influence of wealth and corporate power in state legislatures, which had previously elected senators.

In the state houses, vote-buying was sometimes part of the electoral process. And as the historian Michael Beschloss has noted, there were "members of the Senate . . . who were essentially owned by railroads, took briefcases full of cash. Their colleagues knew that they cast votes that were essentially paid for." And it was this kind of political environment that recalled Mark Twain's barb that "there is no distinctly native American criminal class except Congress." The acid of corruption eating away at the country's democratic machinery has a long history, but so, too, does the work of generations of reformers who have aroused their fellow citizens to repair the damage.

Almost from Feingold's first day in the nation's capital, it became apparent to Fred Yang that Feingold was going to trample on one of the important norms of political Washington, where members of

Congress and their staff, lobbyists and journalists practiced the fine art of trading small and sometimes not-so-small favors in exchange for mutually beneficial "friendships." For Yang, there was a revealing moment at a Capitol Hill restaurant soon after the election when he and his colleague, Geoff Garin, kibitzed with Feingold and a staff member over lunch. When the check arrived, Garin and Yang were going to pay it, but Feingold refused; he said that he and his staffer would pay for their own lunch. Yang remembers saying to himself: "Boy, they're going to love this guy up here"—meaning, of course, they weren't. Feingold, however, knew what kind of senator he wanted to be. Like Jimmy Stewart's Mr. Smith, he came to Washington with high ideals, but after ten years as a state legislator he was not a political innocent. "I didn't come to Washington to be popular," Feingold says more than a decade after his arrival, a comment that might sound innocuous unless one meant it.

From Day One, the strict ethical rules in Feingold's Senate office were different from the rules in probably all the other Senate offices, and that attracted attention. Feingold and his staff followed the rules of the U.S. Senate or the Wisconsin legislature, whichever were more stringent. In most cases, it was Wisconsin's. When lobbyists and others offered gifts, free meals and entertainment, for example, Feingold and his staff followed Wisconsin's nothing of value or zero tolerance prohibition. Not only did they refuse the "gift" of a cup of coffee but when they attended Capitol Hill receptions, they didn't consume a single canapé or ginger ale regardless of whether the reception was sponsored by a big corporation or a little nonprofit group. On one occasion, Mike Wittenwyler recalls, a friend introduced him to a woman who was a lobbyist in Washington. "The woman took me to lunch, but I told her I had to pay for it. She looked at me like I was insane. 'I'm sorry, it's the rule, I have to pay for my lunch,'" he told her, even though it was a modest one in the Senate cafeteria. Wittenwyler also remembers being invited to his first big Washington event, the annual White House Correspondents' Association dinner, by a *Milwaukee Journal* reporter. "He took me as a guest . . . but Russ would not allow me to take the ticket for free from the newspaper," Wittenwyler says. "I had to pay for a ticket and a tuxedo."

Not only did some lobbyists think that the Feingold rules were weird or excessive, but staffers from other Senate offices began to show their resentment, recalls Susanne Martinez, who was Feingold's newly hired but most experienced aide in 1993. A fifteen-year Senate staff veteran, Martinez began to encounter snide remarks from other Senate offices because, she sensed, they didn't appreciate the implications of the Feingold model.

> I remember going late at night to some committee meeting— we were cleaning up a bill. I walked in, and they had Chinese food. They asked if I wanted some. I said, "Did you buy this? I'm not allowed to accept something except if it's from another staff person." They laughed and said, "Don't worry; we ordered it. You [Feingold] guys are such pains in the butt." So I took an egg roll. And after I ate it, they started laughing. It was actually sent up by some restaurant association or some lobbying group. They were just cracking up. "You're contaminated," they said. "Taking food from lobbyists." So I took a dollar out and laid it on the table. "Here's my dollar for my egg roll," I said. It was an interesting illustration . . . of how it was a threat to their culture.

Back in Wisconsin, the political culture was indeed different from Washington's in the 1980s and early 1990s. Wisconsin's renowned image for honest government could be traced to La Follette and other progressives at the turn of the twentieth century. Up to that point, Wisconsin was no different from many other states. Corporate lobbyists had dominated the state capitol—one of their more colorful tricks of the trade was the rigged card games they ran at the Park Hotel in which compliant legislators somehow walked away with the biggest jackpots. The La Follette progressives wielded a stiff broom when they gained power, sweeping away blatant bribery and slightly less poisonous practices, such as the railroads' generous dispensation of complimentary travel passes to legislators and even judges. The railroads' travel passes had been a good-for-business investment, roughly akin to today's practice by corporations of making their executive jets available to busy and, they hope, grateful representatives and senators.

During Feingold's tenure in the Wisconsin State Legislature, not all his fellow legislators adhered to the nothing-of-value rule as strictly as he did. In fact, on one occasion in 1988, the legendary Chicago columnist Mike Royko, who delighted in both celebrating and lampooning Illinois-style political chicanery (he said the city of Chicago's motto should be *"ubi est mea"* or "Where's mine?"), wrote a tongue-in-cheek critique of Wisconsin's "misguided" political ethics and etiquette. Royko had heard that Wisconsin's governor, Tommy Thompson, was in a little hot water because, in a wide-ranging interview, he had made an offhand comment to a reporter that when he was a state legislator, some lobbyists might have bought him drinks. Thompson's "confession" turned out to be the focus of the reporter's story and provoked an investigation by the secretary of state. Royko wrote:

The governor, sounding genuinely confused, said that he meant no harm and that such things can innocently happen. As he explained, a group of people can be sitting around munching sandwiches and having a beer. The politician might pick up that tab, which is legal. But then the lobbyist might order after-dinner drinks and pay for them, which is illegal. If you think about it, that's pretty stupid. Why should a lobbyist get free sandwiches and beers and not reciprocate by popping for the after-dinner hooch. That's simply common courtesy. In Illinois' state legislature, if a lobbyist didn't buy his share of drinks, or more than his share, he would be considered a moocher and a low-life.

Taking the Illinois worldview, one of Feingold's U.S. Senate colleagues, John Breaux of Louisiana, once told Feingold during a Senate debate on banning gifts and free meals that maybe people in Wisconsin didn't like having a little fun. To which Feingold responded, "Oh, we do, but we pay for it."

Six months after Feingold took office in 1993, he was featured on the front page of the *Wall Street Journal* because his office had taken the highly unusual if not revolutionary step, it was reported, of "getting rid of freebies from lobbyists and special interest groups," sending it all to a local charity. And quite a smorgasbord of goodies it was: everything from candy, cookies and bratwurst to a Waterford crystal obelisk, fancy bookends and a hydroponic plant. "It's time to clean up stuff like this," Feingold said. His office had logged 201 gifts in less than six months. "This is the mother of all perks," he said. "It's potentially worth tens of thousands of dollars a year. And it's been part of the way of life around here."

But now, after the 1992 election, "business-as-usual" was under attack in Washington. It was not only Ross Perot, the political outsider, who had scored points in the 1992 presidential campaign by castigating the ethics of Washington's political insiders. The new president, Bill Clinton, also had embraced political reform. And so, early in 1993 with reform in the air, a gift ban was proposed in the Senate by Feingold and three other Democrats: Paul Wellstone of Minnesota, Carl Levin of Michigan and Frank Lautenberg of New

Jersey. But old ways die hard in Washington, especially when congressional perks are at stake. Many Democrats and Republicans alike enjoyed receiving free meals or trips to "charity" golf events and seminars in luxurious settings that lobbyists paid for. Many felt a sense of entitlement, in part because they believed that they could be making much more money as lawyers or lobbyists if they had not made a sacrifice of holding public office. And then there was the stinginess factor. In the early 1990s in Washington, Susanne Martinez recalls, a number of senators and their wives coveted invitations as honored guests to socially important black-tie charity balls. But if a gift ban were enacted, a senator would have to pay $1,000 or more for tickets, which might be a little more charity than the average senator had in mind. Not surprisingly, the gift ban proposal did not quickly sail through the Senate, nor was a similar proposal allowed to move forward in the House, where first the Democratic speaker, Tom Foley, and then his Republican successor, Newt Gingrich, employed delaying tactics.

Finally, after more than two years and much prodding and shaming by editorial writers and public interest groups, the Senate did adopt a gift ban in the summer of 1995. The new rules allowed gifts up to $50, but no senator could receive more than $100 from an individual per year. Although the reform fell short of Wisconsin standards and there were loopholes, it was generally hailed by reform advocates as an important step, albeit a modest one, toward curbing the influence of special interest money in Washington. The *New York Times* said the "reform would have been buried" without the leadership of Feingold and his three Democratic colleagues, plus two Republicans, William Cohen of Maine and John McCain of Arizona. It was one of the first issues on which Feingold and McCain worked together—and by the time the gift ban was approved, they were already close to unveiling a much more ambitious reform of the campaign finance laws.

★ ★ ★

Washington was an exciting place for Democrats in January of 1993. For the first time in twelve years, one of their own was president. In the Senate, four women, all Democrats, had been newly elected, an unprecedented event that led to stories about "The Year of the Woman" in Washington. But perhaps nobody was more unabashedly excited about being a United States senator than Russ Feingold. At one of the first gatherings of new senators, Feingold could hardly believe he was in the ornate office of the Senate president, Robert Byrd of West Virginia, listening to a lecture by the silver-haired orator on the Senate's two-hundred-year history. When Feingold and his friend Bob Decheine walked out, they were shaking their heads, wondering if it was all real or only a dream.

Even before Feingold arrived in the Senate after the election, the *Washington Post* sent a reporter, Michael Abramowitz, to Wisconsin to learn more about what the reporter would later write was "one of the great political stories" of the year. His long feature not only recounted Feingold's unorthodox run to unexpected victory. It explored the possibility that his political insights and strategies might have implications beyond Wisconsin. Political experts had predicted that incumbents would fare poorly in 1992, but that turned out not to be the case. Only three incumbents lost, one being Feingold's opponent. What had Feingold achieved and what did he represent that might indicate something new or different was happening in American politics? The answer, or so it seemed when the *Washington Post* article ran, was a bit elusive. On the surface, there appeared to be similarities between Feingold and the feisty Minnesotan, Paul Wellstone. But, Abramowitz wrote, "Feingold's politics are actually patterned less after Wellstone and more after Wisconsin's own long line of mavericks that goes back to Robert La Follette and makes it tricky to read too much national significance into his upset victory." Indeed, "tricky" was a good word choice, implying that it was unclear whether independent-minded politicians could have broad voter appeal beyond the Badger State. Abramowitz, using the words "progressive" and "populist" interchangeably, concluded that "Feingold's brand of populist politics is hard to classify on the ideological spectrum. An advocate of both abortion rights and deep cuts in Pentagon programs, he also espouses fiscal conservatism and has sponsored a constitutional amendment in Wisconsin guaranteeing the right to keep and bear arms."

Apart from Feingold's early work on the gift ban, there were two issues more than others that reflected his political values. The first had to do with fiscal responsibility, the budget deficit and government spending. When he moved into his new office on the fifth floor of the Hart Building, he displayed prominently on one wall the deficit reduction plan he proposed during the Senate campaign. "The first thing we did," recalls Susanne Martinez, "was we went through the eighty-two-point plan," looking for programs Feingold could sink his teeth into. It took a while, she remembers, in part because some of the deficit-cutting recommendations were already being worked on by others. They finally targeted a program on international broadcasting. It included generous funding for such Cold War relics as Radio Free Europe. Since Europe was now free, dispassionate observers argued, RFE (and a companion operation, Radio Liberty) should be given an honorable burial. The cost savings over five years was estimated at $1 billion. But this program, like virtually every federal program, had influential supporters and a congressional protector—in this case, Senator Joe Biden of Delaware. He was a senior Democrat on the Committee on Foreign Relations who was about to have an unexpected confrontation with one of the committee's rookies.

Feingold ended up on Foreign Relations by default. When he

didn't land two of his preferred committee assignments, Appropriations or Judiciary, the Democratic majority leader, George
Mitchell, gave him a list of four other committees to choose from:
Armed Services, Commerce, Banking and Foreign Relations. "I
knew that the insiders would tell you," Feingold says, "the last one
you should pick in terms of power and fund-raising was Foreign
Relations. But I just had one of those moments when you really
know who you are." During Feingold's teenage years, when he
dreamed about becoming a U.S. senator, he even fantasized about
the Senate committees he would serve on. Foreign Relations was
at the top of his list—and, in the late 1960s, it was a glamorous,
influential committee. Chaired by one of the giants of the Senate,
J. William Fulbright, the committee's hearings were at the center
of the raging national debate over the Vietnam War. As a newly
elected senator, Feingold still equated serving on Foreign Relations and being "connected with what's going on in the rest of the
world" as the essence of being a senator.

When the Foreign Relations Committee held hearings on the
international broadcasting program early in 1993, Feingold came
armed with juicy examples of budgetary extravagance, not the least
of which were the salaries of top Radio Free Europe officials based
in Germany. A *Washington Post* column captured the flavor of the
proceedings:

> Eyes popped, heads spun and reporters thought about dusting
> off their resumes after a Senate Foreign Relations Committee
> hearing last week when Sen. Russell Feingold (D-Wis.)
> unveiled the pay of top officials at Radio Free Europe/Radio
> Liberty Inc. The president of the Munich-based operation
> receives $316,824 in salary and benefits, according to Fein-
> gold's figures. That includes a $52,056 "post allowance" for liv-
> ing expenses, payments of German taxes, a housing allowance

and other benefits. The director of Radio Free Europe receives a package worth $318,036, while the personnel director gets a package worth $232,704.

Sen. Joseph R. Biden Jr. (D-Del.) said the high salaries do not mean the independent corporation . . . should be put under the control of the U.S. Information Agency, which would whack the pay down to regular federal government levels. Moving RFE/RL under USIA, rather than keeping it an independent grantee, Biden argued, would threaten the operation's journalistic independence and make it a tool of American foreign policy. Feingold and his allies say an organization begun by the CIA and funded by the government need not worry about being seen as a tool of U.S. policy. With the Cold War over, they argue, taxpayers need a break and a corporation setting its own salaries is not the way to go.

Biden wasn't the only guardian of the status quo. Feingold soon discovered he was up against Washington insiders of varying political stripes—the wealthy Republican Malcolm S. Forbes was chairman of the board of the broadcasting program; the AFL-CIO president, Lane Kirkland, was another board member; the writer Bette Bao Lord, wife of a high-ranking Clinton administration official, publicly criticized Feingold's budget cuts; and on and on. Feingold's reaction to this kind of opposition sounded very much like the person he was—a still young man from Janesville who didn't identify with the influential Washington networks and had no aspiration to become part of them. "There are some pretty well-placed people who don't want this to happen," Feingold said. "It has become a classic example of why it's so difficult to cut fat out of the federal budget. Every program has the most surprising set of people supporting it, and it's not the people back home. It's the people here who are tied into the Washington social scene."

Despite Biden's opposition, Feingold won a big victory when the Committee on Foreign Relations voted 15–4 for Feingold's proposal. It was his first legislative battle in the Senate. Today, Martinez, who knew her way around the Senate, recalls how impressed she was. "Early on, I don't think Biden took Russ seriously because he was a freshman and Biden was way up there at the top of the pyramid. But Russ met with everyone on the committee about his concerns. It was his careful, meticulous work of building the case . . . and getting all of the votes lined up. And I remember Biden was shocked." Before the end of the year, much of Feingold's proposal to reshape the international broadcasting program and cut its budget was signed into law. "It was an early example," Martinez says, "that when Russ took one of these things on, he really did his homework . . . [and] had to be taken seriously." As for Feingold, he recalls that winning his first battle was "very instructive because it was a whole different world than fighting this stuff in Wisconsin where you knew all the agencies. You begin to get a flavor of all the back channels, the relationships, the former staffers, the senators, the unbelievable complexity of the special interests and government intersection. But it was fun and exciting."

In his first year, Feingold had begun to assemble the core of a strong staff, although he was the unquestioned, hands-on boss. In addition to Martinez, there were two first-rate, loyal Wisconsinites, Nancy Mitchell and Sumner Slichter. Both knew Feingold from his days at Foley & Lardner and have worked with him ever since. Mary Murphy Irvine was hired after Feingold's election to the Senate, eventually becoming his valued chief of staff. And there were other talented, dedicated aides, George Aldrich and Patti Jo McCann, who have worked with Feingold for much of his political career.

After that first legislative success, Feingold went after an assortment of other inviting budget-cutting targets, such as the federal subsidies to wool, mohair and even helium producers. He attempted to abolish the Uniformed Services University, a little-known but costly medical school in the Department of Defense that had the support of a senior Democratic senator. He made a senatorial ruckus over a behind-the-scenes maneuver by two senators, Howell Heflin, a Democrat of Alabama, and Republican Fred Thompson of Tennessee, to exempt the Tennessee Valley Authority from the impact of a proposed constitutional amendment for a balanced budget. This caught the attention of the *Washington Post*, which editorialized that if Thompson and Heflin "really think the balanced budget amendment is such a good idea, they should be willing to vote for it without [the TVA exemption], which Mr. Feingold refers to as 'constitutional pork.'" The paper concluded that "the entire episode, as Mr. Feingold notes, underscores the folly of trying to deal with budget issues through a constitutional amendment."

At first, some Wisconsinites might have thought that Feingold was following in the footsteps of Bill Proxmire, the state's most successful Democratic politician over three decades until his retirement in 1988. In the Senate, Proxmire, a former journalist with PR flair, became nationally known for his monthly Golden Fleece Awards, throwing a caustic spotlight on a federal government agency or program that, in Proxmire's view, was wasting taxpayer money. One unlucky recipient, for example, was the National Science Foundation, cited for funding a study of why people fall in love. No doubt Proxmire's awards had great popular appeal, but after many years they made some of his more liberal supporters uncomfortable. The cumulative effect, they feared, played into the hands of government-bashing conservatives.

Feingold never traveled very far down the Proxmire path. Even his publicity-seeking, campaign-driven eighty-two-point deficit reduction plan, when put into a larger context, suggested the budget problem was not only about unjustified government spending; it was also about misplaced priorities. His biggest proposed budget cuts were aimed at a bloated Pentagon budget that siphoned money away from domestic programs Feingold strongly supported, such as national health insurance. Moreover, Feingold called for cuts in government spending while opposing middle-class tax cuts; it was an intellectually honest deficit reduction position, grounded in logic and the Wisconsin progressive tradition. The progressives, as noted, were believers in socially beneficial government programs *and* fiscal responsibility. And even Milwaukee's socialist mayors—they reigned from the early 1900s through 1960—were careful administrators. In the 1950s, the last one, Frank Zeidler, presided over the expansion of public works but was cautious if not conservative when it came to financing the new programs. For much of the twentieth century, the ethos of civic life in Milwaukee, the state's most important city, reflected its sizable German population's proclivity for competence, community and thrift. To a large extent, those values were at the heart of small-town Wisconsin, too, including Feingold's hometown. Proxmire, who had the disadvantage of growing up in Illinois, became a successful Wisconsin politician because he was also something of a clever political anthropologist. With Feingold, Wisconsin was always in his bones.

Bill Clinton's hard-fought budget victory in 1993 was one of the most important of his presidency for both economic and political reasons. There was widespread concern that the huge budget deficits of the 1980s and early 1990s were a threat to the long-term stability of the American economy. In fiscal 1993 alone, the deficit was $255 billion. Through a combination of spending cuts and increased taxes on wealthy individuals and corporations, Clinton's goal was to reduce the federal debt by $500 billion over five years. In fact, by 1998, there would be a budget surplus of almost $70 billion, the first surplus in almost thirty years, and the economy was humming.

The Clinton budget victory was a significant factor, among others, for the fiscal and economic improvements that came later in the decade, but in 1993 not a single Republican voted for the president's budget in the House or Senate, where a 50–50 tie was broken by Vice President Al Gore's vote. Politically, some Democrats probably paid a price when they voted for higher taxes—the defeat in the next election of a freshman Democratic congresswoman, Marjorie Margolies Mezvinsky, from suburban Philadelphia was cited as a prime example.

But the political pluses outweighed the minuses for Democrats, many in the party believed, including Feingold. For generations, Republicans stereotyped Democrats as profligate "tax-and-spend" politicians. But in the 1980s, Ronald Reagan's embrace of supply side economics led to billowing budget deficits that gathered and hung over the economy like ominous clouds. Now, in a reversal of roles, Democrats had an opportunity to talk about the virtue of fiscal prudence and responsibility. Although that made some party liberals uneasy because, it seemed, they were behaving like old-fashioned Republicans, the stark reality was that there would not be money for new or expanded social programs until the red ink was dried up. Indeed, in the 1980s, Ronald Reagan's anti-government supply side ideologues envisioned that big tax cuts and large deficits would starve the beast of government—and to a significant extent, they had been right. In August of 1993, Feingold said bluntly on the Senate floor before casting his vote: "The people of this country voted for change . . . because they know we have a problem and that there is only one alternative"—and that was to cut spending and raise taxes.

Feingold gives Bill Clinton high marks for the budget initiative in 1993, applauding his commitment to a balanced budget and calling it "progressive" because Clinton rejected "mindless across-the-board cuts. He did it in a way that worthy programs would continue to grow, but he was willing to take tough steps on other things." Feingold became an advocate of rational if not conservative "pay-as-you-go" budget-making when he joined the Senate Budget Committee during his first term. That committee served as a platform where he could burnish his credentials for fiscal responsibility, an issue that had been so important in his successful run for the Senate.

While Feingold was in Clinton's corner during the big budget fight, he was soon a fervent opponent of the president when it came to a vote on a big trade issue in 1993, the North American Free Trade Agreement or NAFTA. Clinton's predecessor, George Bush, had negotiated the trade agreement with Canada and Mexico, but it had yet to be approved by Congress. It called for creating a free market trading zone among Canada, Mexico and the United States and had the strong backing of major American corporations, congressional Republicans and the Clinton administration. Labor unions opposed NAFTA because they feared jobs would be lost to Mexico and wages depressed in the United States. In Congress, Democrats were divided. In November when the Senate approved NAFTA, twenty-seven Democrats were in favor, twenty-eight opposed. For Feingold, the split reflected not merely differences about trade issues per se, but it also symbolized a fundamental difference over the direction of the Democratic Party.

He was angered by the growing influence of corporate campaign contributions in his party—and those contributions, he believed, were a big factor behind the Clinton administration's support of NAFTA. For him and other progressives and liberal Democrats, the influence of big money was a dispiriting trend that had started in the aftermath of Democratic election defeats in the early 1980s, when moderate and conservative Democrats launched the pro-business

Democratic Leadership Council. The corporate-backed DLC's motto might have been, "If you can't beat 'em, join 'em."

By 1993, the DLC, in collaboration with the Clinton administration, was a leading player in a massive public relations campaign to sell NAFTA in Congress. Feingold said: "I see the DLC as, to some extent, taking the soul away from the Democratic Party. And I see the DLC as having sold American workers down the river." Feingold believed NAFTA was not good for the country, and especially not good for small businesses and millions of blue- and white-collar workers that progressive Democrats should be fighting for. The loss of manufacturing jobs in particular has devastated a number of cities and states. Milwaukee, once known as a prosperous manufacturing center, has a new distinction: it now ranks in the top ten U.S. cities with the highest rates of child poverty. Feingold didn't place blame for the loss of all well-paying American jobs on skewed trade policies, but he believed they were often important factors.

The victorious NAFTA proponents were effective rhetoricians, labeling their opponents as dangerous protectionists who didn't believe in free trade and free markets. In practice, however, the developed countries of the world do not engage in anything that ordinary citizens would think of as "free" trade, according to Nobel Prize–winning economist Joseph E. Stiglitz. Stiglitz, who served on President Clinton's Council of Economic Advisers when NAFTA was pushed through the Congress, now writes that "if any trade agreement were to be a success, it should have been [NAFTA]." But it hasn't been a success, Stiglitz admits, when measured by the biggest promises of its advocates. NAFTA did not close the gap in income between Mexico and the United States, nor did it reduce pressure of illegal immigration from Mexico to the U.S. Indeed, in some cases NAFTA worsened the problem— for example, tens of thousands of poor Mexican farmers were forced off their land and then headed north across the border because they couldn't compete with subsidized American imports. And the growth in manufacturing jobs along the Mexican-U.S. border was short-lived—as Stiglitz notes, 200,000 jobs in the region were lost in 2001–02, many moving to China.

And what about the so-called side agreements of NAFTA that were supposed to protect workers' rights and establish basic health, safety and environmental standards? These were the provisions that, from an American perspective, were supposed to "level the playing field" for U.S. workers. The short answer, Feingold believes, is that neither the Clinton administration nor the Mexican government was ever serious about enforcing these provisions. This political reality was summed up by an American labor union official quoted in David Bacon's book *The Children of NAFTA*: "It was hypocritical for [Clinton] to promise such protection during the debate on NAFTA. The whole reason for the treaty was to guarantee cheap labor in Mexico."

Indeed, NAFTA is yet another reminder that, in the world as it is, trade issues are less about "free market" economics and fairness than they are about the exercise of political power. Stiglitz sees this quite clearly: "Special interests are largely to blame—not special interests in the developing countries resisting trade liberalization, as proponents of trade liberalization complain, but special interests in the developed world shaping the agenda to benefit themselves, while leaving even the average citizen in their own countries worse off." A decade after NAFTA was implemented, Feingold said, "I strongly disagree with the President's characterization . . . of NAFTA as a 'success.'" In Wisconsin alone, he says, 23,000 jobs have been lost mainly because of NAFTA, many of the losses occurring in small, vulnerable towns.

Feingold's vote against NAFTA came at the end of his first year in the Senate where, according to a year-in-review story in the

Milwaukee Journal, "Feingold has adroitly walked the tightrope of becoming effective in Washington while retaining his image of independence in Wisconsin." According to Feingold's colleague Paul Wellstone, who was quoted in the story, "The most important challenge for someone like Feingold, who has a mandate from Wisconsin to be willing to rock the boat and push very hard, is to be effective. He has walked that fine line. What has probably helped him the most is whenever we have a discussion of issues he is so obviously well prepared and so smart and so able to hold his own in debate that he has built up a lot of respect."

The article cited some of Feingold's legislative successes that were called impressive for a first-year senator—in addition to his budget-cutting victories, he also won a temporary moratorium on the marketing of Monsanto's bovine growth hormone, although BGH had been approved for sale by the Food and Drug Administration. The portrait of Feingold highlighted his willingness to go against his president, his party and, on a couple of hot-button issues, popular opinion. "Feingold was one of 33 senators who voted to lift the legislative ban on gays in the military," the newspaper story recounted, "and was one of only four senators" who voted against a major Clinton anti-crime bill because it expanded the federal death penalty, which Feingold vehemently opposed. On foreign policy, the article mentioned that Feingold had criticized the Clinton administration's approach to Somalia before the disaster in Mogadishu on October 3, when eighteen American soldiers were killed.

Even Republicans had to concede, the *Milwaukee Journal* reported, that "Feingold does not duck issues. People may have disagreed with Feingold's vote against the crime bill or for Clinton's budget, but voters 'respect the fact that he's straight-up about issues,' said R. J. Johnson, executive director of the state GOP."

As for Feingold, he said, "I think I'm doing a pretty good job.

I'm working as hard as I can. I'm keeping my promise of staying in touch."

During his Senate campaign, Feingold made a promise that was later ridiculed as impractical, a waste of time and a campaign gimmick that would never really be implemented: if elected, he promised to visit all seventy-two Wisconsin counties every year and listen to what ordinary people had on their minds. The scope and regularity of the endeavor was unheard of in Wisconsin politics and rare for any U.S. senator, especially from a state as large as Wisconsin— where it requires a seven- to eight-hour drive from Feingold's old hometown near the Illinois border to reach one of his favorite vacation retreats, the Apostle Islands in Lake Superior, on the northern tip of the state. But now, after fourteen years as a senator and more than a thousand "listening sessions," as they are called, Feingold says these give-and-take encounters "are probably the overriding influence" on the way he thinks and talks about virtually every important issue facing the country, including the Iraq War. "I can't even imagine not having that influence on me. It's huge."

The idea of the listening sessions was invented in the darkest days of Feingold's run for the Senate in 1992, when he looked dead in the water, registering only single digits in a poll not many weeks before the primary. Feingold and his campaign committee started brainstorming for a good idea—perhaps another promise or two in addition to the promises painted on his garage door. "You should promise never to do any foreign travel," Feingold recalls somebody suggesting. "And I said, 'Absolutely not. That is ridiculous. I'm not going to the U.S. Senate and promise never to leave the country.' Then somebody said, 'You know, Dave Obey, Congressman Obey, had said that once in a while he'd do something, he'd call a listening session.' Somebody else said, 'You know, you should promise to do a meeting like that in every county during your six years.' I said, 'No—every year.' And then somebody said, 'Well, you probably won't win anyway.' We're all in that mind-set [because] we're at 9 percent. But I still thought I could win; I was not at all thinking I'm making an idle pledge. But there's also this part of me," Feingold concedes, and begins to smile. "Well, maybe I'll never have to do it."

The listening session promise didn't receive much publicity during the remainder of the campaign but after Feingold won, the political pros in Wisconsin thought he had committed himself to a dumb idea. In their view, practicing retail politics statewide was a big waste of time. Winning elections and getting reelected was about raising money and building name recognition—and that was accomplished by getting yourself on television, not meeting with small groups of people often in sparsely populated rural counties. And, of course, they had a point. In Wisconsin, about a third of the seventy-two counties have so few people that, in total, their population represents just 6 percent of the electorate. In some far-flung northern counties such as Florence, Sawyer and Taylor, there may be more pine trees, white-tailed deer and wall-eye than voters. And perhaps worse, these tend to be Republican counties! But the promise had been made—and fourteen years later, Feingold has traveled about 140,000 miles—the equivalent of five times around the world—meeting with his fellow citizens in each Wisconsin county every year.

At the end of 1993 when Feingold completed the seventy-second listening session, the *Milwaukee Journal*'s Craig Gilbert wrote that he "had made good on the first installment of his audacious pledge." Countless newspaper headlines such as "Feingold Kept Promise," or "Feingold Session Validates Democracy," have appeared over the years in small-town newspapers after one of Feingold's listening sessions. They have become his trademark in the state. In 1993, he put the political benefits of the listening sessions into perspective. "I hope it's a positive politically, because I think I'm doing something people would think is the kind of representation they want," he said. "But if I were just thinking about politics, I would be doing things differently. . . . I don't go there and give a big talk about what I'm going to do. I go to listen to people."

When Feingold conducted his first session in Racine, he didn't know quite what to expect, he remembers. "I had the notion people would come, say their piece and leave." But that's not what has happened. "They never leave," he discovered. "They stay until the end, and I think that's because there's no place else people go and sit down and hear what their neighbor has to say anymore." Since the first listening session, the scheduling and format have remained much the same. Typically, in early January before Congress convenes, Feingold holds a half-dozen or so sessions in the southern or central counties, saving the northern third for the warmer summer months. Throughout the remainder of the year, he periodically zigs and zags around the state, using congressional breaks and weekends. To be more efficient, he likes to schedule a couple of sessions in adjacent counties on the same day, several hours apart. Between Feingold and his staff, they often select some of the tiniest towns that few people outside of the county have ever heard of—towns such as Casco, Hawkins, Redgranite and Elcho.

Local residents learn about an upcoming listening session because either they read an announcement in the local newspaper or, if they have attended before, they received a notice from Feingold's office. The number of people who attend varies widely—it might be as few as twenty or as many as 150. Driving to a listening session in his navy blue Chevrolet van, Feingold and his staff guess how many people will show up. Most of the time, a safe bet is in the forty to fifty range. The format is simple: anybody who wants to speak on a federal, state or local issue fills out a short form, including his or her name, address and phone number. Feingold's staff—he usually has two or three with him—collects the forms and gives them to Feingold when the session begins.

But even before a word is spoken, Feingold doesn't come across as the typical politician. There is no glad-handing or working the crowd when he walks into the room, which might be in a library, senior citizen center or high school gymnasium. Most of the people have arrived and are seated in rows.

Feingold heads straight for the front of the room. He's dressed in a dark suit or sport coat and tie, although on some weekends and in the summer the clothes are more casual. If he spots people he knows, he gives them a friendly but brief greeting. He begins with: "Hi, I'm Senator Russ Feingold. I'm one of your two U.S. senators." There's a hint of modesty that doesn't sound false. He'll share a brief memory about his last visit to the county—he may mention some local elected officials he met, and one or two of them may be in the room. Sometimes a state legislator, Republican or Democrat, will sit next to him. He rarely fails to note that the annual listening sessions are a promise he made when he first ran for the Senate. At the beginning of the Marinette County listening session in 2006, he added: "We'll hit number one thousand in a few weeks, God willing." He may also take thirty seconds or so to highlight an issue he's been working on in Washington, or an issue that has been discussed at other sessions. In his first years in the U.S. Senate (and even today), health care was one of his major concerns, especially long-term care, which had also been a priority when he was a state senator. Almost every year since 1993, health care ranked as the first or second most discussed topic at the listening sessions, rivaled only in recent years by the Iraq War.

Feingold winds up his short introductory comments by saying: "The purpose is just basically to hear what you have to say. Nobody is going to be called on if they don't want to talk," he assures newcomers.

Typically, about twenty or twenty-five people want to speak. They tend to be older, which partly explains the high interest in health care. Although half might be in their sixties and seventies, most age groups are represented. More young people show up when a listening session is held at a high school or near a college campus. Speakers tend to talk for a few minutes and expect Feingold to respond. Others simply ask him a question. Politically, many if not most of the participants tend to share his views, but it is impossible to know from one listening session to another what the political mix will be—or what issues will be raised. The newspaper in Ripon, a town that bills itself as the "Birthplace of the Republican Party," and which is located in heavily Republican Fond du Lac County, once observed: "These mini-town-hall forums at first seem like a campaign ploy, including a giant map to prove Wisconsin's senator is all over the state working for his constituents. But once the session begins, attendees soon realize Feingold is truly listening and earnestly responding to their concerns. . . . Feingold is respectful without being patronizing. After an emotional outburst by a constituent at the Ripon Library, he explained where he felt the two agreed and then ended his answer by calmly saying, 'I can't agree with you on that last point.'"

One summer afternoon in Hawkins, down the road from Ladysmith in northwest, rural Rusk County, a handful of older men arrived at the community center for the listening session shortly before Feingold appeared and began gossiping. Sitting nearby, a cantankerous contemporary said in a stage whisper to nobody in particular: "It's election time, this is the only time you'll see him for another six years." Actually, Feingold's next election was four years off, but one of the other men quietly corrected him on the basic fact: "No, he comes here every year." The room was nearly full when Feingold appeared at 2:45, and the session soon began although the official starting time was at three. One of the first people he called on was the cantankerous cynic. In a tone mixing equal amounts of sarcasm and belligerence, the man said: "You Democrats want to take all of our arms away from us; I wonder what's behind that? Why do you keep telling everyone that you want our guns?"

"I never say that!" Feingold countered emphatically. Politically, he believes Democrats have paid a big price by allowing themselves to be perceived as the anti-gun enemy among working-class men such as the one who asked him the question. "[I'm one of those] Democrats who believe in the right to bear arms—*strongly*," he continued. "I wrote Wisconsin's Right to Bear Arms constitutional amendment. I'm very proud of that." At other listening sessions, he has told people about his college thesis on the Second Amendment, how he became convinced that the amendment protected the rights of individuals. On this occasion, he said: "I've voted for some things like the Brady Bill, but I also voted against renewing the ban on the semiautomatics. I don't think that confiscating weapons is the way to handle the problem. We have the right to guns for self-defense, for hunting and recreation. That's in the Constitution—the Second Amendment. That is my view. And I think Democrats have made a terrible mistake over the years of letting what you just said become what people *think* is true."

"But it is true," the man countered.

"No, that's only true of a few Democrats," Feingold persisted. "I've said a lot of people don't vote for us because they *think* we're going to take away their guns. So, it's our job as Democrats to show people that that's *not* what we're trying to do. Not *your* senator," he emphasized good-naturedly, resting his case with a friendly smile, trying his best to convince the man he's really on his side.

More hot-button topics surfaced at listening sessions in the mid-1990s, foreshadowing issues in Feingold's reelection campaign in 1998. In Washington, where Republican majorities set the agenda in the House and Senate, party strategists orchestrated up-or-down votes on emotional issues that would motivate grassroots conservatives and others. In Wisconsin, for example, flag desecration became a hot topic at some listening sessions when the Senate debated a constitutional amendment to prohibit burning the American flag. Feingold not only voted against the proposed amendment but spoke eloquently about the American tradition of free speech. "This nation was born of dissent and, contrary to the view that it weakens our democracy, this nation stands today as the leader of the free world because we tolerate those varying forms of dissent, not because we persecute them." But at a listening session in the town of Grafton north of Milwaukee in Ozaukee County, a resident attacked him for his vote against the flag-burning amendment.

"We hired you to do a job for us," said the man, who was wearing an American Legion cap. "You are not doing that job because Russ Feingold is voting his conscience, not the people of Wisconsin. That's a simple statement, as simply stated, Senator, as I can make it. And to me it requires a very simple answer. Why?"

Feingold turned a charged moment into a small civics lesson. "It raises a fundamental issue of representative government," he began. "Is it my job to go out there and simply vote what a poll tells me is a majority view, or is it my job to listen to the people, combine my own conscience and also my own view of the Constitution? My view is the latter."

Another divisive issue, especially in 1997 and 1998, was partial birth abortion. The issue not only came up at listening sessions, but a Wisconsin anti-abortion group launched a campaign to recall both Feingold and Herb Kohl in the spring of 1997 because of their votes on the issue. The recall was unsuccessful, but the issue did not go away. At a listening session in the summer of 1998 in Chilton, the Calumet County seat in east-central Wisconsin, several people angrily complained about Feingold's abortion stand. He told them he'd heard similar comments at other listening sessions and knew

how strongly many people felt about late-term abortions in particular. "I have never pretended to be anything but pro-choice," he
said. "But I'm not 100 percent pro-choice on late-term abortions."
His position, which had changed somewhat he said, was that a late-
term abortion should be permitted only if the mother was in danger of "grievous physical injury." But pro-life advocates were not
mollified, firmly believing that anything broader than an exception
based on saving a mother's life is an unconscionable loophole.

Over the years, listening sessions have generated legislative
proposals, and Feingold has turned some into law. He's proud of
the rural health programs he's enacted, working in some cases
with Republican colleague Susan Collins of Maine. At the same
listening session in Rusk County where the man complained
about anti-gun Democrats, a young dentist from nearby Ladysmith thanked Feingold for legislation that supports dental programs in rural, underserved areas, and noted what a big difference
it's already made in the county. Indeed, unless one takes time and
talks to people who are barely getting by in beautiful northwest
Wisconsin, one might not know how deep and debilitating the
poverty is because, driving along U.S. Route 8 on a near-cloudless
summer day, there is no hint of it among the golden cornfields,
fat rolls of hay and lush green pines lining the highway. But once
inside the village hall in the room where the listening session is
held, a room that doubles as a senior citizen meeting room, there
is a quiet clue on the bulletin board in the form of a short, neatly
typed message: "Beginning June 1, the cost of the senior citizen
lunch will be increased to $3.25, but nobody will be turned away
who cannot pay."

Because the majority of Feingold's listening sessions are in rural
and small-town America, he has spent a lot of time among those
who feel forgotten by an urban-oriented political culture. When
he is asked to share a few highlights from his fourteen years of lis-

Sanford D. Horwitt

tening, Feingold's first recollection is about one in Aurora, a town on the Michigan border in Florence County. The county board chairman, who escorted Feingold into the town hall, sat next to him. "There are only about thirteen people," Feingold says, including an old man. "I won't say curmudgeonly, but he hardly said a word. And we go through this meeting; it takes about forty-five minutes." And then Feingold repeats what the man said: "I just want to say something. I can't believe that you would come here and sit down and listen to us here like this." And, Feingold says, the man began to cry. "The way he said it," Feingold remembers, "made me realize that this is almost like a vision for people of what democracy should be." And there were other emotional displays that stand out. As the cost of health insurance continued to escalate, small business owners, Feingold says, started coming to listening sessions sharing their painful stories. "They came to speak very emotionally . . . about the impact on their businesses . . . and what it means to not be able to cover what they call their 'family' members, the people that work with them." As committed to health insurance reform as he was, these heart-wrenching testimonials pushed him to do more. "I don't forget these stories that people tell about situations they're in," he says. He is deeply affected, he admits, by both "the emotion and the reasoning" that he experiences firsthand.

By the mid-1990s, Russ Feingold had become identified with campaign finance reform more than any other issue, thanks to growing media interest in the issue and his collaboration with John McCain. A generation older than Feingold, McCain was a Navy pilot in the Vietnam War when, in 1967, his A-4 Skyhawk was shot down by an antiaircraft missile. Seriously injured, he was captured by the North Vietnamese, imprisoned and tortured for five and a half

174

years after refusing to be released ahead of other American prisoners when his captors learned that his father was an admiral in the Navy. In 1982, a decade after he returned home, McCain was elected to the House of Representatives, and when Barry Goldwater retired in 1986, he succeeded him in the U.S. Senate.

John McCain and Russ Feingold seem to be unlikely partners. While McCain was a prisoner in the infamous "Hanoi Hilton" in the late 1960s and early 1970s, Feingold was a high school and college student strongly opposed to the Vietnam War. In the Senate, their views on military and war-and-peace issues are often miles apart. Indeed, the first time McCain and Feingold crossed paths shortly after Feingold came to the Senate, an unpleasant confrontation seemed to be in the making. As McCain recalls, "When I first noticed him . . . he was arguing on the Senate floor to cut funding for an aircraft carrier. I asked him in debate whether he had ever been on an aircraft carrier. When he answered in the negative, I suggested that he learn a little more about them before he decided the country needed fewer of them." It was the kind of acid-tongued dressing-down that John McCain was known for in the Senate, the style not universally appreciated. Feingold, however, responded in a way that impressed McCain. "He reacted with typical good humor and observed, correctly, that he didn't need to see a carrier to understand their purpose," McCain writes in his memoir. "As I've come to know him, I realize that my remark was as unfair to him as it was discourteous. Russ didn't take positions that he is not well-informed about. Even when I believe his judgment to be mistaken, it is not for his lack of diligence in studying the issue."

McCain, irascible and glib, found he identified with Feingold because of other things they shared. "From the moment of our first disagreement, I began to notice his independence," McCain says. "He seemed to find earmarks and pork barrel spending as offensive as I did, and I watched him with growing admiration as he frequently fought with appropriators on the Senate floor. He had little more success in those contests than I have had, but his willingness to keep at it, and his ability to remain affable but undaunted in defeat, impressed me."

McCain's and Feingold's independence distinguished them in the Senate. Unlike other senators, neither played the earmark game and the inevitable vote-trading that it required—and, therefore, they were free from much of the pressure to conform to party leadership. A senior staffer for the Democratic Senate leadership in the mid-1990s recalls that when it came time to round up votes, the leadership had to deal, generally speaking, with four kinds of senators: the dependable party-liners; the nervous Nellies who might change their mind at the last moment because they heard from a complaining constituent; the extortionists who always wanted something in return for their vote; and the one senator who more than any other voted on principle, Russ Feingold.

Like Feingold, McCain was troubled by the corrupting influence of big campaign contributions. He had had his own embarrassing brush with the problem in 1989 when he and four other senators were accused of applying pressure on federal regulators to help a campaign contributor, Charles H. Keating, Jr., the chairman of an Arizona-based savings and loan company that ultimately collapsed. The senators became known as the Keating Five. After an investigation, the Senate Ethics Committee recommended in 1991 that the Senate censure one of the senators, while citing McCain and three others for "questionable conduct." For McCain, the episode produced lingering psychic pain and a resolve to clean up the political system.

After the 1994 election, McCain asked Feingold if he wanted to work on some reform issues together—earmarks and lobbying, for example. By the next year, they also joined forces on passing the new gift ban. And then, starting in the fall of 1995, they became the co-sponsors of the most important campaign finance reform initiative since the Watergate era. The McCain-Feingold bill, as it was called, began receiving extensive national press coverage in 1996 and 1997, coverage that peaked when the legislation came up for votes in the Senate. But in both years, although a majority of senators favored the legislation, the total fell short of the sixty votes required to stop opponents from using a filibuster to block it. Eventually, the original, more ambitious McCain-Feingold bill was scaled back—dropped, for example, was a provision for free television advertising if a candidate agreed to voluntary campaign spending limits. But the main focus of McCain-Feingold—the highest priority—remained the same: closing the soft money loophole that allowed corporations, labor unions and wealthy individuals to make unlimited campaign contributions to the political parties, contributions that were often solicited by members of Congress.

The aroma of tainted campaign fund-raising that hung over the 1996 presidential election underscored the need for reform, many believed. Initially, most of the news stories focused on the questionable fund-raising practices of the Clinton White House. Russ Feingold was among the few Democrats who called for the appointment of an independent counsel to investigate alleged improprieties. In February, after the election, he appeared on NBC's *Meet the Press* along with McCain, and said: "Regrettably, I think we've come to the point where, under the discretionary powers of the attorney general, we probably do have to go to a special counsel." He said the investigation should examine both Democrats and Republicans, an evenhanded approach that did not sit well with Republican leaders.

No special counsel was ever appointed, but news coverage of investigations by the Department of Justice and Congress kept the campaign finance issue in the news. By April of 1998, campaign finance reformers were suddenly on the verge of a breakthrough in the House of Representatives, where previously the Republican leadership had prevented a vote on the House version of McCain-Feingold. (In the House, the legislation was referred to as Shays-Meehan, after the House sponsors, Republican Chris Shays of Connecticut and Democrat Marty Meehan of Massachusetts). But even if it passed in the House, the Senate Republican leadership was likely to thwart McCain-Feingold again, if it could. In an impassioned speech, Feingold took to the Senate floor on April 22, in part to shame the Republican leadership but, more broadly, to show how the current system was corrupting Republicans and Democrats alike.

"The distinguished majority leader of our body was asked on Monday, what he will do if the House passes McCain-Feingold," Feingold began. "His answer? 'Nothing.' And everyone laughed. . . . We will see if the American people will stand for this kind of obstructionism if a bill comes back from the House." Feingold rejected "the notion that the scandals we saw in 1996 were just due to lawbreaking," a reference to campaign contributions from foreign sources in China and elsewhere. The main issue and "the biggest scandal," he said,

> stems not from what is illegal today but from what is perfectly legal—soft money. . . . Soft money is the mother of all loopholes. It is the most ingenious money-laundering scheme in American history. Corporations and labor unions are prohibited from giving money directly to candidates. It has been that way for most of the century. Instead, what they do is they give the money to the candidate's party. . . . This laundering scheme allows the parties to dump tens of millions of unregulated dollars into congressional elections and into presidential elections. Just last fall the Republican Party ran an unprecedented issue ad campaign

in the special congressional election for the seat vacated by former representative Susan Molinari of New York. The party reportedly spent $800,000 on ads attacking the Democratic candidate for that office. Much of that money was soft money, money that is supposed to be illegal in federal elections.

Feingold reminded his colleagues that the mad scramble to raise ever-increasing amounts of soft money had led to the spectacle of the Clinton White House charging Democratic campaign contributors $100,000 for a night in the Lincoln Bedroom, and "coffee with the President or dinners with key leaders of the Congress cost people some $50,000 . . . because it is legal to contribute $50,000 or $100,000 or even more to a political party in this country."

And it wasn't only wealthy individuals staying overnight in the Lincoln Bedroom whose contributions added to the record-setting $262 million in soft money that was raised by the political parties in 1996. Feingold listed some of the generous corporate donors: "Philip Morris gave over $3 million in soft money in the 1996 cycle, and RJR Nabisco, Joseph Seagram & Sons, Atlantic Richfield, and AT&T all gave over $1 million. Federal Express gave almost a million. It is still a scandal," he said, "that the tobacco companies contribute millions of dollars to our political parties while the Congress is considering extraordinarily important legislation that will decide the fate of that industry and of the children that its product kills."

Auctioning off access to high-ranking government officials and manipulating the legislative process were increasingly common in Washington, Feingold knew, because of soft money. As depressing as the trend line was, he told his Senate colleagues: "I refuse to accept the judgment that we are doomed to have this kind of campaign finance system in America." And then, in words that were more personal and prophetic than anybody might have imagined that day in the Senate, Feingold said: "We have to take responsibility. We have to do our part as lawmakers . . . to restore the public's faith in our system and in us."

★ ★ ★

At the national level, American politics is like a rigged poker game: the incumbent gets two aces before anybody else gets a card. That's why an incumbent senator or representative almost never loses. And that's why Russ Feingold's decision to throw his aces away was a shocker. In one stunning announcement, he gave up his incumbent's fund-raising advantage and, with it, all the advantages money buys in political campaigns.

In February 1998, Feingold listed "ten promises" that would guide his upcoming reelection campaign. His most significant, eyebrow-raising promise was to limit his overall campaign spending to a dollar per voter, or about $3.8 million, even though he could have raised considerably more. Although there were other significant promises on the list—the vast majority of his contributions would come from Wisconsin and no more than 10 percent from political action committees—limiting his overall spending to a modest one dollar per voter grabbed the most attention. In his statement, Feingold noted that "I do not feel that excessive spending is necessary or appropriate when putting my case before the people of Wisconsin."

Feingold ignored saying anything about a similar proposal his likely opponent, Republican congressman Mark Neumann, had made a few weeks earlier. Neumann had also suggested spending limits of one dollar per voter. Years later, Neumann says he made the proposal because he didn't think that he could match Feingold's fund-raising. Plus, he liked the idea of outmaneuvering Feingold on a campaign finance issue. Neumann quickly agreed to the spending limits, perhaps thinking he would get credit for having initiated the idea. But an editorial in the *Appleton Post-Crescent* saw it differently. While noting that Neumann's acceptance of Feingold's ten promises was good news for Wisconsin voters, the paper added: "But let's be clear about what happened here. Neumann called Feingold's bluff and shouldn't have. Neumann clearly didn't think Feingold would readily agree to campaign spending curbs in the defense of his Senate seat. After all, incumbency brings fund-raising power, and why would Feingold look a campaign gift horse in the mouth? Well, here's why: Much of Feingold's Senate tenure has been based on his leadership on campaign finance reform, notably the McCain-Feingold bill. . . . In other words, Feingold is practicing what he preaches, a refreshing concept." The paper ridiculed Neumann's slick maneuver as "an awkward attempt to shine the light of reform on him[self]," but since Feingold was the real McCoy, it didn't wash.

Almost completely overlooked at the time by newspapers and others was Feingold's addendum to his ten promises. While one of the ten specified that "I will not participate in efforts to raise soft money," he went further and challenged his future opponent to join him in writing a letter "to our respective party leaders and ask that no party-sponsored, soft money–financed, phony 'issue' advocacy ads which mention or portray any of the candidates for the U.S. Senate be aired in Wisconsin." This was a challenge the Neumann campaign had no intention of accepting. In one respect, though, it didn't matter. Feingold wanted to keep his party's soft money issue ads out of the campaign regardless of what his opponent did. Feingold's self-imposed ban on soft money mirrored the key provision in the still-pending McCain-Feingold bill. In Washington political circles, few people could understand why he would do something that would put him at a disadvantage. But Feingold says, "I literally decided that I did not want to be a U.S. senator anymore if it required me to be involved in the process of asking, or benefiting from, what I considered to be corruptly large contributions. This is really how I felt." He realized that good people were playing by the existing rules *and* backing reforms. Be he had reached a point where "given the way my father brought me up to consider money and politics and corruption, I couldn't stomach being a part of it." Such high-minded sentiments were scoffed at or ridiculed in Washington. Feingold "started believing his own bullshit," was the dismissive reaction of a Democratic lobbyist.

Feingold and Neumann were worlds apart in almost every respect, except for one: they were both from Janesville. Unlike Feingold, Neumann had stumbled into politics. He started out as a math teacher, became a successful homebuilder and then ran for Congress, losing to Les Aspin but eventually winning the First District seat after Aspin joined the Clinton administration. A determined, bright, sometimes hotheaded conservative, Neumann went to Congress in 1995 and tangled with Republican leaders on budget issues. He saw himself on a mission to cut big government down to size, much sooner rather than later. He was also known for his strong pro-life views (with some fanfare, he signed the petitions demanding a recall of Feingold and Herb Kohl). In addition to the gulf that separated them on major issues, Feingold and Neumann didn't hit it off personally. Early in the campaign, Mark Neumann needled Feingold by calling him "Russell," which apparently was an attempt to make Russ sound like an Oxford- and Harvard-educated elitist. In a speech to Democrats, Feingold needled back, saying: "Mark, you can call me Russell, you can call me Rusty, you can call me RDF, or you can just call me Russ. Heck, you can call me anything you want just so long as you understand that you'll be calling me 'Senator' on November 4."

By early August, Feingold appeared to be in pretty good political shape. A poll showed him leading Neumann 49 to 30 percent. But then, Neumann's television ads started running, plus attack ads by the Republican Party. The Feingold campaign, saving its limited cash, did not air a single ad in August or early September. By then, Feingold's lead in the polls had melted.

One of the Republican attack ads calling Feingold "slippery" infuriated him. It was a thirty-second commercial in which an older woman says: "You gotta watch that ol' Russ Feingold—he's slippery. Like him supporting that $16 billion bill with all those wasteful government programs and then pretending he opposed it." The ad was "a bald-faced lie," Feingold said, and was part of "a pattern of deception" by the Republicans. According to a *Milwaukee Journal Sentinel* story, "The ad was the third one paid for by the state Republican Party since mid-August. The bulk of the money for the ads has come from the National Republican Senatorial Committee, but a spokesman in Washington for the committee said he would not disclose how much money was being spent on the campaign. Federal law does not require disclosing such spending or the sources of donations to support it. Because the ads do not explicitly refer to the election or tell anyone how to vote, they are not considered campaign expenses." As long as the old lady in the ad merely said: "Call that Russ Feingold and tell him to stop being so slippery," the sky was the limit for how much unregulated money could be spent to defeat him.

At about the time the "slippery" ad ran six weeks before election day, Feingold released a statement saying that if Neumann didn't want the phony issue ads running in Wisconsin, as he had been quoted as saying, then "he should do like I have done and request that no political party, phony issue ads are run on his behalf. While it is impossible to tell a truly independent group what to do, Congressman Neumann should be able to at least stand up to his party. And, while a lot of people have told me that in order to win, I should also take advantage of this campaign finance loophole and have the Democratic Party run unlimited and unregulated phony issue ads, taking the high road is more important to me than winning ugly."

Not surprisingly, the Neumann campaign had no interest in rejecting soft money ads. And at this point, Feingold didn't expect them to. The real purpose of his statement was to help voters understand that there was a sharp difference between the candidates when it came to ethical behavior. Nonetheless, in September Feingold recalls having "terrible arguments with some of my campaign staff who were begging me to take soft money or run ads earlier. I said, 'No. We're going to take our turn in October. Save our money.' That was the best strategic move ever in my career."

But first things got worse in October, starting the night of Feingold's debate with Neumann in Madison. The debate had gone well and afterward Feingold and some friends were enjoying themselves at a restaurant when Feingold's campaign manager, Mike Wittenwyler, phoned. Feingold stepped outside, where he heard the bad news: their pollster, Fred Yang, told Mike the campaign's new poll showed Russ was behind by two points. Generally, it does not bode well when an incumbent is behind with less than a month to go. Realizing that he was on the ropes, Feingold recalls that "I went home and I lay in bed and I thought about the fact that I could lose. I think it's the only time I ever thought I really could lose an election." But there was no time for self-pity, plus many on the campaign staff were in a panic about the bad poll numbers. To boost their spirits, the next day he dreamed up a list of "ten reasons why we would not lose." The number one reason, he told them, was that "it's unthinkable that we'll lose to this guy." Feingold was disgusted by Neumann's relentlessly negative attack ads using emotional issues such as flag-burning and, especially, partial birth abortion. There was ruthlessness about it, Feingold thought, that went beyond the boundaries of tough campaigning. On partial birth abortion, Neumann "wanted to make it look like I was a big fan of the procedure. He was for the babies and I wasn't. It was an attempt to dehumanize the person who would take this position."

No doubt the Feingold campaign's bad poll numbers were being passed along the political grapevine, which was more evidence that Feingold was blowing his reelection and jeopardizing a Democratic Senate seat. In Washington, the message being spread by a Republican polling firm working for Wisconsin's governor Tommy Thompson was that "Feingold is toast." At a White House bill-signing ceremony, Bill Clinton called Wisconsin's other senator, Herb Kohl, into the Oval Office and told him they had to do something to save Feingold from himself.

In Wisconsin, Feingold's closest friends and family members were extremely worried. Russ's sister Dena, the rabbi in Kenosha, gave him a Hebrew-English Bible to keep with him for the remainder of the campaign. She thought it might spur him on, strengthening his resolve and faith.

At the Feingold campaign office, Mike Wittenwyler was fielding numerous nervous and irate phone calls. Wittenwyler remembers a prominent trial attorney "calling up and yelling at me one night, 'Mike, do you know how much money I have invested in this boy? You guys are going to screw this up!'" Far more serious and worrying for the Feingold campaign was a conference call in Wittenwyler's office that included Nebraska senator Bob Kerrey, who was the chairman of the Democratic Senatorial Campaign Committee in Washington. Wittenwyler remembers that "Senator Kerrey himself was yelling at us. And I just remember thinking, 'Thank God we're in Wisconsin and not Washington.'" Either Kerrey or a staff person told Wittenwyler: "You can't do this. You've got to let us go on the air with soft money ads."

In fact, Feingold thought he had a clear understanding with Kerrey that he didn't want the DSCC's soft money ads. "I had a nice conversation with Bob Kerrey on the floor of the Senate. He came up to me and the [Republican] guns were [already] blazing at me, he goes: 'You don't want these soft money ads, right?' I said, 'No, no.' He said, 'Are you winking?' I said, 'No, I'm not. Absolutely not.'" Fred Yang, Feingold's pollster who knew him well, says the Washington political insiders just couldn't understand that "Russ is the exception to the rule. He means what he says."

Not many days after Bob Kerrey's phone call to Wittenwyler, Feingold was in his campaign van, along with his longtime aide Mary Murphy Irvine. They were driving on Interstate 43, near Green Bay, when the phone rang. Irvine picked it up and the color quickly drained from her face. A campaign aide said he had heard from a TV reporter that Bob Kerrey's DSCC was about to start running soft-money TV ads attacking Neumann. Irvine told Feingold what she had just heard. His immediate response was: "So this is how it ends." He thought it meant the end of his Senate career, because he knew his opponent would tar him as a big hypocrite, claiming that Feingold himself was secretly supporting the ads. Among an increasingly jaded, cynical electorate, who was to say that a decisive number of voters weren't primed to believe the worst.

And then Feingold became enraged. "I went wild," he says. He may have thrown the phone against the side of the van; he doesn't quite remember. It was incomprehensible to him that the DSCC thought the ads would help him after he had so emphatically spoken out against soft money. Feingold's campaign quickly put out a press release with the headline: "Feingold Denounces Independent DSCC Soft-Money Phony Issue Ad." In the release, he said: "All throughout my reelection effort, I've attempted to stand up to the Democratic Party—my own political party—and have asked them NOT to exploit the soft-money phony issue ad loophole on my behalf. . . . The last I had heard, the DSCC was going to abide by my wishes. . . . Now, however, it appears that they may run such ads in our state."

Irvine called her contacts at the DSCC, but nobody would talk to her. Then, Feingold says, "I called Daschle and I called up Kerrey and I said, 'Get those things off!' They agreed, and on October 24, three days after he first heard about the DSCC ad campaign, Feingold announced the DSCC's decision. He also urged Wisconsin TV stations to stop running the ads immediately, even though airtime had been purchased. In all, the ads ran for about five or six days, partly because they were already in the pipeline and partly because the DSCC staff was not in a hurry to stop them.

As it turned out, the DSCC ads were not funded by soft money; in that respect, the original report or rumor that was passed along to Feingold had been wrong. The ads were paid for with hard money contributions that were publicly disclosed and limited by federal election law. But in the context of the Feingold-Neumann campaign, it was a distinction that made little difference because Feingold had also made it clear he didn't want his national party to run any kind of ad campaign in Wisconsin. Moreover, the DSCC ads were harsh attacks on Neumann, the kind of boilerplate negative caricatures that Feingold despised.

The Neumann campaign, however, continued to call Feingold a hypocrite, ignoring his efforts to stop the DSCC ads and accusing him of benefiting from other independent expenditures. In fact, two organizations, the League of Conservation Voters and the AFL-CIO, were supporting Feingold in the critical last weeks of the campaign. Although Feingold made it clear through public statements that he didn't want any outside help, he had no control over independent organizations. Deb Callahan, then president of the League of Conservation Voters, says that Feingold's reelection was a high priority because "he had one of the Senate's best environmental records. We didn't want to lose him."

Neumann, too, benefited from campaign spending by independent groups, especially the National Rifle Association and the National Right to Life. But all of the independent expenditures for Neumann's and Feingold's campaigns paled in comparison to the amount of Republican Party soft money that was spent on TV ads attacking Feingold. That was the general consensus among journalists and nonpartisan organizations observing the campaign.

With time running out, Feingold's campaign released a TV ad of its own that Feingold thinks made a big difference. The ad was called "High Road," and Feingold's friend Steve Eichenbaum produced it early on a Sunday morning in a rural setting northwest of Milwaukee. Feingold, dressed casually in a navy shirt and khaki pants, is seen walking uphill on a winding country road while saying: "By now, you've probably seen a lot more commercials for my opponent. And you may wonder how he can outspend an incumbent senator like me. Simple, I volunteered to limit my spending because I believe people, not money, should determine elections. And big-money, out-of-state groups are providing millions in undisclosed funds for ads backing my opponent or attacking me. But we can show the whole country that big money can't drown out our voices." And at this point, Feingold reaches the top of the hill, stops and says: "It won't be easy, but I've always taken the high road."

Too little, too late is what some of the experts were saying about Feingold's chances on election day. On *Meet the Press* two days before the election, all four panelists predicted a Neumann victory. But a harbinger, perhaps, that escaped the attention of the Washington experts was the editorial endorsement by the *Janesville Gazette*. Because it was the hometown paper of both Feingold and his opponent, there was more local interest than usual in the

Gazette's endorsement, although the *Gazette* was reliably Republican. On the morning of October 31, Russ's mother, Sylvia, some people said, shed tears of joy when she saw the glorious *Gazette* headline: "Feingold Deserves a Second Term." Calling its native son "smart and highly principled," the paper cited Russ's commitment to campaign finance reform as an important reason for its endorsement. "Though Congress earlier this year rejected his efforts to change the way money influences politics, Feingold is abiding by the principles of his plan, showing how much he believes in the need to reform the system. . . . We hope Feingold wins another term." The *Gazette* did not endorse Feingold in 1992, so its endorsement now had special meaning. "I wanted to be regarded as somebody from that hometown they could be proud of," he says.

On election night after the votes were in, Feingold's big gamble was vindicated. It was the happiest, most satisfying day of his professional life. He won by more than 35,000 votes and in Janesville, he swept every ward. At midnight at the Marriott in Middleton, he made a short victory speech, with his mother, wife and children behind him and an exuberant ballroom straight ahead. He began by thanking his family for putting up with the life of politics, and he thanked everybody for putting up with "my crazy idea of how I wanted to run for reelection." The audience laughed and applauded. He said he wanted to thank "my opponents" for a hard-fought race—the audience thought he meant Mark Neumann, but after a pause, he said: "You know who I'm talking about—Trent Lott and Mitch McConnell," and the audience laughed again. They were the Senate Republican leaders who blocked McCain-Feingold and, in the case of McConnell, a man who also served as chairman of the Republican Senatorial Campaign Committee. He saw to it that hundreds of thousands of dollars of soft money were spent trying to defeat Feingold—at one point in the campaign, a confident McConnell predicted that

Feingold was "dead meat." Feingold turned serious and told his supporters that the "corrupt system of legalized bribery has to end." The campaign they had all worked on showed there was a better way. In the spirit of Fighting Bob La Follette, Feingold said, he was going back to Washington to win real reforms. "Watch out, Senator McConnell, I'm heading your way!"

CHAPTER 9

PROFILE IN COURAGE

Within three months after his victory in 1998, Russ Feingold went from hero to goat for some Democrats. They had been inspired by his stand against soft money, but now they couldn't fathom his position during the last act of a hero-less national drama starring the president of the United States.

For the first time in 130 years, a president was impeached by the House of Representatives, on December 19, 1998. But the outcome of Clinton's Senate trial that followed was not in serious doubt. It was widely believed that neither of the two articles of impeachment—for perjury and obstruction of justice—would receive the two-thirds majority or sixty-seven votes required for conviction (the Senate was split between fifty-five Republicans and forty-five Democrats). Nevertheless, when the Senate trial began, feelings ran high.

For hard-line Republicans, including those who had taken control of the House proceedings, their hatred of Bill Clinton was all-consuming. Many deluded themselves into thinking that a majority of Americans would share their feelings. Going after Bill Clinton had seemed like good politics for Republican leaders, at once feeding red meat to Republican Party stalwarts and forcing Democrats on the defensive.

Among grassroots Democrats, their fury had been building during the long, futile Whitewater investigation of Bill and Hillary Clinton's Arkansas real estate dealings and the suicide of deputy White House counsel Vincent Foster. To Democrats, independent counsel Ken Starr, a conservative Republican who took over the investigation in 1994, personified the no-holds-barred determination to get Bill Clinton. When Starr's Whitewater work ran into a dead end, it morphed into a new investigation of the Clinton-Monica Lewinsky affair. At first, in January 1998, Clinton publicly denied he had a sexual relationship with Lewinsky, who had been a White House intern. Hillary Clinton appeared on the *Today* show to defend her husband, saying what many Democrats already believed: that the newest charges against him were part of a "vast right-wing conspiracy that has been conspiring against my husband since the day he announced for president."

But seven months later, Bill Clinton confessed he had had an affair. Many if not most Democratic members of Congress were furious with him. His recklessness had not only endangered his presidency, but it complicated their political lives, putting a number of House and Senate seats at greater risk in the November election. At least that was the conventional wisdom in Washington, where only two months before the 1998 election, there were predictions that the Democrats might lose as many as thirty House seats. With House Republicans seemingly in the driver's seat, they refused to consider censuring the president, an alternative to impeachment that representatives of both Clinton and Dick Gephardt, the House Democratic leader, were exploring. But on election day, the Democrats picked up five House seats, the first time since 1934 that the party in the White House gained seats in a midterm election. Enjoying a strong economy, most Americans, it seemed, behaved like pragmatists at the ballot box. In opinion polls, they gave Clinton high job approval ratings and low marks for his personal behavior, but did not want him impeached. Staunchly partisan Republican leaders in the House, however, men such as Tom DeLay of Texas and Henry Hyde of Illinois, refused to back off. For DeLay, it was impeachment or bust, and he had a constituency of Clinton-haters who would have been angry with anything less.

In the Senate, soon after Clinton admitted in August 1998 that he had publicly lied about his affair with Lewinsky, a White House nose count showed that some Democratic Senators might abandon the president. The list included a number of the most respected members: Robert Byrd, Daniel Patrick Moynihan, Fritz Hollings, Bob Graham, Bob Kerrey—and Russ Feingold. At this point, "abandonment" could have taken several forms, including a call for resignation. In Feingold's case, back in January 1998, he said at a listening session in Waukesha County that he had not yet seen all the evidence to make a judgment, "but if the facts made it clear that [Clinton] lied under oath, then my conclusion would be [he] should step down." He was also quoted as saying: "If there is any proof that [Clinton] lied under oath, I will have no trouble voting on his impeachment." His comments were made when Feingold was beginning his reelection campaign, but as the year unfolded, Wisconsin turned out to be little different than the rest of the country: the state's voters were much more concerned with other issues.

After the November election and the House impeachment vote in December, the attention turned to the Senate, where the impeachment trial began in mid-January 1999. A majority of the country continued to believe that Clinton's transgressions did not reach the level of high crimes and misdemeanors specified in the Constitution. Former senator Bob Kerrey believes "the president was being impeached for something relatively trivial." But the trial, Kerrey knew, was going to prolong the agony for him and other senators, especially those who came from politically divided or competitive states. Kerrey says, "I didn't know who to be madder at—Bill Clinton or the Republicans."

Feingold's thoughts ran in a different direction. He thought about the trial, he says, with both the Constitution and history in mind. "The impeachment trial was one where the Constitution commanded [us], in my view, to take an approach to the trial that made it very difficult for me to live up to my oath and not upset Democrats. . . . It's a separate oath from the oath of office. It's an oath to be an impartial juror." Moreover, he felt a keen sense of being part of history and helping to establish precedents. "It's only the second time in American history that the Senate's been sworn to an oath on a presidential impeachment," he says, adding that the concept of something as basic as "impartial juror" had "no other history than the Andrew Johnson [impeachment trial]. . . . I don't think people thought about it very much. I took it very seriously."

Feingold read original speeches from Andrew Johnson's impeachment trial in 1868, and William Rehnquist's history of the trial in his book *Grand Inquests.* He and his staff put together a list of experts, but Feingold ended up talking to relatively few and avoided taking calls from anybody he thought might be lobbying even informally for the White House. He was prepared to treat the trial as a solemn legal proceeding despite its partisan origins. As he had said six months before the Senate trial began: "Should any legal charges come out of this investigation and come before Congress, I will do my duty as a public servant, not as a member of a political party."

Nearly two weeks into the trial, Democrat Robert Byrd introduced a motion to dismiss the case. Byrd, no fan of Bill Clinton's, emphasized that he thought Clinton had caused his family and "the nation great pain. . . . But I am convinced that the necessary two-thirds for conviction are not there and that they are not likely to develop. I have also become convinced that lengthening this trial will only prolong and deepen the divisive, bitter and polarizing effect that this sorry affair has visited upon our nation." If there still remained the slightest doubt about the ultimate outcome of the trial, it vanished in the results of the vote to dismiss on January 27, 1999. While Byrd's motion was defeated, there were only fifty-six votes to keep the trial going—fifty-five Republicans and one Democrat, Russ Feingold. His vote had no impact on the course of the trial, but its symbolism made it one of the most significant in his political career.

On the eve of the vote, Feingold's press secretary, Mary Bottari, asked him how many Democrats in total were going to oppose Byrd's motion. When he raised only one finger, Bottari knew the media would soon bombard their office. The onslaught overwhelmed the staff and office lobby. Phone calls and e-mail messages came pouring in from people not only in Wisconsin but around the country. Most of them probably hadn't seen Feingold's three-page statement defending his position. "My view, as of this moment, is that to dismiss this case would in appearance and in fact improperly 'short circuit' this trial. I simply cannot say that the House managers cannot prevail regardless of what witnesses might plausibly testify and regardless of what persuasive arguments might be offered." Moreover, he maintained that "because I have decided that the House managers probably must be held to the highest standard of proof—beyond a reasonable doubt—I believe that they should have every reasonable opportunity to meet that standard and prove their case" by calling a limited number of witnesses. Feingold stressed he had not yet made up his mind how he would ultimately vote on the perjury and obstruction of justice charges.

His statement didn't mollify angry Democrats. The chairman of the Milwaukee County Democratic Party said, "I am . . . deeply disappointed that the senator would have such a flagrant disregard for the will of the people." And the chairwoman of the Wisconsin Democratic Party said, "We're getting a lot of very upset people calling. Elderly people crying, other people yelling." Feingold's old friend from their days in the state legislature, Joe Wineke, said, "Clearly what he did disappointed the Democratic faithful in a big way."

One of the harshest rebukes came from Dave Zweifel, the editor of the Madison *Capital Times*. It was Zweifel who spotted Feingold during his first term in the State Senate and wrote glowingly of him as a worthy heir to Fighting Bob La Follette. But now he shared the sentiments of those who "would like to hang [Feingold] by his thumbs for betraying what they presumed was a trust they had with him to stand up against the zealots who will stop at nothing to get rid of this president." Zweifel had read Feingold's statement and dismissed it out of hand. "[W]hat Feingold is doing is providing legitimacy to this whole sorry episode—that the Ken Starr probe of sex in the White House and its fallout can rise to an impeachable offense. That's exactly what the vast majority of Americans . . . are saying doesn't wash."

In a *Washington Post* feature titled "The Vote Heard Round the Country," Feingold's lonely act was portrayed as in keeping with his reputation for political courage, as "someone who goes his own way even when the lights are hot." In the *New York Times*, he was characterized as "one of the Senate's most earnest and independent thinkers" whose "political career has been marked by principled stands that flouted conventional wisdom and party unity." In Republican-oriented newspapers in Wisconsin, Feingold was hailed for his nonpartisanship. "How he voted is not as important as why he voted the way he did," the *Wisconsin State Journal* editorialized. "Feingold has grasped the historical significance of the impeachment proceeding. He understands the Senate is setting standards for future generations." And from tiny Chippewa Falls, the local newspaper applauded "independent actions like [Feingold's] that help restore the American people's faith in government. Because it shouldn't boil down to who you know or what side you're on or what position is politically favorable." Conservative Republicans were eager to throw bouquets at him. "An American hero," raved Tucker Carlson, a columnist for the conservative *Weekly Standard.* "A big-time thing," said Orrin Hatch, the Republican senator from Utah.

Although many Democrats were angry with him—it's impossible to say what the percentage was—there were exceptions. After Feingold's vote on dismissal, his Senate colleague Dick Durbin was overheard telling a companion: "You've got to give Russ Feingold credit." A University of Wisconsin professor who had supported Feingold's reelection said he "show[ed] he's not afraid to stick his thumb in the eye of anybody if he thinks it's the right thing to do." And a Milwaukee public-relations executive who worked for Democrats said approvingly that Feingold had "always been willing to buck party leadership and has never been one to apply the 'go along to get along'" philosophy.

If some Democrats were conflicted about what Feingold had done, there was no better example than the editorial page of the *Capital Times.* While the editor, Dave Zweifel, had written a strongly critical column, his paper's editorial gave Feingold the benefit of the doubt. While voicing its disappointment with his vote not to end the trial, the editorial asked whether it is "reasonable to despise this partisan impeachment process and yet to admire Feingold? We think so." The editorial went on to say that it saw the situation much like "our friend, Terry Fritter, a line worker at the Oscar Mayer plant . . . a union man who is no fan of the right-wing clique that has pushed for impeachment." "When I heard the vote was 56–44," Fritter was quoted as saying in the editorial, "I knew it was Feingold who broke ranks. Feingold's just about the only constitutional scholar in the Senate, and he's for sure the only supporter of the Bill of Rights out there. . . . If he thinks there are questions that have to be answered, then I'm proud he voted his conscience."

Feingold says his vote to continue the trial "was extremely difficult. It was something that really upset people. I had just been through a very tough reelection where people felt they had worked hard to carry me across the line, which they had." He admits agonizing about the decision—whether to follow what he thought was the right course or, as he puts it, "was I going to say, 'Look, I can't do this to my supporters.' So it was tough and some people have never forgiven me for that vote."

Feingold believes, of course, that his reputation for political independence is a big asset. In his 1998 reelection, exit polls showed that he won the independent vote decisively—it may have been his margin of victory. He does well with these voters, he stays, because "they expect you to do your homework, listen to people and to vote your own way. And the impression people have of me, which is accurate, is that I am capable of coming down on different sides on different issues depending on what is the best thing to do. . . . They like . . . that I am not an ideologue in the sense that I've been given a play card and I follow that down the line."

His impeachment vote coming only months after his rejection of soft money solidified Feingold's reputation as a highly unusual politician who operated in an exalted atmosphere high above the ordinary political fray. Remarkably, in all the stories about his impeachment vote and breaking ranks with his party, virtually none even hinted that he had cast his vote for political advantage, either because he coveted an independent image or wanted national attention. Newspaper stories, editorials and columnists took what he had done at face value. A writer for a paper in Appleton, Wisconsin, said: "Having watched Feingold over the years . . . I used to wonder whether he was high-minded and principled, or simply clever at appearing high-minded and principled. I don't wonder anymore. The impeachment vote tipped the scale for me."

Ultimately, Feingold voted not to convict the president on either charge, although he said that "as to obstruction of justice, the president did come perilously close." In fact, he had asked his staff to draft both conviction and acquittal statements. Had Feingold been the only Democrat to cross the line and vote to convict, it would have angered Democratic voters all over again, but it would not have come as a big shock to anybody.

A few weeks after the Senate trial ended, Caroline Kennedy called to tell Feingold that he and John McCain had been selected as co-recipients of the annual John F. Kennedy Profile in Courage Award for their work on campaign finance reform. Feingold was thrilled. Not only had President Kennedy and Robert Kennedy inspired him since childhood, but when he made his first speech on the Senate floor, he was introduced by Ted Kennedy. In his acceptance speech at the John F. Kennedy Presidential Library and Museum, Feingold said: "I'm holding in my hand my own original 35-cent copy of *Profiles in Courage* that I read as a young teenager. I loved it. It fueled my not very well hidden interest in going into politics and maybe even becoming a U.S. Senator. But its influence was not simply to make me want to be a senator. Rather, this thin little book spoke volumes about what kind of a senator it is worthwhile to be. What *Profiles in Courage* illustrates is the role risk and sacrifice can or should play in a career in public service." McCain received the award because he took the political risk of bucking his party's leadership that fought relentlessly to block the McCain-Feingold bill. Feingold was cited for risking defeat in the 1998 election by, Caroline Kennedy noted, "unilaterally adopt[ing] the financial restrictions he had proposed in the Senate" rather than participating in a corrupt financing system.

The Profile in Courage Award was added vindication for Feingold. Winning reelection despite the dire predictions of the Washington political establishment was, of course, the sweetest vindication of all. But the establishment, especially the Democratic consultants, lobbyists and fund-raisers, had not celebrated with him. Long after the election, many remained antagonistic if not hostile toward him. "An arrogant shit" is how one former high-level Clinton White House aide thinks of Feingold. Clinton aides had been furious when Feingold voted with Republicans to keep the Senate impeachment trial going. And in the midst of the trial, Bill Clinton himself fired a dart in Feingold's direction, or so some in Washington thought.

The occasion, two days after Feingold's vote, was a memorial service in the Senate Russell Office Building for Lawton Chiles, the late Florida governor, former senator and friend of Bill Clinton. In his tribute to Chiles, Clinton said: "I thank him for being an early supporter of political and campaign finance reform but . . . doing it in a way that made sense and didn't raise people's defenses. I don't think he had a sanctimonious bone in his body. He just didn't want everybody to have to spend all their time raising money. . . . He didn't go around telling you how much better he was than everybody else because he only took $100."

Clinton's remarks were noted in a gossipy *Washington Post* column by Al Kamen, who wrote: "Let's see now. Who might Clinton be thinking of? Someone in the last election who made much of the fact that he would accept contributions of no more than $100? Would that be the junior senator from Wisconsin, Russell Feingold, the only Democrat to vote against dismissing the charges against Clinton and the only Democrat who voted in favor of deposing witnesses? Sanctimonious? Nahhh. Must be someone else."

Although Feingold had not limited individual contributions to $100, Clinton's comment led many in the audience to assume the president was comparing Feingold unfavorably to Chiles. That is what Peter Baker writes in his book, *The Breach*, an account of the Clinton impeachment and trial. Feingold was apparently not sure; he told Baker that he talked with his staff about it and decided to treat Clinton's remarks as if they weren't aimed at him. So, only three months after the impeachment trial, Caroline Kennedy's stirring summation served as a rebuttal to his critics: "Senators McCain and Feingold demonstrated the kind of political courage my father admired most," she said. "They defied the extraordinary pressures of partisan politics and special interests and stood up for what they felt was best for the country. In doing so, they suffered the displeasure of their party leaders and key constituency groups and even risked reelection to office. In a time when politics and government have been marked by incivility and partisanship, these senators distinguished themselves by their political courage and by their vision of what was right for the country."

Emboldened by his reelection victory and the Profile in Courage Award, Feingold was more determined than ever to pass the McCain-Feingold bill. As Ted Kennedy had said at the award ceremony in Boston, it was time to "close the most scandalous loopholes festering in our election laws and end the corrosive and corrupting power of big money in federal elections." But since Feingold and McCain introduced the first version of their legislation in 1995, perhaps the biggest hurdle they faced, apart from opposition by Senate Republicans, was the assumption in Washington that not many voters cared about the issue. To be sure, the pro–McCain-Feingold coalition of nonpartisan organizations—Common Cause, the League of Women Voters and Public Citizen, among others—was doing a good job of rounding up newspaper endorsements and bipartisan testimonials from prominent civic leaders and former members of Congress. But while that support was prestigious and lofty, did it connect with ordinary Americans? At election time, how many voters really cared?

After Feingold narrowly won reelection, one critic, Peter Beinart, wrote in the *New Republic* that Feingold nearly blew his reelection because he campaigned on the issue. "In this era of liberal confusion about economic policy, the quest for political reform often becomes an end in itself," Beinart argued. "Feingold staked his fate on distinctions between honest and dishonest fundraising that struck many voters as arbitrary and abstract. And it quite nearly did him in."

Feingold strongly disagrees. "That's completely wrong," he says. "Campaign finance is a window to show people that you're on their side in this issue. And when you make the point that these big contributions [were instrumental in] passing NAFTA, or [they] blocked health care . . . people get that." It was true, as Beinart observed, that Feingold's campaign ran TV ads toward the end on bread-and-butter issues such as Social Security, but how much of a difference that made is difficult to say. In the home stretch when the vast majority of major newspaper endorsements went Feingold's way, the common thread was his fight for campaign finance reform.

On June 16, 1999, several weeks after receiving the Profile in Courage Award, Feingold announced on the Senate floor that he was going to begin shining a spotlight on the too often unspoken, hidden connection between big-money contributions and Senate votes. He was going to start "calling the bankroll," a tactic inspired by La Follette's famous roll call, or calling the roll, a century ear-lier. La Follette had arrived in the U.S. Senate the year before landmark legislation was enacted in 1907, banning corporations from making political contributions in federal elections. More than ninety years later, the soft money loophole had compromised that long-standing prohibition. And now Feingold saw himself standing shoulder to shoulder with La Follette in the great pro-gressive reform tradition. "To me, I was a descendant of it and doing exactly what I would hope Bob La Follette would have wanted me to do."

In a brief history lesson, Feingold told his colleagues that "La Follette's calling the roll was part of an effort to expose corporate and political corruption. His view was that powerful economic interests controlled the Senate." Today, Feingold continued, "the power of corporate and other interests in the Senate is still too strong." Senators knew that soft-money contributions and gener-ous PAC donations influenced the legislative process, Feingold said, but there was a gentleman's agreement, so to speak, not to say anything about it. "Campaign money is the 800-pound gorilla in this Chamber every day that nobody talks about. . . . In our debates here," Feingold said, "we are silent about that influence and how it corrodes our system of government."

Feingold announced that in the coming months, when major legislation was debated on the Senate floor, he intended to break the silence by calling the bankroll, by which he meant identifying the special interests that had a stake in the outcome and how much campaign money they had contributed. He wasn't suggesting that campaign contributions per se indicated that a legislative payoff was in the works, but that large contributions in particular raised that possibility and shouldn't be ignored when debating the mer-its of legislation. At a minimum, the public should have a better chance to know what the link might be. Feingold gave a few recent examples of what he had in mind, citing the large campaign contributions that preceded Senate consideration of an amendment to legislation delaying the implementation of new mining regulations. The mining industry, he pointed out, had contributed more than $29 million "to congressional campaigns during the last three election cycles, and $10.6 million . . . in soft money contributions during the same period."

On nearly two dozen occasions over the next year, Feingold called the bankroll, delighting campaign finance reform advocates and irritating lobbyists and some colleagues. The irritation and anger became public on the Senate floor in September 1999 when he spoke against an oil-industry-backed legislative amendment offered by Republican senator Kay Bailey Hutchison of Texas. The issue was about royalty payments on the sale of oil—the oil companies were fighting revised regulations by the Interior Department, with many millions of dollars at stake.

Feingold first spoke about the pros and cons of the issue and then started calling the bankroll of oil industry campaign contributions, noting how soft money might be influencing the Senate's deliberations. "Why might Congress not act to allow these regulations to move forward?" he asked. "One cause of this inaction may be the soft money contributions these same oil companies that are impacted by this rule are making to the political parties." He showed that in the preceding two years, four multinational oil companies that would benefit from the Hutchison amendment had made large campaign contributions: Exxon gave more than $230,000 in soft money and more than $480,000 in PAC money; Chevron more than $425,000 in soft money and more than $330,000 in PAC money; Atlantic Richfield more than $525,000 in soft money and $150,000 in PAC money; British Petroleum and Amoco, two oil companies that had merged, gave a combined total of $408,000 in soft money and $295,000 in PAC money.

"That's more than $2.9 million just from those four corporations in the span of only two years," Feingold said. "They want the oil royalties. . . . And as powerful political donors, I'm afraid they're far too likely to get their way."

Feingold's performance did not sit well with Hutchison and two of her allies. Hutchison told the Senate that Feingold's criticism "borders on a personal attack," a violation of senatorial rules. Her oil state colleague Louisiana Democrat Mary Landrieu claimed Feingold's insinuations "were offensive to members of the Senate on both sides of the aisle," and added that "I just feel compelled to say how disappointed I am in my colleague from Wisconsin." And another senator, Craig Thomas, a Republican from Wyoming, perhaps gave the reform advocates the best gift of all when he leapt to his feet and tried to rule Feingold out of order because Feingold's remarks about campaign finance reform were not germane to the oil royalties debate. Feingold's office quickly put out a press release that included his colleagues' morally indignant statements. To which he added his own parting promise: "When the public sees that big oil companies contribute millions of dollars to the political parties, and then get their way on the Senate floor and avoid their responsibility to pay their fair share of oil royalties, it has every right to be suspicious—and offended. What I said today about the pernicious influence of soft money needs to be said. And I am going to keep saying it for as long as I serve in this body."

Heading into the 2000 presidential election, it often looked as if campaign finance reform might never pass in the Senate, at least not as long as the Republicans were in control. Although there had been an encouraging breakthrough in the House in 1998, when the Shays-Meehan reform measure passed after a drawn-out battle, the Senate was still a graveyard. But both McCain and Feingold were tenacious, their determination contagious and inspiring to reform groups and their members, who, after five years of countless phone-calling and letter-writing, might have grown discouraged about Senate prospects.

Also inspiring because of her distinctive determination was an eighty-nine-year-old New Hampshire grandmother, Doris Haddock, who walked across the country, about ten miles a day, promoting the McCain-Feingold bill. On one occasion in the midst of her long journey, Feingold flew to join Granny D, as she was called, at a news conference in Nashville. It was one of his periodic appearances around the country, often with McCain, to rally the reform troops and broaden public support. After Granny D had walked over two thousand miles, she stopped in Washington for a publicity event, meeting with McCain and Feingold and telling them and reporters, "No one put me up to this. I put myself up to it. Actually, the Senate put me up to it. They say people don't care about this issue. But I can tell you they do care."

In August of 2000, Feingold attracted considerable media attention at the Democratic National Convention in Los Angeles. But it was not because of his minor, mid-afternoon speaking assignment at the convention. Indeed, it was a small wonder that he was allowed to speak at all since convention organizers, led by Terry McAuliffe, were not eager to hear Feingold or anybody else blow the whistle about the spectacle of soft money. Nonetheless, because the party ostensibly supported campaign finance reform, at least some deference was due, and Feingold's assignment was to say that a big difference between the Democrats' presidential nominee, Al Gore, and his opponent, George W. Bush, was that Gore would sign a reform bill if he were president and Bush would not.

To his surprise, Feingold was also able to slip in a more pointed remark that the convention editors did not delete from the

TelePrompTer: "I cannot stand before you without mentioning my concern and dismay that soft money fund-raising has become so much a part of this convention," he told a sparsely filled Staples Center. "It should not be. I, therefore, urge the [Democratic National Committee] to prohibit soft-money fund-raising at all Democratic conventions from now on."

Inside the convention hall, Feingold's rather mildly stated criticism attracted little attention. Outside, however, when he spoke to reporters and at a Shadow Convention organized by a coalition of various reform-minded organizations, he took off the gloves. The Democratic and Republican conventions had degenerated into "corporate trade shows," he said angrily. "The real story of the Democratic convention is influence buying and peddling," and Feingold listed fund-raising events around Los Angeles sponsored by a who's who of corporate America—FedEx, Prudential, BellSouth, US West, Texaco.

To reporters, McAuliffe tried to cover up the magnitude of the fund-raising arching over the convention, asserting that it was nothing like what the Republicans had done at their convention in Philadelphia. But Feingold said McAuliffe's spin was absurd. "In room after room, hotel after hotel, and private home after private home, there are scores of fund-raisers that include contribution levels as high as $50,000 and $100,000," he told the *New York Times*. In fact, *Times* reporters uncovered a rich array of lavish events—in one case, for example, a $100,000 contribution entitled the donor to "four days and nights of invitation-only meals, receptions and intimate events with party leaders, including the president, Al Gore, and first lady Hillary Rodham Clinton." Corporations sponsored glitzy luncheon and dinner "tributes" for leading Democratic senators.

All of this, reporters noted, recalled the Democrats' fund-raising scandals four years earlier, such as the so-called donor maintenance White House coffees for big contributors leading up to the 1996 presidential election, and the infamous Hsi Lai Buddhist Temple fund-raiser attended by Al Gore, who lamely tried to legalize it by saying it was a "community outreach" event. At its 2000 convention, Democratic leaders easily convinced themselves that there was no shame or downside in doing whatever was necessary to keep up with the Republicans' fund-raising prowess. Feingold, however, told reporters he was ashamed of his party's pandering, and that prompted two *Los Angeles Times* reporters to write: "Feingold finds himself like Diogenes, who traveled the land in broad daylight with a lighted lamp searching for an honest man. In Feingold's case, he is hunting for someone at the convention without a palm out."

Feingold left Los Angeles disappointed but a willing trouper, and began campaigning for the Al Gore–Joe Lieberman ticket. On election day, the ticket won Wisconsin by a whisker. But in one of the country's closest presidential elections ever, it all came down to a near–dead heat in Florida, where the state's twenty-five electoral votes would determine the next president. After six tense, acrimonious weeks of recounts and court cases, a 5–4 ruling by the U.S. Supreme Court halted the post-election legal maneuvering, allowing Florida's secretary of state to certify that Bush was the winner by 537 votes. In such a close election, a number of factors could have affected the outcome. In Florida, Ralph Nader received 95,000 votes as a third-party presidential candidate. Many if not most of those votes came from disaffected Democrats who had lost confidence in the party's direction and were repelled by its coziness with corporate America. Some observers thought that was a significant factor costing Democrats the White House in 2000, Russ Feingold among them.

★ ★ ★

FEINGOLD

The Apostle Islands are about as far away from Washington, D.C., as any place in Wisconsin, but that's not the only reason they are one of Russ Feingold's favorite destinations. The quietly enchanting archipelago of twenty-two islands, with mysterious sea caves shaped and reshaped by ten thousand years of waves and weather, rest in the cold, colorful waters of Lake Superior, a twenty-minute car-ferry ride from the delightfully unspoiled fishing village of Bayfield. The Apostles and Bayfield, too, evoke many of the things that Feingold holds dear—family and fun; history, the environment and conservation; and, yes, even the progressive tradition.

Feingold promised to spend most of his time in Wisconsin when he ran for the Senate in 1992, and he did. Like Feingold, more members of Congress spend their weekends and congressional recesses back home compared to the old days. According to the Senate's associate historian Don Ritchie, the time spent back home began to increase in the 1950s when air travel made commuting easier. And in today's two-career families, when a spouse has a hometown-based job, it's less likely that the entire family will pull up stakes and come to Washington. After Feingold was elected to the Senate, Mary Feingold had no interest in moving to Washington, and Russ had no interest in staying there beyond the three or four days per week the Senate was typically in session. So for him, spending most of his time in Wisconsin with Mary and their children was ideal, although some on his Washington staff thought he was missing opportunities to become better known among the national media.

Until the mid-1980s, Feingold knew little about the Apostle Islands. After his father died, his mother, Sylvia, thought it would be a good idea to gather the Feingold family for an annual summer reunion. One of Sylvia's acquaintances told her about the Apostle Islands and, specifically, about one of them, Madeline, where the Feingolds could rent cottages. Nobody in the Feingold

209

family had ever been there, Russ says, so it was going to be part adventure and part experiment. Sylvia told her four children: "I'm going up there, and you're all invited with your families. If nobody comes, that's fine. If you all come, that's fine too." That first summer Feingold brought his two daughters, Jessica and Ellen (he had not yet remarried). His brother and sisters came the next year and most years after that. But for the last twenty years, Russ is the only one who has never missed coming to Madeline Island in July. At first, he loved spending time with his mother and siblings and watching his daughters become closer to their cousins and grandmother. And then he fell in love with the Apostle Islands and began thinking about it "as my home away from home."

The Ojibwe were the first Apostle Island inhabitants. The Apostles occupy a sacred place in Ojibwe culture, for one of their deities, Winneboujou, is credited with creating them while pursuing a large, clever beaver that escaped from a dam he was building on Chequamegon Bay. By the eighteenth century, French missionaries and fur trappers and traders arrived and one of them married the daughter of an Ojibwe chief. Madeline Island was named for her. British trappers and explorers came next—and it is this long, layered history and the influence of several cultures that Russ finds fascinating.

When Senator Gaylord Nelson began his campaign in the 1960s to protect the Apostle Islands and create a national park, the islands were not unblemished or pristine. Historically, there had been logging and quarrying—in the late nineteenth century, the construction of New York City's iconic walk-ups relied on tons of brownstone shipped from the Apostle Islands. However, the islands had remained uninhabited or sparsely populated—even today, not many more than two hundred hardy souls live year-round on Madeline, the only island with a modicum of commercial activity (and the only one not within the boundaries of the

National Lakeshore park). In the winter when Lake Superior freezes, Madeline residents get to Bayfield by driving their vehicles on a makeshift ice road marked off on both sides by discarded Christmas trees "planted" in the snowbanks.

In 1970, Nelson's campaign bore fruit when Congress established the Apostle Islands National Lakeshore. Nearly a quarter of a century later, one of Feingold's proudest achievements as Nelson's successor is the role he played, together with Congressman Dave Obey, in passing legislation in 2004 that established the Gaylord A. Nelson Wilderness within the Apostle Islands National Lakeshore, providing added protection for some 80 percent of the land. And the following year, the Apostle Islands National Lakeshore, although still relatively unknown to Americans, was ranked as the best national park in the United States by a panel of National Geographic experts.

There are a lot of simple pleasures during Feingold's week on Madeline Island—reading on the beach, hiking and especially eating, which is a serious Feingold family tradition, Russ frequently notes. Once or twice during the Feingolds' stay, Russ and other family members take the ferry to Bayfield on the mainland for breakfast at the Egg Toss Bakery Café, or dinner at Maggie's, where the specialties include whitefish and trout from Lake Superior and a flamingo-dominated decor from the vivid imagination of the owner and artist, Mary Rice. Another of Feingold's favorite activities is exploring the other islands, such as Devil's, where there are dramatic sea caves, sphagnum moss and old-growth forests of hemlock and white pine, and Long Island with its pebble nests of endangered piping plovers. He sometimes checks out the old lighthouses scattered around the perimeter of the islands; he has enacted legislation to preserve the most fragile structures.

Both Madeline Island and Bayfield have exceptionally pretty golf courses, which rank among Feingold's favorites. Often people who do not know him well are surprised to learn that Feingold is an avid golfer. His public image seems to give people the impression that he is a very serious man who wouldn't waste his time in a sand trap. And for that very reason, Feingold says, he took up golf in the 1980s. He didn't want people to think that he was merely a driven, humorless workaholic because, he says, that "makes people uncomfortable." Feingold's friend Joe Wineke takes credit for getting him addicted to golf. "He is not real good, but he is addicted," Wineke says. He remembers the first time he saw Feingold with a golf club in his hand; it was a Wineke fundraiser at the Evansville Country Club between Madison and Janesville. "He comes out with this . . . old bag [that] had a metal seat on it that must have belonged to his father. He got the award for the worst score."

Over the years, his game has improved, better than it was in 1993 when President Clinton invited him to play and Feingold shot 102. Apart from the fact that he was playing with the president, that round was notable because the journalist Elizabeth Drew wrote that Clinton had nailed down Feingold's vote for the administration's budget by inviting him to play golf. But Feingold, taking no chances that there was even a hint of an ethical breach on his part, asked Drew for a public correction: "That's just not so," he said. "There was absolutely no connection. I was on record for the budget in June. The vote and the invitation to play golf came in August."

With that lone exception, Feingold's golf career has been non-controversial, the outings on public courses filled with a little competition and much ribbing among friends and staff. Especially when he's with his contemporaries, like Wineke, there's a lot of locker room needling and banter. "He's a yapper," one of Feingold's friends says, "he talks constantly." And he likes to be in control, driving the golf cart and keeping score. Although he's under no illusions about his golf talent, he's as competitive about the game as he is about almost everything else. He carefully grades each of his drives, for example, still striving to get all As. But as much fun as he has on the golf course, the high point of his athletic career, Feingold may concede, was in the sixth grade when he could beat anybody in the forward crab race.

In the summer of 2001, Feingold not only visited the Apostle Islands in July, but he came back to the area in the waning days of August, finishing up a batch of listening sessions in nearby counties. From Hayward in Sawyer County, he drove over to Rick Dale's innovative Highland Valley Farm on the edge of Bayfield, where Dale grows blueberries and raspberries, makes honey and syrup and is a leader in the small-scale sustainable farming movement. The previous summer at a listening session, Feingold promised Dale he would visit the farm to see the techniques Dale was pioneering. It was the last day of August, a Friday afternoon, and as close to perfection as a late-summer day could be. The September weekend called for more of the same. On such days, whether one was a golfer or not, the best view of all was from the third hole of Bayfield's Apostle Highlands course because it was five hundred feet above Lake Superior. Looking to the east, you could see all the way to Michigan and the Porcupine Mountains. Looking beyond Bayfield's little harbor, you could see Feingold's peaceful Madeline Island and the rest of the old Ojibwe homeland. From this vantage point, the islands looked like dark blotches, not nearly as tantalizing as the shimmering Lake Superior. As much as Feingold loved the islands, it was the lake that made a powerful impression. "There's something mystical about it," he says. "That lake changes color about forty times a day. It's such a beautiful lake, but it's also incredibly *dangerous*. It can change in a minute."

Indeed, the many shipwrecks are proof of that. But on such a beautiful early September weekend in 2001, a sudden violent storm was the last thing on anybody's mind.

A week later on an early Tuesday morning, the flawless blue sky over the East Coast from Washington to New York City looked like a copy of the sky above the Apostle Islands. Feingold, who was in his Washington apartment across from the Capitol, had the TV on while he was on the phone talking with a *Newsweek* reporter. Before the conversation had started, shortly before 9 A.M., he saw the first horrifying scene on his TV set: smoke and fire coming from the upper floors of the North Tower of the World Trade Center in New York. A passenger plane had struck the building, according to reports. But minutes later, a second plane smashed into the South Tower. Clearly, now, these were no accidents, and there was more horror to come. About an hour after the North Tower was hit, a third plane crashed into the Pentagon in Northern Virginia, not far from the White House and the Capitol. From Capitol Hill, members of Congress and their staffs could see the black smoke, and many feared the Capitol might be next. Indeed, another hijacked plane west of Washington may have been headed toward the Capitol or the White House. But it crashed in a Pennsylvania field when passengers fought with the terrorist-hijackers for control of the plane. Meanwhile, the U.S. Capitol and nearby congressional office buildings were evacuated. Feingold's staff joined him across the street at his apartment. But then the apartment building was evacuated, too. Eventually, Feingold and others went to the Capitol Police headquarters.

The mood in political Washington was a mix of shock, anger and fear. Some compared the attacks to Pearl Harbor on December 7, 1941, "a date which will live in infamy," President Roosevelt said. But others said the terrorist attacks on the World Trade Center were much worse—cruelly immoral—because some three thousand innocent civilians were targeted and killed. On one point, however, there was virtual unanimity: the United States must respond militarily, and soon. Less than seventy-two hours after the attacks, Congress approved a resolution authorizing President Bush to take military action. The resolution passed the House 420–1, and the Senate 98–0. Specifically, the resolution stated the president could "use all necessary and appropriate force against those nations, organizations, or persons he determines planned, authorized, committed or aided the terrorist attacks that occurred on September 11, 2001, or harbored such organizations or persons, in order to prevent any future acts of international terrorism against the United States by such nations, organizations or persons." Feingold supported a U.S. retaliatory strike. He said the September 11 attacks were "acts of war" that called for a "strong and aggressive military response."

It was widely assumed in Washington that the American military retaliation would be in Afghanistan, aimed at the terrorist leaders responsible for the attacks, Osama bin Laden and his Al Qaeda network, as well as Afghanistan's ruling Taliban movement that provided Al Qaeda with an operational base. Less than a month after the terrorist attacks, on October 7, the first U.S. and British air strikes in Afghanistan were launched. They were accompanied by a strong show of political unity when leaders of both parties in the House and Senate issued a statement supporting President Bush's actions while emphasizing that these "actions and any future actions are directed against those who perpetrated the heinous attacks on the United States on Sept. 11, not against Islam or the people of Afghanistan."

Unity was suddenly a major theme in the Congress, at least temporarily replacing partisan division. The unity was driven mainly by fear. Fear was pervasive in the nation's capital. Armed soldiers were on city streets and F-15 and F-16 fighter jets were patrolling the skies. Many people, in and out of government, feared for their lives, thinking other attacks were imminent. But there was also political fear. Politically, perhaps the most vulnerable was the president and his administration. The country had been blindsided on the president's watch. To what extent the Bush administration was responsible remained to be seen (several years later in 2004, the bipartisan 9/11 Commission would cite a "failure of imagination" in both the Clinton and Bush administrations to foresee the real possibility of a 9/11 catastrophe, as well as the failure to make anti-terrorism a priority).

But in the immediate aftermath of 9/11, decisive action was the best method of communicating that the president was in charge, not out to lunch, as some critics would suggest. Step one was his plan to go on the offensive in Afghanistan. Step two was his urgent call for legislation that would give law enforcement agencies new anti-terrorism tools. Of course the clear implication was that had the tools been available, the World Trade Center would still be standing. Questions and doubts about whether the FBI, CIA and other agencies used their existing tools competently would be saved for another day.

With much public relations fanfare, the Bush administration whipped up a package of anti-terrorist measures that Attorney General John Ashcroft rushed to Congress on September 19, demanding it be passed within forty-eight hours. The package was cleverly called "Uniting and Strengthening America by Providing Appropriate Tools Required to Intercept and Obstruct Terrorism"—or, simply, the USA Patriot Act.

The USA Patriot Act did not fly through Congress quite on Ashcroft's timetable, but the legislative skids were sufficiently greased that the job was done before too many in Congress had a chance to read the final product. In the Senate, this was accomplished by short-circuiting the legislative process—and that was a turning point for Russ Feingold. At first, however, when the proposed legislation landed on his desk, he assumed "I was going to be with everybody else, voting for it. And that's where I wanted to be. I didn't want to be voting against the anti-terrorism act any more than I wanted to vote against the Afghanistan resolution. "I [wasn't] looking for trouble, as my mother might say."

A number of Patriot Act provisions were not controversial. But after reading the proposed legislation, Feingold and his staff put together a list of Patriot Act provisions that were troubling and that worried civil liberties organizations. Some of his colleagues on the Judiciary Committee had the same concerns. But even after the original administration proposal was modified by Senate staff, Feingold believed there were still serious problems, such as the so-called sneak-and-peek authority that would allow law enforcement to search a person's residence or office without his or her knowledge until after the search was carried out. Other constitutionally dubious provisions had to do with expanded government power to access a citizen's library records and other personal information, and broad, unprecedented authority to wiretap phones and monitor personal computers. These provisions violated basic constitutional protections or at least raised serious questions, Feingold believed, and he planned to offer amendments to remove them when the Judiciary Committee held its customary mark-up before the legislation went to the Senate floor.

But suddenly, the Democratic leadership announced there would be no committee mark-up, that the legislation was going straight to the Senate floor for an up-or-down vote, no amendments allowed.

"What?" Feingold blurted in disbelief when he heard the news.

When he was younger, his temper sometimes flared, but he had learned to control it. Not this time. "I was shocked, and I objected," which resulted in a heated shouting match in a corner of the Senate chamber with Tom Daschle, the Democratic majority leader. "He was demanding that I not pursue these things," Feingold says. Daschle was fearful that Democrats would be seen as soft on terrorism if they slowed things down or broke ranks and "weakened" legislation supported by the president.

On October 9, Daschle pushed for a vote on the Patriot Act, but Feingold blocked it until he was allowed to offer his amendments. But each of his amendments was quickly tabled and, late on Thursday night, October 11, a month after the attacks, the Senate prepared to vote. Feingold and his staff talked about what he was going to do. "I can tell you as honestly as I can, I didn't care what the politics were," he recalls. "All I could think about when I was standing over there [on the Senate floor] was three thousand people were just murdered, and this is one of toughest moments in the history of the country. The soldiers are doing their job, the police are doing their job, and I have a job to do. *And my job is to get this right.*" He was now chairman of the Constitution Subcommittee of the Judiciary Committee. "If I'm not going to [do the right thing], who is?"

Before his vote on the final legislation, Feingold spoke on the Senate floor and placed his vote in a democratic framework. He recalled a Supreme Court case he had read in law school, *Kennedy* v. *Mendoza-Martinez*, in which evasion of the military draft during the Vietnam War was the issue. In coming down on the side of civil liberties even during wartime, Justice Arthur Goldberg wrote that while the Constitution "is not a suicide pact," it was conceived to ensure "fundamental constitutional guarantees" when the temptation to suppress civil liberties was greatest—namely, when governments fear that constitutional guarantees "will inhibit government action." Feingold explained that his decision to vote against the Patriot Act was made "in this spirit. . . . I believe we must redouble our vigilance . . . to ensure our security and prevent further acts of terror. But we must also redouble our vigilance to preserve our values and the basic rights that make us who we are." In the final analysis, he said, the legislation did "not strike the right balance between empowering law enforcement and protecting civil liberties."

Already, Feingold told the Senate, he found disturbing signs that the Bush administration was heading down a road littered with historic violations of constitutional rights—the suspension of habeas corpus during the Civil War, the internment of Japanese-Americans and others during World War II, the surveillance and harassment of antiwar protesters during the Vietnam War. "As it seeks to combat terrorism," Feingold said, "the Justice Department is making extraordinary use of its power to arrest and detain individuals, jailing hundreds of people on immigration violations and arresting more than a dozen 'material witnesses' not charged with any crime. The government has not brought any criminal charges related to the attacks with regard to the overwhelming majority of these detainees." And he expressed great concern about a new, dangerous kind of racial profiling that had emerged. Warning that "we who don't have Arabic names or don't wear turbans or headscarves may not feel the weight of these times as much as Americans from the Middle East and South Asia do," Feingold said that "even as America addresses the demanding security challenges before us, we must strive mightily . . . against racism and ethnic discrimination. . . . Preserving our freedom is one of the main reasons that we are now engaged in this new war on terrorism. We will lose that war without firing a shot if we sacrifice the liberties of the American people."

The Senate voted for the USA Patriot Act by a vote of 98–1, with Feingold the only senator opposing a bill that other members admitted was flawed and eroded liberties. The legislation was sent immediately to the president for his signature.

As to the public reaction to his vote, Feingold says he hoped most people might be supportive. "I thought I'd have to explain [why I voted against it], and that I could explain, and people would be pleased that I raised questions." But he had no idea that in the months and years ahead, as public concerns grew about the Bush administration's controversial anti-terrorism and Iraq War policies, his vote would become a symbol that defined him to a wide audience as an uncommonly courageous politician in the post-9/11 world. In fact, the immediate reaction to his vote was overwhelmingly positive across much of the political spectrum, his mail running two to one in favor. Back home in Madison, he received several standing ovations at the Wisconsin Academy of Sciences, Arts and Letters, when he spoke passionately about his fight to protect civil liberties and his vote against the Patriot Act. It was a rousing performance that should "rank on the list of 'profiles in courage' addresses," wrote the journalist John Nichols.

In Washington, Feingold was hailed on the floor of the House of Representatives by Dick Armey, the conservative Republican leader. The breadth of the political benefits for Feingold might have been foreshadowed weeks earlier in the House Judiciary Committee, where some of the most conservative *and* liberal members of Congress joined forces and agreed on a pro–civil liberties, greatly altered version of the Patriot Act. This across-the-spectrum consensus was remarkable, observers noted, and it produced a bill Feingold probably could have supported. Although the House Judiciary Committee approved it unanimously, the Bush administration prevailed on House leaders to kill it.

Several months later, Feingold was invited to speak to a large audience of Arab-Americans who had come to Washington for the Arab American Institute Foundation's annual convention. This was no ordinary time for people of Middle Eastern descent. In the weeks after 9/11, federal agents arrested and detained more than a thousand people, refusing to reveal their identities or the charges against them. In early November 2001, Feingold and five other senators sent a letter to the Attorney General. "The Department of Justice should aggressively investigate and prevent future terrorist attacks," the letter began, "but should at the same time act with constitutional restraint." Feingold added his own comments later, saying, "My concern is based on the incredible scope of the detainments. Maybe there's a perfectly good explanation for it, but it's time to start hearing it." When Feingold was introduced to the Arab-American audience by the foundation's president, Jim Zogby, the audience applauded loudly when Zogby said Feingold was the only senator who voted against the Patriot Act.

Feingold said that he accepted the invitation to speak because "I wanted to join you to show my support, not only as an elected official, but as a Jewish-American, reaching across an ethnic and religious divide that at times, unfortunately, seems like a great abyss." Although he talked about foreign policy and the Israeli-Palestinian conflict, he was especially concerned with addressing the fear many in his audience felt about federal law enforcement practices in their communities. "I know Arab-Americans have borne an especially heavy burden during these very trying times," he said. "Your patriotism was questioned. And, most troubling, the freedom you have the same right to enjoy as every other American . . . continues to be threatened today. But I want you to know that you are not alone in this struggle." As Zogby said later, Feingold and his heartfelt words "were extraordinarily well received."

Feingold's stand against the USA Patriot Act probably repaired his damaged reputation among some liberals around the country. A year earlier, when the new Bush administration was being formed, they were angered by his vote to confirm John Ashcroft as attorney general.

From the day that Ashcroft was nominated, he was the Bush administration's lightning rod when it came to civil rights, civil liberties and other important, often emotional issues. Going back to his days as Missouri governor and then as a U.S. senator, Ashcroft was a darling of the political right wing and despised by the left. His confirmation process turned into an epic tug-of-war over a presidential cabinet nomination. The considerable money and emotion that scores of organizations on the right and left invested in this fight were about much more than Ashcroft's record, however. He was nominated only weeks after the bitter 2000 presidential race was decided, the outcome leaving the political right elated and the left seething. Five Republican-appointed U.S. Supreme Court justices had departed from precedent and concocted a rationale that gave the White House to George W. Bush. Their behavior was nothing less than "judicial lawlessness," the writer and lawyer Scott Turow said. From the perspective of the political left, Bush's presidency was illegitimate to begin with, but to add insult to injury, he started to act as if he had a conservative mandate. Rather than to try to unify the country, his highest political priority was to reward his right-wing base. The Ashcroft nomination was a dry run for the next nomination to the U.S. Supreme Court. How many votes Ashcroft could get, or could be denied, in the Senate would be an early indication of how a similar Supreme Court nominee would fare.

The lobbying on both sides of the Ashcroft nomination was intense. The Senate Judiciary Committee approved the nomination, 10–8, on a strict party-line vote—with one exception. Feingold voted for the nomination because, he said, the president should have the right to select his own team. There were virtually no examples in U.S. history, Feingold said, of a cabinet nominee being rejected because of his political views or ideology. And he didn't believe that Ashcroft's opponents had made the case that he suffered from serious ethical deficiencies or was unlikely to uphold the law, the only legitimate grounds for rejecting a cabinet nominee, Feingold thought. Those were his reasons for his controversial vote. But it didn't hurt Ashcroft's cause that he and Feingold had a cordial relationship. They served on two subcommittees together and although they had little in common politically, they hit it off personally. In Congress, these seemingly unlikely friendships are more common than outsiders might think.

Feingold's vote in the Judiciary Committee enraged some organizations and individuals on the left (in the final Senate vote, seven other Democrats also voted for Ashcroft). "I have never been more disappointed in a U.S. senator than I am in Russ Feingold," said Ralph Neas, president of the liberal People for the American Way. To liberals, Feingold said that Ashcroft would take his marching orders from the White House, so it was Bush they should hold accountable, an argument that many furious liberals at the time were not interested in hearing. Some of Feingold's young staff that handled the blizzard of phone calls were reduced to tears because many of the callers were so nasty. In Wisconsin, one letter writer said old Fighting Bob La Follette would be "gagging in his grave" over Feingold's embarrassing vote. Some people were looking for ulterior motives, perhaps a deal Feingold struck with Republican leaders to bring the McCain-Feingold bill to the floor for a vote. "Anyone who knows me knows the one thing I have never done in my career and will never do is make any such deal," Feingold told the now merged *Milwaukee Journal Sentinel*. "It has cost me dearly on occasion that I don't horse-trade, but I just don't do it."

In a written statement, Feingold expanded on the main reason for his Ashcroft vote. Not only did any president deserve broad latitude when selecting a cabinet, but "above all, I believe that a real commitment to bipartisanship demands that we make difficult decisions if we are going to work together for the American people. For me, supporting John Ashcroft was one of those difficult situations." Some Wisconsin editorial writers, including liberals and conservatives, agreed with Feingold's reasoning. The headline "Courageous Vote" over the editorial in the Republican-oriented *Beloit Daily News* best captured the political benefits that Feingold probably picked up with his Ashcroft vote: "Feingold rejected raw partisanship by breaking ranks with his fellow Democrats." To be sure, a politician can't break ranks too often, but in contemporary American politics, where independent-minded voters are increasingly a bigger portion of the electorate, Feingold's Ashcroft vote was probably a political winner. Feingold does not acknowledge that such political considerations might have affected his decision-making, but a University of Wisconsin political science professor, David Canon, said the Ashcroft vote would appeal to independent voters not only in Wisconsin but nationwide. If, for example, Feingold decided to run for president, Canon observed, "I think this was a shrewd move on his part."

Seven years after John McCain and Russ Feingold joined forces on campaign finance reform, the landmark McCain-Feingold legislation banning soft money won approval in both the House and Senate and was signed into law by President Bush in March 2002.

The big breakthrough occurred in the Senate, where the Republican leadership had stymied all previous attempts. A number of factors changed the political dynamics, but several were especially significant. First, John McCain made the McCain-Feingold bill a centerpiece of his unsuccessful but widely admired run for the 2000 Republican presidential nomination, giving the campaign reform cause new prominence and luster. Second, Democrats picked up five seats in the Senate in 2000, providing the McCain-Feingold forces a better chance of stopping a Republican filibuster. Third, a conservative Republican, Thad Cochran of Mississippi, surprised many when he announced his support of the legislation in early 2001.

But when the debate over McCain-Feingold came to the Senate floor in March 2001, the outcome was not assured. In fact, the debate went on for two weeks, and every morning McCain and Feingold met to plot strategy with a bipartisan group of colleagues—senators such as Democrats Carl Levin, John Edwards, Chuck Schumer, Joe Lieberman and Maria Cantwell, and Republicans Olympia Snowe, Susan Collins, Fred Thompson, and Jim Jeffords. The group's top priority was to keep the pro-reform senators together and defeat unfriendly amendments. Toward that end, virtually every day the group distributed a fact sheet to colleagues on pending amendments, and McCain and Feingold tried to maintain the overall solidarity by voting the same way on the amendments (an exception was public financing of federal campaigns, which Feingold supported but McCain didn't).

Finally, on March 20, the McCain-Feingold legislation passed the Senate by a vote of 60–40. When McCain first met with reporters, he was uncharacteristically subdued. "It's not often that I'm rendered speechless," he said, "and I'm sure that the affliction will not remain with me very long." Feingold, calling his partnership with McCain "the highlight of my professional life," adding, "This bill won't miraculously erase distrust and suspicion of the Congress overnight. It won't completely end the primacy of money, but it's a big step in the right direction." In that vein, McCain said: "Campaign contributions from a single source that run to hundreds of thousands or even millions of dollars are not healthy to a democracy. Is that not self-evident?"

Sanford D. Horwitt

The *New York Times* called the passage of McCain-Feingold "an extraordinary victory." It was also something of a miracle because the legislation was not only opposed by the Republican Party leadership, but also by much of Washington's lobbyist-business establishment, the AFL-CIO, and potent advocacy organizations such as the National Rifle Association and the American Civil Liberties Union. On the other side, much credit went to the indefatigable Fred Wertheimer, president of Democracy 21, Meredith McGehee at Common Cause, and many others who sustained grassroots and newspaper editorial support over many years. But in the Senate, a leading opponent of reform, Phil Gramm of Texas, believed the key to success was not popular pressure but McCain's and Feingold's tenacity.

As soon as the Bipartisan Campaign Reform Act (or BCRA as McCain-Feingold was now called) was signed into law, there was a race to the courthouse by opponents to see who could be first to file a constitutional challenge. The National Rifle Association won, but it willingly deferred to an equally zealous opponent, Senator Mitch McConnell, who had memorably predicted that Feingold was "dead meat" in his 1998 reelection campaign. The landmark case that would end up in the Supreme Court would be known as *McConnell v. Federal Election Commission*, although McConnell would be joined by a similar coalition of organizations that had opposed McCain-Feingold in the Senate.

From the beginning of the case, Feingold was optimistic about the outcome, and like many Supreme Court watchers, he thought that Sandra Day O'Connor was the key swing vote. Although the case was exceedingly complex, at the heart of it was the question of political corruption. Broadly speaking, did the appearance and reality of corruption justify placing some restrictions on speech? In addition to banning unlimited soft money contributions to political parties, the new legislation also placed restrictions on issue ads.

Advocacy organizations could no longer spend unlimited amounts from their general treasuries to run ads mentioning a federal candidate's name thirty days before a primary or sixty days before a general election. Such ads, however, could be aired if they were paid for with funds subjected to the federal campaign limits, such as the funds contributed to an organization's political action committee.

Before the case went to court, both Feingold and McCain were deposed by lawyers representing McConnell and the other plaintiffs. The lawyers pressed them for concrete examples of political corruption, not only stories they had heard, but corruption they witnessed. And both McCain and Feingold gave examples. Feingold recounted an incident involving Federal Express that was partially reported in the *New York Times* in 1996. The *Times* story revealed the Senate had stayed in session for two extra days until language was inserted into an obscure law that benefited FedEx. In the article, Feingold, who had been in the Senate for only three years, was quoted as saying: "I was stunned by the breadth and depth of their clout up here." He was one of thirty-one senators who ended up voting against the FedEx position but when he had attempted to organize more opposition, he got "the sense . . . that this company had made a real strong effort to be friendly and helpful to Congress." Indeed it had, the *Times* reported, through "a generous political action committee, the presence of popular former congressional leaders on its board, lavish spending on lobbying, and a fleet of corporate jets that ferry dozens of officeholders to political events around the country."

But there was something else, too: the large FedEx soft money contributions to the political parties. And what the *New York Times* did not report was the name of at least one senator who knew about FedEx's soft-money largesse and the company's interest in pending legislation.

In his deposition, Feingold recalled the episode when questioned by one of the plaintiffs' lawyers, Floyd Abrams. Abrams wanted Feingold to name the Democratic senator who said that his colleagues should go along with the FedEx provision because "it just gave us 100,000." Feingold said: "Let me first say that it's necessary for me to state the name of the senator which I'm about to do because generally speaking, of course, that's not the way we do business. We try to respect private conversations, though this is an exceptional situation where the [BCRA] statute is being challenged. So I simply want to put on the record and indicate that it was Senator Wendell Ford." That testimony, and other testimony like it, was persuasive because, in a 5–4 decision, the Supreme Court upheld all the major provisions of the new campaign finance law. The Court's dissenters tried to define corruption narrowly, implying that it only meant buying votes for cash or something akin to it. But the majority opinion said "this crabbed view of corruption, and particularly of the appearance of corruption, ignores precedent, common sense, and the realities of political fundraising exposed by the record in this litigation."

Feingold was on his way to a listening session in Fennimore, Wisconsin, when the call came about the great news. He was ecstatic, shouting out some wildly exuberant expletives that may have surprised a few young staff members in the van with him, he says. He was also thrilled to hear that Sandra Day O'Connor had been the key, decisive vote. "I felt that she would not want in her closing years . . . to put a stamp of approval on what was objectively a corrupt system. Even though she was a conservative, she said, 'Wait a minute. It can't be that unlimited million-dollar contributions are perfectly fine.' Thank God she did the right thing. It was a very courageous thing, and I'm eternally in her debt."

For Feingold, the entire process leading up to the Court's decision gave him a great deal of lawyerly satisfaction—working with the legal team that included his old Wisconsin friends David

Harth and Chuck Curtis; going up against some of the country's foremost legal minds during his long deposition; sitting with McCain at the Supreme Court and watching an extraordinary four hours of oral argument about their historic efforts. And then, "the wonderful moment," as he calls it, when five justices provided the exclamation point to Russ Feingold's and John McCain's long, noble quest for a more honest, democratic political system.

CHAPTER 10

IRAQ

"We are about to make one of the weightiest decisions of our time," Russ Feingold said from the Senate floor on October 9, 2002, the day before he and his Senate colleagues voted on whether to give President Bush the authority to launch a preemptive war in Iraq.

With the Senate poised to vote, Bush was in a strong political position. According to an NBC News/*Wall Street Journal* poll, the president's job approval was at 64 percent, and 67 percent said he was doing a good job on terrorism. A majority, 58 percent, supported military action in Iraq.

But a few weeks before the Senate vote, Democratic antiwar activists around the country had applauded Al Gore, the Democratic Party's presidential candidate in 2000, when he sharply criticized Bush's Iraq war plan in a California speech. Midterm elections were coming up, however, and inside the Beltway, the reaction was different. Democratic strategists thought Gore's criticism could hurt the party's prospects.

The Democratic campaign consultants subscribe to the maxim "Winning isn't everything, it's the only thing," made famous by the Green Bay Packers coach Vince Lombardi. And the coaching advice the consultants provided to Senate Democrats was this: it was not a great time to be a Democrat; in post-9/11 America, there was a shift among voters toward the Republican Party. Any Senate Democrat who was thinking about opposing the president's Iraq war resolution should understand that he or she was flying in the face of public opinion—going against a popular president and the public's desire for aggressive action against terrorists. Whether in the 2002 midterm or 2004 presidential election, any Democrat running in a competitive political environment would be taking a big risk voting against the war resolution. In the heat of a campaign, it would be difficult to defend an anti–Iraq War position and counter Republican TV attack ads that, for example, might feature an image of President Bush on one side of the screen and Osama bin Laden and the antiwar Democrat on the other. In that contest, fear trumps reason, the consultants warned.

Based on this kind of advice, Democratic Senate leaders wanted to get the Iraq war resolution out of the way as quickly as possible so that Democratic candidates could focus on economic issues in the last month of the 2002 election campaign. Moreover, they didn't feel a moral obligation to strongly contest Bush's policies.

To be sure, while Feingold had not exaggerated the historical importance of the decision the Senate was about to make, there was little suspense about the results. Everybody in Washington knew the war resolution was going to pass overwhelmingly despite gaping holes in the administration's pro-war arguments and evidence. Even some critics with solid Republican credentials, such as Brent Scowcroft, saw a disaster in the making. Nonetheless every Republican senator except Lincoln Chafee sided with the administration. But hugely disappointing to many Democratic activists was that only twenty-one Democratic senators out of fifty opposed going to war in Iraq. It is impossible to say how many of the twenty-nine Senate Democrats voted for the Iraq war resolution because they were persuaded by the consultants' warnings. However, political observers did not think it was a coincidence that nearly all the Democratic senators who were thinking about running for president in either 2004 or 2008 voted with the Bush administration on the war—senators such as John Kerry, John Edwards and Hillary Clinton.

But Russ Feingold, too, had been thinking about running. He had dipped a toe in presidential waters, making a round of college speeches while telling reporters in early 2002 that it was nevertheless unlikely that he'd become an official candidate in 2004. Probably in 2008, his friends guessed, but first he had to be reelected in 2004, which could be difficult. After all, he was the lone Senate vote against the USA Patriot Act—and now, on the Senate floor, he was about to deliver a scathing attack of the Bush administration's Iraq war plan. "The administration's arguments just don't add up," he said. "They don't add up to a coherent basis for a new major war in the middle of our current challenging fight against the terrorism of al Qaeda and related organizations. Therefore, I cannot support the resolution for the use of force before us."

In his lengthy speech, Feingold emphasized two issues that he found especially objectionable about Bush's Iraq scheme. First, he rejected the Bush administration's key contention of a link between the 9/11 terrorists and Saddam Hussein's Iraq. Both Bush and Vice President Dick Cheney had gone to great lengths to make the connection—and public opinion polls showed they had succeeded. But Feingold wasn't buying it and while he was not alone, most Democratic senators did not push the issue as he did. With a touch of sarcasm, Feingold told the Senate that the president had "to do better than the shoddy piecing together of flimsy evidence that contradicts the very briefings we've received by various agencies. . . . [T]he administration appears to use 9/11 and the language of terrorism and the connection to Iraq too loosely, almost like a bootstrap." Second, Feingold believed the Bush administration had completely failed to develop a realistic post-invasion strategy for Iraq. If Saddam Hussein's regime falls, Feingold said, the aftermath was not only likely to be costly but "could involve the occupation of a Middle Eastern country [which] is no small matter." Feingold talked about the difficulty of "extricat[ing] ourselves" from Iraq—and "after all of the briefings, all of the hearings and statements, as far as I can tell, the administration apparently intends to wing it when it comes to the day after or, as others have suggested, the decade after. And I think that makes no sense at all."

After his vote against the war resolution, Feingold told reporters that Wisconsin residents supported his position. That might have been wishful thinking, however. Public opinion in Wisconsin was little different than it was nationwide, the results of the Badger Poll showed. Unlike Feingold, Wisconsin's other senator, Democrat Herb Kohl, voted for the war resolution, as did one of the state's Democratic congressmen, Ron Kind, plus all of the state's Republican representatives. In political terms, Feingold had cast a tough vote. And that was the implication of an editorial in the Madison *Capital Times*: "In a Senate where most members are this week compromising their ethics, their duties and their intelligence in order to support the Bush administration's attempt to gin up war fever on the eve of an election, Feingold is part of the minority that has chosen to speak truth to power. . . . What sets [him] apart . . . is the fact that he is willing to speak truth when others lack the courage to do so."

Finding the right words and speaking effectively in post-9/11 America was an important challenge, Russ Feingold knew. Nationally, he thought his party was making a big mistake by ceding the issues of national security and terrorism to Bush and the Republicans. These issues were not going away. Terrorism was the number one issue facing the country, Feingold told audiences in the years after 9/11. At his listening sessions, he was blunt: "The terrorists want to kill us and our children." The bluntness, and the hardheaded tone, seemed to startle some of the dovish attendees. But Feingold doesn't see himself as a pacifist or antiwar politician. After all, he voted for the military strike in Afghanistan, and he also believed that Iraq with chemical and biological weapons under Saddam Hussein was a danger. He supported the concept of regime change, but not through the ill-conceived, unjustified rush-to-war proposal of the Bush administration.

Feingold's foreign policy ideas were affected by 9/11, but he doesn't think they have changed in a fundamental way. In a recent interview, he explained how, as a young man, he read extensively about the post–World War II period and tended to be critical of how the U.S. often engaged in "unilateral military force, from the Dominican Republic to Vietnam, in situations where it wasn't necessarily the wisest thing to do. . . . I came into the Senate with skepticism about that, plus the history of the La Follette era and of states in this part of the country being a little more skeptical about military adventurism."

He believes that military force should be used judiciously. "Generally speaking, military force should be the last choice," he says. "The downside of it is so significant that unless it's essential, or truly the best thing in our national interest, we shouldn't do it." In recalling the involvement of American troops in Bosnia, which he opposed, Feingold says: "When we start talking about holding the bag for the Europeans because they wouldn't do the job in Bosnia, and misrepresenting to the American people that it was only going to be $2 billion and the troops would be home by Christmas—I see that kind of thing and I resent not only the cost but the dishonesty of it. I believe in a more regional approach and a good example . . . is East Timor where I was the most active member of the Senate trying to free East Timor from Indonesia. When it came time to have a force there, it was led by the Australians. They asked us for a couple hundred troops, but we weren't 'the guy' there, the policeman."

He is adamant that all foreign policy considerations must flow from the top goal of protecting the lives of the American people. "And our first priority right now," he says, "is to stop Al Qaeda and their affiliates and sympathizers. . . . It is the preeminent responsibility of the government of the United States. Now, whether it should be done more militarily or less is an important question. I think there is a tendency to look at it almost exclusively as military and to me that is just wrong. Of course it includes the military, but that's way too narrow a vision if we really want to succeed in terms of turning people's minds and hearts more positively toward us. There are too many people out there who are being convinced to do us harm."

One of the sources of anti-Americanism, Feingold believes, is that too often the U.S. allies itself with repressive regimes. He recalls that soon after 9/11, he dropped into an open house in Madison for the Islamic community. "They were mostly students and other young people from all over the Middle East," Feingold says. He thought they'd want to talk with him about Israel or Iraq. But what he heard "was their anger at the United States for supporting regimes in their home countries that were against human rights, women and democracy." For the United States, Feingold thinks there is no other acceptable choice than to be committed to using its diplomacy, economic leverage and other persuasive methods to push authoritarian regimes toward democracy. He's under no illusions about how difficult and risky that may be. "There's a legitimate fear," he says, "that if we push real hard for a 'real democracy,' which is what we have to do, that radical groups will take over a country who are very antagonistic to the United States. It happened in the Palestinian area, it's what arguably happened in Lebanon and in other places. And that's the risk. But I think the greater risk is to be associated . . . with a regime that is ultimately going to collapse unless they move toward democratization. . . . It's extremely complicated . . . but we simply cannot be perceived as propping up the Egypts and Saudi Arabias of the world. It plays into this disastrous reputation we had even before 9/11, and worse after Iraq, of course."

The Iraq War is a national security fiasco not only because it has reinforced anti-American attitudes in Islamic countries, Feingold believes, but especially because it has diverted American resources from fighting terrorism in breeding grounds around the world. These are often the poorest, most politically fragile countries where Feingold has visited over the years as a member of the Foreign Relations Committee and its African Affairs subcommittee. To maximize the chances of succeeding in a fight against the global terrorism network, Feingold said in a recent speech that "we must build a comprehensive national security strategy that seeks to bring stability and progress to people in places like Somalia, Mali and Indonesia. Those people must believe that their communities and governments will protect them by, for example, stamping out corruption, respecting human rights and enforcing the rule of law."

The enormity of the challenge, which Feingold acknowledges, is not only because it requires the United States to be engaged in far-flung locales. "In fact, being the most powerful nation in the world may make this approach even tougher, because we need to understand the hopes and fears of people who feel powerless and voiceless. But we are up to this challenge, and we can muster serious resources, and creative diplomatic strategies, to meet it head-on."

In the 2004 presidential election, Wisconsin was a key battle-ground state, as it had been four years earlier. Too close to call was the consensus, a coin flip between George W. Bush and John Kerry. Neither Democrats nor Republicans held an advantage. The eight congressional districts were split between the two parties. The Republican Tommy Thompson had been a four-term governor but was succeeded by the Democrat Jim Doyle. Independent voters had long been important in Wisconsin, but more than ever they determined the outcome of elections, as was now also true in other states.

As for Feingold's reelection prospects in 2004, starting out he had an edge as the incumbent but, from the vantage point of his opponent's campaign strategists, his record was a big, fat target. It was not only his votes against the Patriot Act and the Iraq War, although those were the most inviting targets. Feingold also had called for a national moratorium on the death penalty and led Senate hearings on capital punishment and racial profiling. He had opposed Bush's tax cuts and private savings accounts for health care. All of these supposedly controversial positions could be exploited in TV ads. And Feingold's Republican opponent, Tim Michels, had an appealing biography. He was a former Army Ranger, a business executive and a multimillionaire. Although he won the Republican primary, he was not well known but had the money, it seemed, to overcome that disadvantage.

Not surprisingly, the Michels campaign went after Feingold hard on his Patriot Act vote and national security. The Michels campaign was one of the few in the country that ran TV spots showing the images of the burning ruins of the World Trade Center towers. In the last days of the campaign, Michels continued to hammer away on the national security message, running an ad featuring former New York City mayor Rudolph Giuliani.

Feingold never backed away from his votes on the Patriot Act and the war. In one of his earliest TV ads, he said, "We can fight terrorism without sacrificing our freedoms." In another ad, military veterans endorsed Feingold for his courageous stand protecting the freedoms they fought for. The Veterans of Foreign Wars Political Action Committee also supported him because of the work he had done on veterans issues. Other campaign ads zeroed in on health care and trade. He favored state-based universal health care funded in part by the federal government. An organization of mainly Republican small business owners endorsed Feingold because he had spoken out against unfair trade agreements and demanded a better deal for them and their employees.

On election night, the prognosticators were right about the Bush-Kerry race in Wisconsin: it was even closer than the razor-thin margin by which Al Gore carried the state in 2000. Kerry, who had voted for the Patriot Act and had vacillated on the war, eked out the win, 49.70 to 49.32 percent, the smallest margin of any state he carried.

Feingold , on the other hand, rolled up a near-landslide victory, winning more than 55 percent of the vote and carrying twenty-seven counties that Bush won. After twelve years, people had a better sense of who he was. Not only did they like his populist touch—he kept his old promise and has returned more than $70,000 in Senate pay raises to the U.S. Treasury—but he also comes across as down-to-earth.

Exit polls revealed three key reasons for Feingold's decisive victory.

First, he won 90 percent of the voters who wanted to see change or reform.

Second, 77 percent who said Iraq was the most important issue supported him.

Third, and most important of all, Feingold won a whopping 62 percent of the independent vote. By definition, independent voters are not political insiders and, Feingold says, "they sense that I'm not either. And they like that." His longtime aide George Aldrich, who managed the 2004 campaign, says he heard scores of voters give essentially the same explanation about why they were voting for Feingold: "I don't agree with him on everything, but I respect him and he's honest."

At the spirited election victory party at the Marriott in Middleton, Feingold said: "This election is about something bigger than ourselves. It's about our freedoms. Sometimes a person has to stand alone for our freedoms, but you're never alone for long." And in Wisconsin that night, he was hardly alone, having just received the largest number of votes in state history. Russ Feingold, who had boldly challenged the Bush administration's 9/11 policies, demonstrated he had important political insights and lessons to share with his Democratic Senate colleagues and party leaders in Washington. Whether they were ready to listen remained to be seen.

EPILOGUE

Following his breakthrough election victory in 2004, Russ Feingold became the strongest, clearest voice in the U.S. Senate demanding an end to the Bush administration's increasingly unpopular Iraq War, and a leading critic of its assault on civil liberties in post-9/11 America. On the Internet, antiwar bloggers were singing his praises and contrasting his boldness with the fecklessness of other Democrats. Many were urging him to run for president in 2008, and he was thinking seriously about it.

Feingold was the first senator to call for a timetable for withdrawing U.S. troops from Iraq. He made the proposal in mid-August 2005, after a round of listening sessions in northern Wisconsin. He was impressed and a little surprised by the breadth of antiwar fervor he encountered in the rural counties. In the town of Lake Tomahawk, for example, a resident said she was "totally upset with this war," and an elderly woman added emphatically: "I think we should be out of there." Over and over, this was what he heard. Days later, back at his house in Middleton early one morning, he sat in his cozy family room and sketched a proposal calling for a timeline for redeploying U.S. troops from Iraq. On August 18, he announced his plan at a listening session in the town of Marquette and in a press release. Three days later, he was on *Meet the Press* explaining it to a national audience.

Feingold was proposing that U.S. troops be withdrawn from Iraq by the end of 2006. Citing various experts who said the prolonged U.S. military presence in Iraq was a magnet for terrorists and insurgents and was fueling violence and instability, he said, "I am putting a vision of when this ends on the table in the hope that we can get the focus back on our top priority and that is keeping America and the American people safe." He acknowledged that U.S. economic, political and some military support would continue after the troops left Iraq. "But it's almost as if talking about completing the [military] mission in Iraq has become taboo," he said. "It's time for senators and members of Congress, especially those from my own party, to be less timid while this administration neglects urgent national security priorities in favor of staying a flawed policy course in Iraq. We need to refocus on fighting and defeating the terrorist network that attacked this country on September 11, 2001, and that means placing our Iraq policy in the context of a global effort, rather than letting it dominate our security strategy and drain vital security resources for an unlimited amount of time."

The White House accused Feingold of undermining U.S. troops and sending "the wrong message to the enemy." He responded to that accusation by recounting an exchange he had on a recent trip to Iraq with a top U.S. general. "I said, 'Off the record, your own view, would it help if we had a timeline to let the world know that we're not staying here forever?' And this is what he said, verbatim: He said, 'Nothing would take the wind out of the sails of the insurgents more than to have a timeline in place.' So this is a false argument. It's a phony argument that doesn't really address the reality that we are actually causing more insurgents, more terrorism . . . from all around the world coming into Iraq because we don't have a vision for success and completion of the mission."

Epilogue

Two months later, senior Pennsylvania congressman John Murtha stunned Washington when he made a similar proposal. A retired Marine colonel who earned a Bronze Star and two Purple Hearts for his service in Vietnam, Murtha, a Democrat, was known for his pro-defense views. But he had been talking to his military friends who convinced him it was time to get out of Iraq. The White House tried to discredit Murtha by calling his timeline for redeploying the troops a plan "to surrender to the terrorists." But once Murtha joined the antiwar ranks, it was more difficult for the administration and pro-war pundits to marginalize congressional critics by calling them soft on terrorism, extreme or left-wing. And in Feingold's case, after all, he was representing the views of a very nonradical heartland state where the most important beverage was milk.

Nearly a year passed before there was a vote in the Senate on an amendment by Feingold and John Kerry, who had joined him in pressing the Senate and the administration for adopting an exit strategy in Iraq. It seemed an odd pairing, since Kerry's cautious, tortured position on the war had helped doom his presidential run. But now he sought to redeem himself and was refreshingly candid and concise when he recalled the original Senate vote on the Iraq War resolution: "Russ made the right vote, I made the wrong vote, it's that simple." The amendment, which called for redeploying most of the 126,900 troops in Iraq by July 2007, received only thirteen votes. Twelve Democrats supported it along with the Independent Jim Jeffords. Within days of the vote, Feingold was back on *Meet the Press* and this time his frustration and anger were aimed more at his own party than at the Bush administration and its Iraq policies. "The White house has done a terrible job of running the fight against terrorism [and] a terrible job in Iraq," he began, "but they've done a brilliant job of intimidating Democrats. Somehow Democrats are afraid to say, 'Look, not only was this a mistake, but it continues to be a mistake and it's being run in a mistaken way.' And I cannot understand why the structure of the Democratic Party, the consultants [who] are here in Washington, constantly advise Democrats not to take a strong stand." Tim Russert, the program's moderator, asked Feingold if he was suggesting that "the majority of the Democratic Senate is out of touch with the American people." He did not hesitate. "Those who vote against bringing the troops home don't get it. . . . I saw two or three polls, Tim, in the last week that showed that a majority of the American people favor a timetable. You know, we lost in 2000, we lost in 2002, we lost in 2004. Why don't we try something different, like listening to the American people?"

Finally, in the 2006 election, Americans frustrated and angry about the Iraq War and corruption in Congress voted enough Republicans out of office to give control of both the House and Senate to the Democrats. Democratic campaign leaders congratulated themselves on their winning strategy, but the larger truth was that Republicans were responsible for their own demise. And after the election, when it came to the Iraq War, the Democratic Party remained divided and timid. Early in 2007, while Russ Feingold became the first in the Senate to introduce legislation to stop funding the Iraq War, a majority of his Democratic colleagues were working up the courage to pass a "nonbinding" resolution expressing disapproval of the administration's last-gasp "surge" of more troops in Iraq.

In addition to taking the lead on the Iraq War, Feingold also was one of the few senators who forcefully challenged the Bush administration's real and alleged violations of civil liberties and human rights in the name of fighting terrorism. These ranged from the administration's military commissions to the indefinite detention of "enemy combatants," secret prisons, the use of torture, national security letters and wiretapping without court approval. It was the warrantless wiretapping issue in particular that Feingold seized on in December 2005 to dramatize the administration's power grab and disregard for the rule of law.

The *New York Times* broke the story reporting that the president had secretly authorized the National Security Agency to wiretap the international calls of American citizens without obtaining approval, as the law required, from the special FISA court, named for the Foreign Intelligence Surveillance Act of 1978. The president used his weekly Saturday radio program to justify the warrantless wiretaps. Feingold was the first to respond in his own radio commentary, calling it "shocking . . . that [the president] authorized the NSA to spy on American citizens without going to a court. . . . The president believes that he has the power to override the laws that Congress has passed. This is not how our democratic system of government works. The president does not get to pick and choose which laws he wants to follow. He is a president, not a king."

Feingold made it clear in interviews that while he supported wiretapping terrorists, the president's blatant disregard of the law was such a fundamental violation of democratic government that the Congress couldn't look the other way and ignore it. But that's essentially what Senate Democrats were doing—they made a quick political judgment that it was not a good public relations move to complain about the law breaking if it would make them look weak on terrorism. But civil liberties organizations and Russ Feingold thought otherwise. One organization filed a lawsuit challenging the president's authority. And Feingold introduced a resolution calling on the Senate to censure the president.

The reaction to his censure proposal was enormous, both in the mainstream media, on the Internet and in calls to Feingold's office. He said it was the biggest, "most explosive" reaction to anything he had done to that point in his career. Interview requests came pouring in; he was on most of the national TV and cable news programs. From grassroots Democrats, the response was overwhelmingly positive, Feingold says, because they wanted somebody in Washington to stand up and hold the administration accountable. For most of the first six years of the Bush presidency, the Republican-controlled Congress smothered criticism and provided no oversight of even dubious administration practices. Therefore in Feingold's opinion, the censure proposal very quickly served its main purpose. "The primary objective was to make sure that illegality was not swept under the rug, which everybody in Washington was complicit in," he says, "Republicans for obvious reasons, Democrats because they were too afraid to touch the fact that this president had thumbed his nose at the law."

Russ Feingold was criticized by some Democratic strategists for even raising the issue, while others said he should have organized more support before he introduced the censure proposal. But he believed that the Democratic leadership of both houses would have tried to derail his idea had they known about it. "The Democratic Party is structured right now," he said in an interview in April 2006, "to destroy a progressive approach by saying it's the way to lose. So I was determined to do this in a way that would force them to own up to their historic responsibility to stand up for the rule of law." A Judiciary Committee hearing was held on the censure resolution. Although only a handful of senators cosponsored the resolution, a federal district court decision in 2006 came down on Feingold's side of the issue. And after the 2006 election, the White House announced it would no longer circumvent the FISA court. Even before the court decision, Feingold was "extremely pleased . . . because I know that forever it will be in the history books that a senator proposed a censure resolution . . . to make sure that our system of government is maintained."

Not everybody thought Russ Feingold had been motivated

only by a textbook defense of the Constitution and rule of law. Soon after his 2004 reelection, he formed the Progressive Patriots Fund to support his presidential explorations. But no sooner was he out on the early presidential trail than he and his wife, Mary, announced they were divorcing after fourteen years of marriage. Many friends were surprised by the news, and a few political pundits speculated about whether the country was ready for a twice-divorced Jewish president. Nonetheless, Feingold made the rounds to New Hampshire, Iowa and more than a dozen other states in 2005 and 2006. At Democratic Party events, he was already a heroic figure, drawing enthusiastic, emotional responses. He moved audiences with the "eloquence of authenticity," as the writer David Kusnet calls the best contemporary speaking. But when he appeared at a meeting of a few hundred Democrats in Rockingham County, New Hampshire, the audience responded before he even said a word. The man introducing Feingold was rather blandly reciting his background, but when he mentioned that Feingold was the only member of the U.S. Senate who voted against the Patriot Act, the audience rose as one and gave him a standing ovation. And this happened in many other venues. On the Internet, Feingold was becoming a favorite Democratic candidate of liberal, antiwar bloggers.

Back in Washington, an old political friend sat down with Feingold one day and gave him a little advice. He liked and admired Russ, but he told him that if he happened to catch fire in the early caucus and primary states, Iowa and New Hampshire, that "they're going to stop you." By "they" he meant the Washington Democratic establishment, which didn't appreciate Feingold's independent thinking and passionate commitment to progressive politics. Feingold laughed and said, well, if he won Iowa and New Hampshire, "it would be a hell of a couple weeks." And by the fall of 2006, many of Feingold's good friends assumed he was going to take the plunge and make his candidacy official after the midterm elections. He had to become better known beyond a core group of Democrats, civil libertarians and other activists. And there was a question of how much money he could raise. Although he'd start as a dark horse, people who knew him best thought that if anybody could figure out how to win, Russ Feingold could.

But on the Saturday after the 2006 midterm elections, Feingold surprised and disappointed a lot of friends and fans when he said he was not going to be a candidate. He didn't come right out and say it, but he had discovered that he didn't have the burning desire to run this time. And he had no interest in merely using a presidential campaign as a platform for his ideas or to increase his stature. He could use the Senate for that, especially now that his party was in the majority. The Senate majority leader, Harry Reid, had brought Feingold into his weekly leadership meetings, and Feingold would chair subcommittees and help set agendas on civil liberties and civil rights, and in foreign affairs. Plus, he was also one of the few senators who served on the three committees—Judiciary, Foreign Relations and Intelligence—that had overlapping responsibilities for the most important post-9/11 issues facing the country.

Each of Russ Feingold's Senate elections symbolized something important to him. His first race showed it was possible for a little guy who had no money but a big dream to run and win. His second race, the extraordinary reelection campaign in 1998, was his attempt to dramatically expose the corruption of a soft-money-dominated political system. When the McCain-Feingold reform bill was enacted, Hillary Clinton and many others thought it was going to be a disaster for their party. Nothing of the kind happened, however, and the Democratic Party was arguably strengthened when it was forced to find new, broader support among less affluent Americans.

Feingold's reelection in 2004, he believes, validated his assumption that strong, thoughtful opposition to the Bush administration's post-9/11 blunders on the Iraq War, terrorism and civil liberties would be valued by voters, not rejected.

His winning formula has been tested in what the political scientist Thomas Schaller calls "America's most competitive state." Russ Feingold's appeal has a strong "back to the future" quality. He lives simply, both in Washington and Middleton. In Wisconsin, he spends much of his time in small towns and celebrates the community-centered virtues reminiscent of his Janesville youth. And, of course, there is his identification with Fighting Bob La Follette and Progressive Era reformers. Much of the major domestic agenda of that era continues to resonate because it addresses timeless tensions and challenges in American democracy—issues of corporate power and big-money influence on the political system; income inequality and support of workers' rights; investment in public education, health and infrastructure; conservation and environmental protection; government efficiency, transparency and the rule of law. The early-twentieth-century reformers such as La Follette tackled all these challenges, in many cases producing landmark legislation and influencing succeeding generations to continue the unfinished work. Today, the writer Joel Kotkin observes that a significant segment of the American electorate "offers a potential base for creating a new, viable progressivism. Independent by nature, pragmatic and public-minded, they resemble the very classes that fostered and nurtured the first progressive movement and could also be the key to its 21st-century revival." In fact, these are the kind of independent voters who have elected Feingold to the Senate—and in his 2004 election, when the key issues included the Iraq War and fighting terrorism, they backed him overwhelmingly.

Epilogue

Time and again, Russ Feingold has turned conventional political wisdom on its head, succeeding politically by speaking boldly, sometimes taking controversial but principled positions and fighting corporate power when it's exercised to the detriment of ordinary Americans and the common good. In short, it is the kind of politics that used to be more characteristic of the Democratic Party before many of its leaders lost their moral compass and became obsessed with raising large sums to pay for expensive, TV-dominated political campaigns. Within the Democratic Party, Russ Feingold represents a serious, authentic alternative to his party's Washington establishment. Perhaps his own electoral successes, prominence and reformer's vision will inspire many others to become Feingold Democrats.

NOTES

Beginning in 2001, I had informal conversations and a series of interviews with Russ Feingold. Unless otherwise noted, Feingold's quotes come from my interviews that were conducted on July 10, 2002; August 23, 2002; December 4, 2002; April 17, 2003; May 12, 2005; July 19, 2005; November 19, 2005; December 31, 2005; April 14, 2006; June 29, 2006; August 12, 2006; November 4, 2006; December 13, 2006; February 24, 2007.

INTRODUCTION: LIVING IN THE REAL WORLD

1 *"You're not living in the real world":* Frederic J. Frommer, "Sens. Clinton, Feingold in Shouting Match," Associated Press, Jul. 20, 2002.

2 *"the White House is like a subway":* Marc Lacey, "House Subpoenas Torrance Businessman; Donations: Johnny Chung Is Expected to Invoke 5th Amendment Before Fund-raising Panel," *Los Angeles Times,* Nov. 8, 1997.

3 *On election day:* John McCain with Mark Salter, *Worth the Fighting For;* (New York: Random House, 2002), p. 363.

3 *"Don't worry":* Interview with Mary Murphy Irvine, Jun. 7, 2006, and Russ Feingold.

3 *"Idealism lives":* "No Third Term!," William Safire, *New York Times,* Nov. 5, 1998.

4 *"the country owes Feingold"*: "A Principled Win," *Washington Post*, Nov. 5, 1998.

4 *"Senator, I do live in the real world"*: Associated Press, Jul. 20, 2002; interview with Russ Feingold.

4 *"Hillary Clinton's 'Real World'"*: *New York Times*, Aug. 2, 2002.

CHAPTER 1. "I'M FOR KENNEDY!"

8 *"their allegiance"*: "50 Year History of the Rock County 4-H Fair," undated booklet, p. 7.

8 *"The big reason for"*: "Come to the Fair," *Janesville Gazette*, Jul. 29, 1960.

10 *"Coy Mangram, the bearded snake charmer"*: "Storm Frightening Event for Those on Fairgrounds," *Janesville Gazette*, Aug. 4, 1960.

11 *"centered largely on"*: Ibid.

14 *"immediately prepared to establish"*: "Historical Sketch of the City of Janesville, Wis.," *Holland's Janesville Directory*, p. 3.

14 *"the county of Rock"*: Ibid., p. 19.

15 *"Janesville's political culture"*: J. Rogers Hollingsworth and Ellen Jane Hollingsworth, *Dimensions in Urban History* (Madison: University of Wisconsin Press, 1979), p. 90.

16 *"the epitome of fiscal conservatism"*: Ibid., p. 92.

17 *"No new general"*: Mike DuPré, *Century of Stories: A 100-Year Reflection of Janesville and Surrounding Communities* (Janesville, Wisc.: Janesville Gazette, 2000), p. 45

18 *"was filled with warmth and love"*: Interview with Voltairine Bock, Jun. 28, 2006.

19 *"My dad was"*: Interview with Deborah Aronson, Jul. 25, 2006.

20 *"Chevrolet Plant Closing"*: *Janesville Gazette*, Sept. 2, 1932.

CHAPTER 2. "RENEGADE BY NATURE"

24 *"We hit it off pretty well"*: Sylvia Feingold, oral family history, undated.

24 *"one of the best things":* Interview with Voltairine Bock, Jun. 28, 2006.

25 *"I had a scholarship":* Sylvia Feingold oral family history, undated.

26 *"the kind of person":* Interview with Voltairine Bock, Jun. 28, 2006.

26 *"Leon was the finest person":* Interview with David Feingold, Aug. 19, 2005.

27 *"The first time I ever saw":* Interview with Thomas Fairchild, Jun. 20, 2006.

29 *"Jim assured me":* Ibid.

32 *"He was a custom-home builder":* Interview with Pete Duester-beck, Jun. 16, 2006.

35 *"I was one of the only Democrats":* Russ Feingold oral history interview with Bob Lange, Dec. 27, 2005.

CHAPTER 3. THE SIXTIES COME TO 1207 VISTA AVENUE

38 *"My brother and I":* Interview with Tim Cullen, May 11, 2006.

39 *"one of [his] biggest thrills":* Russ Feingold oral history interview with Bob Lange, Dec. 27, 2005.

39 *"I was honored":* Ibid.

41 *"Okay, let's play for Vista Avenue":* Interview with Dave Feingold, Jun. 21, 2006.

41 *" 'Rusty, I hate to tell you this' ":* Ibid.

44 *"We must take a look":* "Keep City Open for Negroes, Student Urges at YMCA Meeting," *Janesville Gazette,* Mar. 1, 1967.

44 *"To relieve Janesville":* DuPré, *Century of Stories,* p. 38.

47 *"For my father":* Interview with Dave Feingold, May 12, 2006.

47 *"endured some of":* DuPré, *Century of Stories,* p. 77.

49 *"I have bad news for you":* quoted in Arthur M. Schlesinger, Jr., *Robert Kennedy and His Times* (Boston: Houghton Mifflin, 1978) p. 874.

52 *recalls that maintaining control:* Interview with Tom Joynt, Apr. 17, 2006.

53 *"I marched into the guidance":* Interview with Chuck Arneson, Jun. 12, 2006.

56 *"He was just a brilliant student":* Interview with Bill O'Brien, Feb. 7, 2006.

56 *"Russ was the one":* Interview with Jackie Kinnaman, Aug. 17, 2005.

58 *"the source of Russ's popularity":* Interview with Mickey Crittenden, Sept. 13, 2006.

59 *"one of the strengths":* Interview with Pete Duesterbeck, Jun. 16, 2006.

60 *"You had to know something":* Interview with Tom Joynt.

60 *"We have a report here":* Interview with Russ Feingold, May 12, 2006.

61 *"You know, I think":* Ibid.

61 *"I can't wait until":* Ibid.

62 *"Toto":* This is the way it appeared in the *Daily Cardinal*. The actual utterance is, "Toto, I've a feeling we're not in Kansas anymore."

63 *"May we have the inner":* Rabbi Manfred E. Swarsensky, *Intimates and Ultimates: A Selection of Addresses* (Madison: Edgewood College, 1981), p. 174.

64 *"grave calm"* and *"CBS News":* Dan Schwartz, "Pomp and Circumstance," *Daily Cardinal*, fall registration issue, p. 3.

65 *"We're going to ride":* Interview with Ron Luskin, May 10, 2006.

67 *"Russ had a pathway":* Ibid.

67 *"He'd have this big stack":* Interview with Pete Duesterbeck, Jun. 16, 2006.

68 *"Russ was inquisitive":* Interview with Mike Hughes, May 8, 2006.

68 *"much better place":* Russ Feingold oral history interview with Bob Lange, Dec. 27, 2005.

68 *"I did not want":* Ibid.

69 *"That's not me":* Interview with Joel Grossman, Jul. 11, 2006.

70 *"Nor was my"*: Russell D. Feingold, The Armed Amendment: The Bases and Prospects for the Modern Significance of the Second Amendment to the United States Constitution, unpublished senior honor thesis, p. v.

71 *turning it into a book:* In addition to his senior thesis in political science, Feingold wrote a second thesis in history, a comparative analysis of congressional attitudes toward Israel in 1947, 1956, 1967 and 1973.

71 *"The courses were early"*: Russ Feingold oral history interview with Bob Lange, Dec. 27, 2005.

74 *"just a plain kid"*: "2 Area Men Rhodes Scholars," *Wisconsin State Journal*, Dec. 23, 1974.

75 *"this looks like Wisconsin"*: Russ Feingold oral history interview with Bob Lange, Dec. 27, 2005.

78 *"one of the worst"*: Ibid.

CHAPTER 5. THE F.L.

80 *"we didn't have a seasoned"*: Interview with David Harth, Jun. 20, 2006.

80 *"Poor Nancy"*: Interview with Harvey Temkin, Jun. 20, 2006.

81 *"I thought Russ"*: Interview with David Harth, Jun. 20, 2006.

82 *"I remember looking"*: Interview with Mike Hughes, May 8, 2006.

82 *"What are you"*: Interview with Dave Travis, May 10, 2006.

84 *"undeviating commitment"*: "Leon Feingold," *Janesville Gazette*, Dec. 5, 1980.

84 *"They're going to kill you!"*: Interview with Harvey Temkin, Jun. 20, 2006.

84 *"But, Russ"*: Interview with Russ Feingold, who quoted Nancy Mitchell.

86 *"an Afro out to here"*: Interview with John (Sly) Sylvester, Jun. 21, 2006.

87 *"really stuffy law firm"*: Ibid.

87 *"What is a young"*: Paul A. Rix, "Senate Dems Have High Vote Hopes," *Wisconsin State Journal*, Oct. 31, 1982.

Notes

88 *"I've had experiences"*: Virginia Mayo, "Experience the Issue in 27th," *Capital Times*, Oct. 28, 1982.

89 *"I didn't think it would"*: Virginia Mayo, "Feingold's Hard Work May Pay Off in Tight Senate Race," *Capital Times*, Nov. 5, 1982.

89 *"high stakes drama"*: John Patrick Hunter, "Recount Process High-Stakes Drama," *Capital Times*, Nov. 23, 1982.

90 *"he smiled at Feingold"*: Ibid.

90 *"You've got to give the kid credit"*: Interview with John (Sly) Sylvester, Jun. 21, 2006.

91 *"It was an exemplary campaign"*: "An Exemplary Race," *Capital Times*, Nov. 23, 1982.

CHAPTER 6. A TRUE PROGRESSIVE

95 *"No lobbyist came to me"*: Janet Bass, "Legislative Aid Coming, but Slowly," *Capital Times*, Jul. 9, 1985.

95 *"There were a lot of people"*: Ibid.

96 *"Enemies of the Republic"*: Lincoln Steffens, *McClure's Magazine*, March 1904.

97 *"placed Wisconsin in"*: John D. Buenker, *The History of Wisconsin, Volume IV, The Progressive Era, 1893–1914* (Madison: State Historical Society of Wisconsin, 1998), p. 491.

98 *"Nothing else ever"*: Robert M. La Follette, *La Follette's Autobiography* (Madison: University of Wisconsin Press, 1963), p. 65.

99 *"spoke forty-eight days"*: Ibid., p. 144.

100 *"We went in as a lobbying group"*: Interview with Lee Swanson, Oct. 20, 2006.

101 *"Russ was always"*: Ibid.

102 *"The bankers always win"*: Paul A. Rix, "Senate Approves Interstate Banking," *Wisconsin State Journal*, Mar. 25, 1986.

102 *"The question is whether"*: Mike Stamler, "Feingold Balking at Bank Bill," *Capital Times*, Mar. 14, 1986.

103 *"legal financial extortion"*: Ibid.

104 *"Feingold Takes"*: "Feingold Takes a Courageous Stand," *Capital Times*, Mar. 20, 1986.

104 *"the only reason"*: Mike Stamler, "Feingold Defies Dems, Will Sit on Banking Bill," *Capital Times*, Mar. 18, 1986.

104 *"Senate Democrats designed"*: Mike Stamler, "Dems Ploy Revives Banking Bill," *Capital Times*, Mar. 21, 1986.

105 *"It just shows"*: Ibid.

105 *"I cared about Russ"*: Interview with Tim Cullen, Jun. 22, 2006.

106 *"Feingold the Bold"*: Charles E. Friederich, "Feingold the Bold: He Fought the Tide," *Milwaukee Journal*, Mar. 25, 1986.

107 *"State Senator Russell"*: Dave Zweifel, "Russell Feingold: A True Progressive," *Capital Times*, Dec. 20, 1985.

108 *and throughout the country:* In 1994, Congress passed an interstate banking bill, known as the Riegle-Neal Interstate Banking and Branching Efficiency Act, removing almost all the remaining barriers to bank consolidation that had not been removed by state legislation in the 1980s. The legislation was not only a high priority of the Clinton administration, but it was pushed hard by banking lobbyists and, most notably, by NationsBank of Charlotte, North Carolina. President Clinton and NationsBank's wily, aggressive chief executive, Hugh L. McColl, Jr., had become pals, attending the national championship basketball game together several months before the final vote on the banking bill in the U.S. Senate. That bill sailed through with only four senators voting against it. One was Russ Feingold.

108 *"From the 1950's"*: Otis White, "Support Your Local Banker," *New York Times*, Jun. 1, 2006.

110 *"The property tax"*: Thomas W. Still, "Politicos Scramble to Shuffle Tax Deck," *Wisconsin State Journal*, Jan. 25, 1987.

112 *"I saw the terrible"*: Interview with John Kinsman, Oct. 31, 2006.

113 *"It consumed a lot"*: Interview with Jeffrey Remsik, Jun. 19, 2006.

113 *"vehicle to allow consumers"*: David Blaska, "Feingold: Label Milk Made Utilizing BGH," *Capital Times*, Jul. 17, 1988.

114 *"little question that"*: "Our Free Market System Requires BGH Labeling," *Milwaukee Sentinel*, Sept. 6, 1989.

114 *"Why Rush?"*: "Why Rush? Cows Can Wait," *Milwaukee Journal*, Aug. 20, 1989.

Notes

114 *"Small towns are picking"*: Keith Schneider, "Biotechnologies Cash Cow," *New York Times*, Jun. 12, 1988.

115 *"Feingold has been orchestrating"*: Judith Klusman, "US Mugs Monsanto on BGH Facts," *Milwaukee Journal*, Mar. 31, 1991.

115 *"secret BGH research"*: Neil M. Shively and Richard Bradee, "UW Urged to End Secret BGH Tests," *Milwaukee Sentinel*, Aug. 15, 1989.

115 *"Wisconsin Temporarily"*: Keith Schneider, "Wisconsin Temporarily Banning Gene-Engineered Drug for Cows," *New York Times*, Apr. 28, 1990.

CHAPTER 7. HOME MOVIES

118 *"He had to bring it up"*: Ruth Conniff, "U.S. Sen. Russ Feingold: Regular Guy Among Millionaires," *Express*, Jul. 31, 1997.

120 *"Russ didn't have"*: Interview with Al Madison, Dec. 12, 2005.

120 *"What amazed me"*: Interview with John (Sly) Sylvester, Jun. 21, 2006.

120 *"I'm going to win"*: Interview with Dave Zweifel, May 8, 2006.

121 *"a lot of people"*: Interview with John (Sly) Sylvester, Jun. 21, 2006.

122 *"I had to call"*: Interview with Mike Wittenwyler, Feb. 10, 2006.

122 *"We argued"* and *"Yeah, maybe"*: Ibid.

123 *"Some Democrats said"*: Craig Gilbert, "Feingold Claims Grass-Root Lead," *Milwaukee Journal*, Jun. 13, 1992.

124 *"wide open"*: Robin Estrin, "Feingold Goes to D.C. to Push for Senate Bid," *Capital Times*, Jun. 27, 1992.

126 *"What the fuck"*: Interview with Steve Eichenbaum, Sept. 23, 2005.

126 *"Let's just shoot"*: Ibid.

128 *"repulsive"*: Craig Gilbert, "Opponents' Spat Gives Feingold Lift," *Milwaukee Journal*, Aug. 28, 1992.

128 *"I think that both"*: Rick Romell, "Feingold May Not Have Time for Upset," *Milwaukee Sentinel*, Aug. 29, 1992.

128 *"The ad probably will"*: Jeff Mayers, "Feingold's 'Home Movies' Mixes Message, Humor," *Wisconsin State Journal*, Aug. 18, 1992.

130 *"What he seems to have"*: Romell, "Feingold May Not Have Time for Upset."

130 *"There just isn't that much time"*: Ibid.

132 *"The blunt fact is"*: Steve Schultze, "Checota Gives Boost to Feingold," *Milwaukee Journal*, Sept. 5, 1992.

133 *"what it could mean"*: "State Primary: Feingold," *Wisconsin State Journal*, Sept. 6, 1992.

134 *"that people do count more"*: Dave Callendar, "Feingold Does It," *Capital Times*, Sept. 9, 1992.

134 *"What did Joe Checota"*: "It Serves the Pit Bulls Right," *Milwaukee Journal*, Sept. 9, 1992.

134 *"In a jujitsu match"*: "State Primary: Feingold."

134 *"She offered a"*: Francis X. Clines, "Underdog in Wisconsin Slips the Blade Nicely," *New York Times*, Sept. 18, 1992.

136 *"You know what"*: Interview with Steve Eichenbaum, Sept. 23, 2005.

137 *"Russ, you gotta"*: Interview with David Harth, Jun. 20, 2006.

138 *"looking like a cat"*: Kenneth R. Lamke, "2 Debate Taxes and TV Ads," *Milwaukee Sentinel*, Sept. 12, 1992.

138 *"The senator correctly"*: Ibid.

140 *"in bed with"*: Craig Gilbert, "Kasten, Feingold Debate Feisty, but Not Nasty," *Milwaukee Journal*, Oct. 16, 1992.

142 *"Is there no limit"*: Dave Daley, "Use of Dahmer's Name in Survey Has Senate Challenger Crying Foul," *Milwaukee Journal*, Oct. 10, 1992.

143 *"surprisingly strong"*: Jeff Mayers, "Feingold Positively Overwhelms Kasten," *Wisconsin State Journal*, Nov. 4, 1992.

143 *"There's something seriously"*: Craig Gilbert, "Feingold Proves Strategists Wrong," *Milwaukee Journal*, Nov. 4, 1992.

144 *"The conventional wisdom"*: "Feingold Did It His Way the Right Way," *Milwaukee Journal*, Nov. 4, 1992.

CHAPTER 8. MR. FEINGOLD GOES TO WASHINGTON

147 *"The furniture was junk"*: Interview with John (Sly) Sylvester, Jun. 21, 2006.

148 *"members of the Senate"*: Transcript of *The NewsHour,* Jan. 8, 1997.

148 *"there is no"*: See www.twainquotes.com.

149 *"The woman took"*: Interview with Mike Wittenwyler, Feb. 10, 2006.

150 *"He took me"*: Ibid.

150 *"I remember going"*: Interview with Susanne Martinez, Dec. 19, 2006.

151 *"The governor"*: Mike Royko, *Chicago Tribune,* Dec. 19, 1988.

152 *"Oh, we do"*: Interview with Patti Jo McCann, Jan. 3, 2007.

152 *"getting rid of freebies"*: Jackie Calmes, "His Special Interest Is Ban on Gift Giving by Special Interest," *Wall Street Journal,* Jul. 2, 1993.

153 *"reform would have"*: "Now, Gifts to the House," *New York Times,* Jul. 30, 1995.

154 *"one of the great"*: Michael Abramowitz, "The Foreseen Rise of Russ Feingold," *Washington Post,* Nov. 30, 1992.

155 *"The first thing"*: Interview with Susanne Martinez, Dec. 19, 2006.

156 *"Eyes popped"*: Al Kamen, "Radio Free Europe Gets Static on Pay," *Washington Post,* Jul. 21, 1993.

157 *"There are some"*: Patrick Jasperse, "Welcome to Washington: Feingold Learns Lesson with Very First Bill," *Milwaukee Journal,* May 3, 1993.

158 *"Early on"*: Interview with Susanne Martinez, Dec. 19, 2006.

159 *"really think the balanced budget"*: "Constitutional Pork," *Washington Post,* Feb. 23, 1995.

161 *"The people of this country"*: Senate speech, Aug. 6, 1993.

163 *"if any trade agreement"*: Joseph E. Stiglitz, *Making Globalization Work* (New York: W.W. Norton, 2006), p. 61.

164 *"It was hypocritical"*: David Bacon, *The Children of Nafta* (Berkeley and Los Angeles: University of California Press, 2004), p. 164.

165 *"Feingold has adroitly"*: Patrick Jasperse, "Feingold: Year in Senate Earns Him Respect," *Milwaukee Journal,* Jan. 23, 1994.

165 *"Feingold does not duck issues"*: Ibid.

165 *"I think I'm doing"*: Ibid.

Notes

167 *"has made good"*: Craig Gilbert, "Feingold Meets Goal on Visits to All 72 Counties," *Milwaukee Journal*, Dec. 1, 1993.

167 *"I hope it's a positive"*: Ibid.

169 *"We'll hit number one"*: Author's notes, Aug. 14, 2006.

170 *"These mini-town-hall forums"*: "Feingold Session Validates Democracy," *Ripon Commonwealth Press*, Jan. 8, 2004.

172 *"We hired you"*: Michael Tackett, "Senator Goes to Wisconsin—for Reality Check," *Chicago Tribune*, Jun. 4, 1996.

175 "When I first noticed him": McCain with Salter, *Worth the Fighting For*, p. 357.

175 *"He reacted with"*: Ibid.

175 *"From the moment"*: Ibid.

177 *"Regrettably, I think"*: Stephan Labaton, "Voices in Each Party Call for Special Counsel on Fund Raising," *New York Times*, Feb. 24, 1997.

178 *"The distinguished majority leader"*: Senate speech, Apr. 22, 1998.

180 *"I do not feel that"*: "U.S. Senator Makes 10 Campaign Promises," *Herald Times Reporter*, Feb. 11, 1998.

180 *Years later*: Interview with Mark Neumann, Nov. 16, 2006.

181 *"But let's be clear"*: "Feingold the Clear Winner in Spending Agreement," *Post-Crescent*, Feb. 10, 1998.

182 *"Mark, you can call"*: Amy Rinard, "Democrats Rally Around Feingold, Hope for Repeat of 92," *Milwaukee Journal Sentinel*, Jun. 13, 1998.

183 *"slippery"*: Text of ad in *Milwaukee Journal Sentinel*, Oct. 25, 1998.

183 "a bald-faced lie": Alan J. Borsuk, "Feingold Blasts GOP Ad," *Milwaukee Journal Sentinel*, Sept. 26, 1998.

183 *"The ad was"*: Ibid.

183 *"he should do"*: "Feingold Challenges Congressman Neumann to Stand Up to the Republican Party," copy of press release, Sept. 28, 1998.

185 *"Feingold is toast"*: Author's notes from a meeting at the Tarrance Group, approximately Oct. 20, 1998.

185 *"calling up"*: Interview with Mike Wittenwyler, Mar. 6, 2006.

186 *"So this is how it ends":* Interview with Mary Murphy Irvine, Jun. 7, 2006, and Russ Feingold.

186 *"Feingold Denounces":* "Feingold Denounces Independent DSCC Soft-Money Phony Issue Ad," campaign press release, Oct. 21, 1998.

188 *But all of the:* According to the nonpartisan Center for Responsive Politics, the AFL-CIO independent expenditures totaled $133,544; the League of Conservation Voters, $196,673; the National Rifle Association, $116,415; and the National Right to Life, $74,579.

188 *"High Road":* Text from a recording provided by Russ Feingold.

189 *"my crazy idea":* Videotape of Feingold election-night speech.

190 *"dead meat":* R. W. Apple, Jr., "Wisconsin: Campaign Funds at Center of Wisconsin Race," *New York Times*, Oct. 23, 1998.

CHAPTER 9. PROFILE IN COURAGE

193 *"but if the facts":* Dennis A. Shook, "Feingold Will Support Action If Clinton Lied," *Waukesha Freeman*, Jan. 27, 1998.

193 *"the president was being":* Interview with Bob Kerrey, Nov. 30, 2006.

194 *"The impeachment trial":* Interview with Russ Feingold; also, he returned to the topic at the University of Wisconsin when he delivered the 2005 Thomas E. Fairchild Lecture titled, "Upholding an Oath to the Constitution: A Legislator's Responsibilities," Apr. 22, 2005.

194 *"Should any legal":* David Espo, "Fallout from Confession Begins," *Milwaukee Journal Sentinel*, Aug. 19, 1998.

195 *"the nation great pain":* Peter Baker, *The Breach* (New York: Scribner, 2000), p. 335.

195 *"My view":* Russ Feingold, "Senate Should Not Short-Circuit the Impeachment Trial," *Milwaukee Journal Sentinel*, Jan. 28, 1999.

196 *"I am . . . deeply":* Jim Stingl, "Feingold's Reputation Precedes Him," *Milwaukee Journal Sentinel*, Jan. 28, 1999.

196 *"We're getting a lot":* Ibid.

196 *"Clearly what he did":* Mike Flaherty, "Democrats Don't Like

Vote, but Go Easy on Feingold," *Wisconsin State Journal*, Jan. 28, 1999.

196 *"would like to hang"*: Dave Zweifel, "Feingold Threw Us an Impeachment Curve," *Capital Times*, Jan. 29, 1999.

196 *"The Vote Heard"*: Kevin Merida, *Washington Post*, Jan. 29, 1999.

196 *"one of the Senate's"*: Frank Bruni, "Democrat Joins the G.O.P on 2 Impeachment Votes," *New York Times*, Jan. 28, 1999.

196 *"How he voted"*: "A Vote on Principle, Not Partisanship," *Wisconsin State Journal*, Jan. 29, 1999.

197 *"independent actions like"*: "Feingold Courageous for Breaking Ranks," *Chippewa Herald*, Jan. 29, 1999.

197 *"An American hero"*: Bob Vitale, "Feingold Supported from Unlikely Sources," *Oshkosh Northwestern*, Jan. 29, 1999.

197 *"A big-time thing"*: Ibid.

197 *"You've got to give"*: Bruni, "Democrat Joins the G.O.P on 2 Impeachment Votes."

197 *"show[ed] he's not afraid"*: "Feingold Shows Independence," *Green Bay News Chronicle*, Jan. 28, 1999.

197 *"always been willing to"*: Stingl, "Feingold's Reputation Precedes Him."

197 *"reasonable to despise"*: "Feingold's Principles," *Capital Times*, Jan. 28, 1999.

199 *"Having watched Feingold"*: Jim Meyer, "The Real Thing," *The Scene*, Mar. 1999.

199 *"as to obstruction"*: Feingold's statement from the Senate's closed deliberations on the articles of impeachment against President Clinton, excerpts of which senators were allowed to publish in the *Congressional Record* for Feb. 12, 1999.

199 *"I'm holding"*: Remarks of U.S. Senator Russell Feingold, 1999 Profile in Courage Award recipient, May 24, 1999.

200 *"unilaterally adopt[ing]"*: Remarks delivered by Caroline Kennedy on presenting the 1999 Profile in Courage Award, May 24, 1999.

200 *"An arrogant shit"*: Interview; anonymous.

200 *"I thank him for being"*: Peter Baker, *The Breach*, p. 362.

Notes

200 *"Let's see now"*: Al Kamen, "A Dearly Departing Shot," *Washington Post*, Jan. 29, 1999.

201 *"close the most scandalous"*: Remarks of Senator Edward M. Kennedy on the presentation of the 1999 Profile in Courage Award to Senator John McCain and Senator Russell Feingold, May 24, 1999.

202 *"In this era"*: Peter Beinart, "Wisconsin's Modern Mugwump, Fussy Russ (Russell Feingold)," *New Republic*, Nov. 23, 1998.

203 *"the power of corporate"*: Senate speech, Jun. 16, 1999.

204 *"Why might Congress"*: "Feingold Refuses to Back Down on Influence of Money in Senate," Feingold press release, Sept. 23, 1999.

205 *"borders on a personal attack"*: Craig Gilbert, "Following the Money: Feingold's Push for Campaign Reform Angers," *Milwaukee Journal Sentinel*, Oct. 3, 1999.

205 *"were offensive to members"*: Ibid.

205 *"When the public"*: "Feingold Refuses to Back Down on Influence of Money in Senate."

206 *"No one put me up"*: Lloyd Grove, "Little (Dangerous?) Old Lady from Pasadena," *Washington Post*, Oct. 15, 1999.

207 *"I cannot stand before you"*: Richard Simon and Greg Krikorian, "Senator Seeks an End to Soft Money," *Los Angeles Times*, Aug. 16, 2000.

207 *"corporate trade shows"*: John Nichols, "Feingold Raps Own Party Over Corporate Cash," *Capital Times*, Aug. 14, 2000.

207 *"In room after room"*: John M. Broder and Don Van Natta, Jr., "Contributors in a Giving Mood," *New York Times*, Aug. 15, 2000.

208 *"Feingold finds himself"*: Simon and Krikorian, "Senator Seeks an End to Soft Money."

212 *"He is not real good"*: Interview with Joe Wineke, Jun. 20, 2006.

212 *notable because the journalist*: See Elizabeth Drew, *Citizen McCain* (New York: Simon & Schuster, 2002).

212 *"That's just not so"*: Kenneth R. Lamke, "Feingold Says Vote Not Tied to Golf: Senator Denies Allegation in Book About Clinton," *Milwaukee Sentinel*, Oct. 25, 1994.

215 *"use all necessary"*: "After the Attacks: Text of Joint Resolution Allowing Military Action," *New York Times*, Sept. 15, 2001.

215 *"acts of war"*: Russ Feingold, "Statement on the Terrorist Attacks of Sept. 11, 2001," Sept. 12, 2001.

215 *"actions and any future actions"*: David E. Rosenbaum, "The Lawmakers; Congressional Leaders Offer Strong Endorsement of Attack," *New York Times*, Oct. 8, 2001.

218 *"is not a suicide pact"*: "Statement of U.S. Senator Russ Feingold on the Anti-terrorism Bill," Oct. 25, 2001.

218 *"in this spirit"*: Ibid.

220 *"rank on the list"*: John Nichols, "Feingold Upholds Dissenting Tradition," *Capital Times*, Oct. 16, 2001.

221 *"The Department of Justice"*: Dave Umhoefer and James H. Burnet III, "Feingold, Colleagues Seek Information on Detainees," *Milwaukee Journal Sentinel*, Nov. 3, 2001.

221 *"I wanted to join you"*: From text of Feingold's speech at the Arab American Institute Foundation's Kahlil Gibran "Spirit of Humanity" Awards Gala, Washington, D.C., Apr. 10, 2002.

221 *"were extraordinarily well received"*: Interview with Jim Zogby, Nov. 29, 2005.

222 *"judicial lawlessness"*: Scott Turow, "A Brand New Game: No Turning Back From the Dart the Court has Thrown," *Washington Post*, Dec. 17, 2000.

223 *"I have never been"*: Katrina van den Heuvel, "Feingold Tries to Explain His Vote for Ashcroft: An Exclusive Interview," *Nation*, Jan. 31, 2001.

223 *"gagging in his grave"*: Letter by Ed Kuharski, *Capital Times*, Feb. 8, 2001.

223 *"Anyone who knows me"*: Craig Gilbert, "Feingold's Supporters Question Ashcroft Vote," *Milwaukee Journal Sentinel*, Feb. 1, 2001.

224 *"above all, I believe"*: Russ Feingold, "Don't Reject Nominee on Philosophy," *Daily Tribune* (Wisconsin Rapids), Feb. 13, 2001.

224 *"Courageous Vote"*: Feb. 1, 2001.

224 *"I think this was"*: Allison Vekshin, "Feingold Support for Ash-

croft Puts Him Under Scrutiny," *Wisconsin State Journal*, Feb. 18, 2001.

225 *"It's not often that"*: Alison Mitchell, "Campaign Finance Bill Wins Final Approval in Congress and Bush Says He'll Sign It," *New York Times*, Mar. 21, 2002.

225 *"the highlight of my"*: Craig Gilbert, "Divided Senate Passes Campaign Finance Reform," *Milwaukee Journal Sentinel*, Mar. 21, 2002.

225 *"Campaign contributions from"*: Ibid.

226 *"an extraordinary victory"*: "An Extraordinary Victory," *New York Times*, Mar. 21, 2002.

227 *"I was stunned"*: Neil A. Lewis, "Federal Express Knows Its Way Around Capital," *New York Times*, Oct. 12, 1996.

228 *"it just gave us 100,000"*: From McConnell v. FEC: District Court: Witness Depositions and Cross Examinations, Sept. 9, 2002, posted on the website of the Campaign Legal Center, http://www.campaignlegalcenter.org/McConnell-49.html.

228 *"this crabbed view"*: McConnell, United State Senator, et al. v. Federal Election Commission et al., Dec. 10, 2003; and Linda Greenhouse, "Justices, in a 5-to-4 Decision, Back Campaign Finance Law That Curbs Contributions," *New York Times*, Dec. 11, 2003.

CHAPTER 10. IRAQ

231 *"We are about to"*: "Statement of U.S. Senator Russ Feingold on Opposing the Resolution Authorizing the Use of Force Against Iraq," Oct. 9, 2002.

233 *"The administration's arguments"*: Ibid.

234 *"In a Senate where"*: "Speaking a tough truth": *Capital Times*, Oct. 10, 2002.

235 *"The terrorists want to"*: Author's notes.

237 *"we must build"*: "Beyond Iraq: Refocusing Our National Strategy," prepared text of his remarks at the Center for Strategic and International Studies, May 19, 2006.

Notes

240   *"I don't agree with"*: Interview with George Aldrich, Feb. 7, 2007.

240   *"This election is about"*: Graeme Zielinski, "Maverick Feingold Secures Easy Victory," *Milwaukee Journal Sentinel*, Nov. 3, 2004.

EPILOGUE

241   *"totally upset with"*: Author's notes, Aug. 11, 2005.

242   *"the wrong message"*: "Bush Rips Feingold Plan," Associated Press, *Capital Times*, Aug. 19, 2005.

242   *"I said, 'Off the record'"*: Meet the Press, Aug. 21, 2005.

243   *"to surrender to"*: David E. Sanger, "Defending The War; Iraq Dogs President as He Crosses Asia to Promote Trade," *New York Times*, Nov. 17, 2005.

243   *"Russ made the right vote"*: Frederic J. Frommer, Associated Press, Jun. 27, 2006.

243   *The White House has done"*: Meet the Press, Jun. 25, 2006.

245   *"shocking . . . that"*: Text of Feingold's response to the President's radio address, Dec. 17, 2005.

247   *"they're going to stop you"*: Private conversation confirmed by both participants.

249   *"America's most competitive"*: Thomas E. Schaller, *Whistling Past Dixie* (New York: Simon & Schuster, 2006), p. 152.

250   *"offers a potential base"*: Joel Kotkin, "Rethinking Progressivism," Pat Brown Institute, Nov. 14, 2005, p. 2.

ACKNOWLEDGMENTS

Putting words on paper is a solitary exercise, but creating a biography is a collaborative adventure. I'm grateful for the help of many people.

Over the past five years, Russ Feingold was generous with his time, agreeing to numerous interviews and sharing recollections about his youth, education and politics. I appreciated his willingness to cooperate while recognizing that I was interested in writing an independent account of his political career. He never asked to see a word of what I wrote before the book was completed.

I also appreciated the helpfulness of Russ Feingold's siblings—Nancy, Dena and Dave, as well as Dave's wife, Julie. They provided valuable insights about family and community life in Janesville, and much more. One of my regrets is that I did not write more about each of them because they, too, are leading significant, productive lives—Nancy as a psychotherapist, Dena as a rabbi, and Dave as a civically engaged lawyer in Janesville. Not the least of their accomplishments is that they are all proud parents.

At Simon & Schuster, I was privileged to have as my editor the gifted Alice Mayhew, and I am grateful for her guiding hand, impeccable judgment and enthusiasm. I also want to thank Alice's assistant, Serena Jones, for her support, patience and good cheer. The manuscript benefited from the fine work of Fred Chase and Mara

Acknowledgments

Lurie. I appreciate the creativity and thoughtfulness of designer Paul Dippolito, and of Victoria Meyer and Rebecca Davis in publicizing the book.

My agent, Mary Evans, was a passionate progressive and Feingold Democrat before I met her. Every writer should have Mary in his or her corner. We were introduced by our mutual friend, Nicholas von Hoffman, who encouraged me to write about Feingold. Nick's wit and wisdom are only two of the many reasons I value his friendship.

Many of the people whom I interviewed are cited in the text; I am grateful for their recollections and thoughts. But many others not mentioned, or only briefly, also shared important reflections and ideas, or helped in other ways. I want to thank them, too. They include: Dick Meltzer, Nadine Cohodas, Jim Zogby, Peter Baker, Craig Gilbert, Eleanor Engel, Lynn Adelman, Ted Bornstein, Ed Greelegs, Mary Frederick, Tom Osmond, Lois and Jay Larkey, Gary Hilt, Mike Kuehne, Saul Cornell, Nancy Mitchell, Pete Duesterbeck, Sheldon Lubar, Trevor Miller, Ruth and Len Zubrensky, Geoff Garin, Fred Yang, Mary Bottari, John Nichols, Barbara Block Paterick, Bruce Cohen, Bob Green, Thomas Schaller, Nan Aron, Marilyn Cooper, Mary Murphy Irvine, Mike McCabe, Bob Schiff, Steve Shimshak, John Sylvester, Charlie Cook, Don Ritchie, Enid Brenner, Al Madison, Meredith McGehee, Bob Bauer, Joel Kotkin, Sumner Slichter, Ron Luskin, John Norquist, Curt Gans, Ellen Warren, Larry Sabato, Zack Lowe, Zoe Gratsias, Betty Steele, Amanda Jonas, Matt Freeman, Elsie Freeman Finch, Andy Muzi, Tom Cain, Michael Smith, P. J. McCann, George Aldrich, Louise and Frank Haiman, Bill Christofferson, Ken Guenther, Steve Cooper, Bob Kerrey, Dave Travis, Mike Hughes, Mike Wittenwyler, Theodore and Jan Kinnaman, Jay Heck, Fred Wertheimer, Joe Wineke, Trevor Potter, Tim Elverman, Jeffrey Remsik, Laura Murphy, Brady Williamson, Kathy Kozer, Mark Neumann, Susan Wexler Crater, Barbara Wexler Cooper, Sally Davis, Bill Lofy, and Cole Leystra. I also want to recognize the important contributions of two men I interviewed who have recently died: Tom Fairchild and Frank Zeidler. Both were extraordinary citizens who left inspiring legacies.

In Janesville, Wisconsin, I benefited from the assistance of Mike DuPré, the veteran reporter at the *Janesville Gazette*. Mike not only shared his deep knowledge about local history, but he guided me through the newspaper's files. His book, *Century of Stories: A 100 Year Reflection of Janesville and Surrounding Communities*, is a great resource and community treasure.

Also in Janesville, the accommodating staff at the Hedberg Public Library made my visits enjoyable and productive. At the Rock County Historical Society, I want to thank Ruth Anderson, the assistant archivist, for her exceptional effort and diligence.

Ron Larson, library director at the *Capital Times* and *Wisconsin State Journal*, provided valuable assistance, as did the staffs at the University of Wisconsin–Madison libraries, the Wisconsin Historical Society and the Milwaukee Public Library.

Elsewhere in Wisconsin, I want to thank Jim Nepstad, Chief of Planning and Resource Management at the Apostle Islands National Lakeshore; Julie Van Stappen, Branch Chief of Natural Resources at the Apostle Islands National Lakeshore; Sheree Peterson, Curator of Collections, Madeline Island Museum; John LaCourse, President, Mosser Lee Company; Patrick Geoghegan, Senior Vice President of Corporate Communications, Wisconsin Milk Marketing Board; Laura Mason, Wisconsin Agricultural Statistics Service.

Colleen Cooney, Archives Specialist at the John F. Kennedy Museum and Library, provided timely assistance.

Finally, I could not have written this book without the wise counsel, encouragement and love of three of the most talented people I know: my wife, Joan, and our sons, Dusty and Jeff. Countless times I relied on their keen insights and inspiration. They are a terrific trio!

INDEX

Index

Index

Index

Index

Index

Index

Index

Index

Index

Index

Index

Whitewater, 192

Wilderness Society, 132

Wineke, Joe, 196, 212–13

Winneboujou (Ojibwe deity), 210

Wisconsin:

  dairy industry in, 109–16

  Democratic Party in, 27, 29, 96

  direct primary in, 99

  ethics in politics, 149, 150,
    151–52, 153

  jobs lost in, 164

  listening sessions in, 166–74

  mandatory retirement age in,
    94–95

  poverty in, 173

  presidential elections in, 64–66,
    99

  Progressive Party in, 26–27, 29

  progressive tradition in, 17, 97,
    99, 107, 121, 155, 160

  public financing system in, 91

  Republican Party in, 10

  right to bear arms in, 171

  small-town values in, 160

  taxation in, 110

Wisconsin Bankers Association, 103

Wisconsin Election Campaign
  Fund, 91

"Wisconsin Idea," 97

Wisconsin Senate:

  and banking industry, 100–109

  committee assignments in,
    93–94

  Committee on Aging, 94–96

  and dairy industry, 109–16

Wisconsin State Journal, 128, 133,
  134, 196

Witte, Edwin, 28

Wittenwyler, Mike, 122–23,
  147–48, 149–50, 184, 185,
  186

World Trade Center attacks,
  214–15

World War II, 219

Yang, Fred, 124, 148–49, 184, 186

Zeidler, Frank, 160

Zionism, 19

Zogby, Jim, 221

Zweifel, Dave, 106–7, 120, 196,
  197

ILLUSTRATION CREDITS

Courtesy of David Feingold: 1, 2
Courtesy of Pete Duesterbeck: 3
Courtesy Bill O'Brien and the Janesville Gazette: 4
Courtesy of Russ Feingold: 5, 8, 13, 14, 17, 18
Courtesy of Cole Leystra: 6, 7
Courtesy of John Sylvester: 9, 12
Courtesy of Dena Feingold: 10
Courtesy of the Janesville Chamber of Commerce: 11
Courtesy of the John F. Kennedy Library and Museum: 15
Courtesy of Mary Murphy Irvine: 16
Tribune Media Services, Inc.: 19
Associated Press: 20

ABOUT THE AUTHOR

Sanford D. Horwitt is an author, book critic and policy advisor to foundations and nonprofit organizations concerned with promoting civic engagement and strengthening democratic institutions. He is the author of *Let Them Call Me Rebel,* a biography of Saul Alinsky. His book reviews and essays have appeared in the *New York Times, Washington Post, San Francisco Chronicle, Chicago Tribune* and other publications. In Washington, he was a speechwriter for Congressman Abner Mikva. Born in Milwaukee, he received his bachelor's and doctoral degrees at Northwestern University. He lives in Arlington, Virginia with his wife, Joan. They have two sons, Dusty and Jeff.